REUSING OPEN RESOURCES

Every day, learners use and reuse open, digital resources for learning. *Reusing Open Resources* offers a vision of the potential of these open, online resources to support learning. The book follows on from *Reusing Online Resources: A sustainable approach to e-learning*, published in 2003 by Littlejohn. At that time focus was on the creation, release and reuse of digital learning resources modeled on educational materials. Since then the open release of resources and data has become mainstream, rather than specialist, changing societal expectations around resource reuse. Social and professional learning networks are now routine places for the exchange of online knowledge resources that are shared, manipulated and reused in new ways, opening opportunities for new models of business, research and learning.

The goal of this book is to extend the debate on how open, online resources might support learning across diverse contexts. Twenty-four distinguished experts from nine countries distributed across Europe and North America contribute empirical evidence and ideas. Collectively they provide a vision of the potential of open, online resources to support learning across everyday contexts of education, work and life.

Professor Allison Littlejohn is Director of the Caledonian Academy and Chair of Learning Technology at Glasgow Caledonian University, UK.

Dr. Chris Pegler is a UK National Teaching Fellow and formerly a Senior Lecturer in the Institute of Educational Technology at the Open University, UK.

Advancing Technology-Enhanced Learning

Series Editors Chris Pegler and Allison Littlejohn

Technology-Enhanced Professional Learning, edited by *Allison Littlejohn and Anoush Margaryan*

Reusing Open Resources, edited by *Allison Littlejohn and Chris Pegler*

REUSING OPEN RESOURCES

Learning in Open Networks
for Work, Life and Education

Edited by Allison Littlejohn and Chris Pegler

Routledge
Taylor & Francis Group

NEW YORK AND LONDON

First published 2015
by Routledge
711 Third Avenue, New York, NY 10017

and by Routledge
2 Park Square, Milton Park, Abingdon, Oxon OX14 4RN

Routledge is an imprint of the Taylor & Francis Group, an informa business

Library of Congress Cataloging in Publication Data
Library of Congress Cataloging-in-Publication Data
Reusing open resources: learning in open networks for work, life and
education/edited by Allison Littlejohn, Chris Pegler.
pages cm. — (Advancing technology enhanced learning)
Includes bibliographical references and index.
1. Internet in education. 2. Electronic information resources.
3. Computer network resources. I. Littlejohn, Allison, 1962–editor of
compilation. II. Pegler, Chris, 1956–editor of compilation.
LB1044.87.R49 2014
371.33′44678—dc23
2014001395

ISBN: 978-0-415-83868-9 (hbk)
ISBN: 978-0-415-83869-6 (pbk)
ISBN: 978-0-203-78019-0 (ebk)

Typeset in Bembo
by Swales & Willis Ltd, Exeter, Devon, UK

CONTENTS

FIGURES

TABLES

FOREWORD

The New Age of Open
Learning Opportunities

Education is frequently criticized as a field that rarely changes. Some variation of "classrooms look like they did 100 years ago" is presented when would-be innovators and reformers attempt to motivate their audience. For anyone involved in the education sector, this argument is nonsensical.

Teachers and education systems are rapid adopters of new technologies and innovations. Distance education has its roots as far back as 1833, when a Swedish newspaper ran an advertisement for a course in "Composition through the medium of the post." Scribes and scholars dating millennia into the past used the technologies of books and scrolls to capture and share important ideas and make them available to others. Wherever new communication innovations exist, educators are not far behind in adapting them for teaching and learning: learning via post, radio, television, and the internet.

The last decade has produced stunning opportunities for educators to use technologies to enlarge classrooms and increase access opportunities for formal learning, learning for personal development, and for work performance. At the forefront of these trends are open education resources and open learning.

Innovations are combinatorial in nature, making it difficult to trace a direct lineage between a concept as it exists today and its earliest formation. In the 1960s, the Open University UK launched on the ideals of access and the use of technology to increase the learning opportunities for students who might not have been able to attend a physical campus. Today, millions of students around the world complete their education—from certificates to PhDs—through distance education.

More recently, in 2002, MIT launched the OpenCourseWare (OCW) initiative to make course content available to anyone without fees. In the decade since, hundreds of universities from around the world have launched similar projects and open education resources (OERs) have entered the vocabulary of students, academics, and university leaders.

Openness is infectious. What MIT's OCW did for content, massive open online courses (MOOCs) are now doing for teaching and learning. Rarely has an educational trend developed as rapidly as MOOCs. Since 2011, MOOCs have been featured prominently in TV programs, documentaries, evening news programs, and newspapers. New companies such as edX, FutureLearn, and Coursera were founded with the goals of democratizing education and expanding the profile of already prestigious higher education institutions. Other projects, such as OERu and P2PU, promote openness through innovative pedagogy and assessment models.

The growth of openness in education, reflected by OERs and MOOCs, has been impressive. Of equal significance are the ways in which openness and transparency are changing pedagogical practice around the world. The traditional classroom and subject boundaries are blurring as learning takes place in global classrooms and social networks. I've personally been surprised by how dramatic this shift has been in courses that I teach. Peer-based and self-organized networked learning have impacted dramatically the role of the teacher. Students, with easy access to information and resources, are increasingly contributors to, rather than only consumers of, learning materials. Openness has changed curriculum, teaching, and learning. In the future, assessment and accreditation will quite possibly be added to this list.

The long-rumored arrival of a knowledge economy has finally occurred as economies shift to knowledge-intensive work as routine labour is increasingly performed by robots or automated technologies. The rise of knowledge work places additional constraints on higher education as the profile of students now includes greater numbers of individuals returning to university after decades of employment. In corporate contexts, learning happens through informal social networks as much as through structures of formal training and development. More than at any previous point in history, the learner is in control and openness is the driving agent.

Clearly, we are entering, if not already in, a golden age of learning and learning opportunities.

The substantial developments facing education—MOOCs, OERs, learning networks, emerging pedagogies, and knowledge work—present challenges and opportunities for academics and administrators. Fortunately, Littlejohn and Pegler have edited a roadmap and path forward to enable individuals to embrace these opportunities while navigating around challenges. This text includes a nuanced analysis of how openness influences learning across the range of life, work, and formal education. The reader is introduced to leading educators and academics who are at the forefront of evaluating and researching the changes buffeting education. Learners, academics, administrators, and business leaders will welcome this valuable resource. Littlejohn and Pegler's text weaves together a range of changes and trends and presents a holistic overview of what is happening across the multiple dimensions of personal, formal, and work learning, why it's important to pay attention, and how to respond.

Dr. George Siemens, Executive Director of the Learning Innovation and Networked Knowledge Research Lab (LINK), University of Texas, Arlington, USA.

PREFACE

Researching the reuse of resources in learning can expose an apparent dichotomy. Reusable resources are increasingly and obviously abundant, available in online digital forms suited to both formal and informal learning, yet the research evidence for reuse in practice remains elusive. We also understand little about what significance, if any, availability of reusable resources, including open online resources, has on learning.

The way in which resources are shared online has changed markedly from a decade ago, when Reusing Online Resources (Littlejohn, 2003) appeared. Then the emphasis was on sharing through large, central repositories, looking forward to federated global repositories of 'learning objects'. In this book the focus has moved from resource management to resource use and to how *social interactions around online, reusable learning resources* can promote learning. The move towards open networks and open resources has shifted the pattern of sharing and, with it, users, towards a far more distributed and unpredictable model. One of the challenges of the *diversification of how open online resources are created and released* is that the creators of the resources may be as unfamiliar as the form of the resource. We now talk about social resources as going 'viral' and courses as both massive and open, with reuse happening through recontextualisation across far wider groups of users, but also offering better fit with the needs of personal learners who are sufficiently self-directed. It is difficult to appreciate how the newer forms of open online resource such as the massive open online courses (MOOCs) will evolve as entire courses are developed and refined collaboratively with learners. What is perhaps even more challenging to predict is the *new social organisation of learning with open resources*, such as groups, networks and 'sets', and how these might support learning. By *removing conventional controls and boundaries around learning environments and sites* we are truly opening up learning. No longer can we clearly distinguish the teacher from the learner, the classroom from the workplace, or the creator from the users of knowledge. The *changing societal expectations around open access to learning resources and courses* present new opportunities, not just for learners and educators, but for people in all areas of society.

What these five social trends—changing expectations around learning, new social organisation of learning, increased online social interactions, opening up of controls and boundaries and diversification of how resources are created—may be leading to, whether learning in work, education, or more widely, remains uncertain and is a central concern of this book.

Why Write a Book About Open Resources?

The push to write this book came from the ORIOLE[2] (Open Resources: Influence on Learners and Educators) retreat in 2011. Whether to produce a book that would be available in physical form and published through a conventional academic publisher was something that we needed to consider carefully. Some authors whom we wished to invite seek to change societal attitudes towards copyright by writing only for fully open publications. We respect this stance, but our strategy has been different. We have been working with the publisher to move towards a hybrid model of publication. Why did we decide to do this? The short answer would be because we recognise we are in a transition period between conventional publishing with established quality controls and open publishing with new (more dynamic) methods to ensure quality. This decision has been bold and exploratory and has not been without cost. Our position straddles the worlds of conventional 'publishing' and 'open access', so we have spent long hours in negotiations with authors and the publisher around copyright and access.

We planned a book which would appear in conventional publication as part of the Advancing Technology-Enhanced Learning series and also be represented in open access publication: a special edition of the *Journal of Interactive Media in Education* (*JIME*). This move mirrors the production of *Reusing Online Resources* in 2003, where the book chapters were subject to open commentary and review through a special edition of *JIME*.[3] The original 'hybrid' model was in itself an experiment in open learning, knowledge creation and open resource release and reuse. The new hybrid model allows further experimentation. The open, online journal environment allows this work not only to be 'broadcast' to diverse 'audiences', but enables anyone, anywhere, to reuse and reshape the knowledge. Therefore the book and journal itself is an open resource and how its own reuse morphs to support learning and build knowledge is also of interest to us. The end result is a *learning resource* that was designed for you—the reader—whoever and wherever you are. We hope that you benefit from and contribute to this resource (www-jime.open.ac.uk).

Chris Pegler and Allison Littlejohn, January 2014

Notes

1 Littlejohn, A. (2003) *Reusing Online Resources: A Sustainable Approach to eLearning.* Routledge: London.
2 Open Resources: Influence on Learners and Educators http://orioleproject.blogspot. co.uk/p/project.html.
3 Littlejohn, A. and Buckingham-Shum, S. (2003) Special issue—Commentary and Debate on book: Littlejohn, A. (2003) *Reusing Online Resources: A Sustainable Approach to eLearning.* Kogan Page, London. ISBN 0749439491 http://www-jime.open.ac.uk/ jime/issue/view/28.

ACKNOWLEDGEMENTS

From the initial meetings during a set of conversations in a coaching inn in Woburn, England through to the wonderful writing retreat facilitated by Lou McGill in Wigtown (Scotland's book town), many people have contributed ideas and support to this book. Lou helped us frame our ideas for this new book, with Nina Pataraia then providing editorial assistance throughout the months of contacting authors, reviewers and liaising with the publishers. This book could not have happened without all of them.

The commitment and interest of our authors and reviewers has been impressive throughout and we appreciate the time and expertise that you have brought to the 'ROR II' book project. With such a wide-ranging area of research to draw on we have had to make many difficult choices in editing the book, but we are delighted with what we have all achieved and thank you for your insightful contributions.

Alex Masulis, our Routledge editor, has been massively supportive in brokering the agreement that we could publish authors' drafts for some of these book chapters in an open access journal. We are delighted that *JIME*, based at the Open University, will be that journal and thank its editorial board for this opportunity, especially Martin Weller and Eileen Scanlon.

Our families and friends have, as always, had to lend personal support and their willingness and understanding is very much appreciated. Thanks are particularly due to George, Rhys, Steve and Ying.

CONTRIBUTORS

Editors

Professor Allison Littlejohn (PhD) is Chair of Learning Technology and Director of the Caledonian Academy, a research centre exploring technology-enhanced professional learning in the public and private sectors at Glasgow Caledonian University, UK. Allison leads industry–academic research with multinational companies, most notably Royal Dutch Shell, for whom she was Senior Researcher 2008–10. She has been Principal Investigator or Senior Scientist in research in technology-enhanced professional learning funded by research councils, funding councils, professional bodies and industry associates. Funders include the European Commission, the UK Economic and Social Research Council, the Bill and Melinda Gates Foundation, Shell International, British Petroleum, the Higher Education Funding Council for England, the Scottish Funding Council, the UK Joint Information Systems Committees (Jisc), the UK Higher Education Academy, the Energy Institute. She has been Series Editor with Routledge (Taylor and Francis) since 2005 and has published around 200 academic articles, including three books on technology-enhanced learning. Allison is a Fellow and former Scholar of the Higher Education Academy and has received international fellowships from ASCILITE (Australasia), and the Churchill Trust (UK). www.gcu.ac.uk/academy/people/allison-littlejohn/.

Dr Chris Pegler has over 35 years of experience in education, working in voluntary, vocational, further education, university and local education authority contexts. She has managed and led a number of projects and courses in distance and online education at Warwick University and the UK Open University, most recently as a Senior Lecturer in the Institute of Educational Technology. Her research interests are in reusing online digital resources, including open educational resources (OERs) and Chris was Academic Director of the national Support Centre for Open Resources in Education and co-chaired OER13. She takes particular pride in her National Teaching Fellowship, awarded for work in online learning and resource reuse.

Authors

Jesús Alquézar Sabadie has been working at the European Commission since 2009, both on education and training and on research and innovation policies. Before that, he was employed by the European Training Foundation and Eurydice, amongst others. His fields of expertise include social sciences research techniques and labour market analysis. He is co-author of books such as *Migration and Skills: Moldova, Albania, Egypt and Tunisia* (World Bank-ETF, 2010), *Labour Markets and Employability: Trends and Challenges in Armenia, Azerbaijan, Belarus, Georgia, Republic of Moldova and Ukraine* (ETF, 2012) and several papers. He holds degrees in Sociology and Political Sciences and in European Politics.

Professor Terry Anderson is a professor at Athabasca University—Canada's Open University at the Centre for Distance Education—and is a former Canada Research Chair in Distance Education. Terry teaches education technology and research courses in the Masters and Doctorate of Distance Education programs. He is the past editor of the *International Review of Research in Open and Distance Learning* and the Director of the Canadian Institute for Distance Education Research. For more detailed information about Terry and his research publications see https://landing.athabascau.ca/profile/terrya/.

Helen Beetham is a long-standing advisor on e-learning issues to the UK Joint Information Systems Committee. She was a member of the Beyond Current Horizons programme, commissioned by the UK's New Labour government to advise on education beyond 2025, and has written or contributed to key national reports on e-portfolios, e-learning and pedagogy, digital literacy and open educational practices. A widely cited researcher and author, she co-edited *Rethinking Pedagogy for a Digital Age* and *Rethinking Learning for a Digital Age* (both published by Routledge), which are standard texts at master's level. She is currently synthesising outcomes from a UK-wide programme on Developing Digital Literacies.

Dr Magnus Bergquist is associate professor in Informatics at the University of Gothenburg, Sweden. He has published extensively on open sources in relation to competence and knowledge management as well as organizational innovation. Another research stream is digitalization of education and how the use of laptops in educational settings reconfigures space and place, integrating the physical and the virtual, which creates challenges for both teaching and learning.

Lorna M. Campbell is an Assistant Director of Cetis, the Centre for Education Technology, Interoperability and Standards (www.cetis.ac.uk). She has over 15 years' experience of working in education technology, where her main areas of expertise include digital infrastructure for open educational resources, open education policy, technologies for supporting the management and distribution of educational content, metadata, vocabularies, e-textbooks and digital repositories. Lorna has supported a large number of Joint Information Systems Committee development programmes and she maintains a highly regarded professional blog providing insight and commentary on issues relating to open education policy and technology.

Dr Jonatan Castaño Muñoz has been working at the Information Society Unit of the European Commission's Institute for Prospective Technological Studies (JRC-IPTS) in Seville since November 2012. He is currently involved in the Open Educational Resources in Europe project, which analyses current trends and future opportunities for Open Education in Europe. Before joining IPTS he participated in various research projects on the use of information and communication technology (ICT) in education, with a focus on higher education. His research interests include: open education, open educational resources and the economics of online education, e-learning, the digital divide and the link between ICT, process innovation and educational outputs.

Dr Jon Dron is a member of the Technology Enhanced Knowledge Research Institute and an Associate Professor in the School of Computing and Information Systems, Athabasca University (Canada's open university), where he teaches various graduate and undergraduate courses. He is also an Honorary Faculty Fellow in the Centre for Learning and Teaching, University of Brighton, UK. Jon has received both national and local awards for his teaching, is author of various award-winning research papers and is a regular conference keynote speaker. Jon's research in learning technologies is highly cross-disciplinary, including social, pedagogical, technological, systemic and philosophical aspects of technology and learning design and management. Website: http://jondron.athabascau.ca. Blog: https://landing.athabascau.ca/blog/owner/jond.

Dr Isobel Falconer is a Senior Lecturer at Glasgow Caledonian University, with interests in learning design, sharing practice, and open educational resources (OERs). She led the European OER4Adults project investigating OER in adult learning across Europe in 2012–13, and was a member of the Joint Information Systems Committee- (JISC) funded UKOER Evaluation and Synthesis team, 2009–13. Previously she was a consultant on the National Teaching Fellowship

Scheme-funded SHARE project exploring practice change among higher education teachers; led evaluation on the Planet project, which took a community-based approach to developing pedagogic patterns; and was Co-Investigator on the JISC-funded Mod4L project, which evaluated ways of representing learning designs for sharing and reuse.

Dr Sebastian H.D. Fiedler is a research fellow at the HTK Centre for Educational Technology, Institute of Informatics, Tallinn University, Estonia. He holds a PhD in Education (Educational Technology) from the University of Turku, Finland; a Master of Education in Instructional Technology from the University of Georgia, USA; and a professional Master degree in Psychology from the University of Erlangen-Nürnberg, Germany. His current research focuses on the emergence of historically new forms of digitally mediated learning activity in the creative economy. Sebastian is one of the co-founders of CERColl—the Creative Economy Research Collective in Tallinn.

Martin Hawksey has extensive experience of supporting innovation in teaching and learning within the further and higher education sector, working for a number of national advisory services, and is currently affiliated to the Association for Learning Technology. His current work covers multiple aspects of open education and digital scholarship, his knowledge of social networks and analytics being applied in a number of varying contexts including open online courses.

Professor Patrick McAndrew is Professor of Open Education and Director of the Institute of Educational Technology in the Open University. He has taken a leading part in the research and development of approaches to open and free learning. Recent projects in this area include OpenLearn, OLnet, Bridge to Success and the OER Research Hub. These examined a mix practice and research around the impact of openness. He has had an active role in over 40 funded projects across technology-enhanced learning. Professor McAndrew has a degree in Mathematics from the University of Oxford and a PhD in Computer Vision from Heriot-Watt University.

Lou McGill has over 20 years' experience as a Librarian in the field of learning and teaching. She became involved with learning technology in the early 2000s and has since worked as a learning technologist/educational developer, working on a range of high-profile programmes and projects including Digital Libraries in the Classroom (DLiC), Exchange for Learning (X4L), Repurposing and re-use of digital university-level content and evaluation (RePRoduce) and the Scottish Funding Councils for Further and Higher Education eLearning Transformation Programmes. Lou is currently an independent consultant and writer and has worked for several higher and further education institutions on digital literacies, open education resources, open badging and learning repositories.

Sheila MacNeill is a Senior Lecturer in Blended Learning at Glasgow Caledonian University. Previous to this post she was an Assistant Director for Cetis (Centre for Educational Technology, Interoperability and Standards, www.cetis.ac.uk), where her main areas of interest and work were around the user experience of using and implementing technology for teaching and learning. Much of her work at Cetis involved supporting a number of Joint Information Systems Committee (Jisc) programmes, including curriculum design and delivery, distributed learning environments and developing digital literacies. Sheila is active in exploring the implications and potential of analytics to support teaching and learning; the learner experience of massive open online courses, exploring the notions and realities of 'digital' institutions.

Dr Anoush Margaryan is a Senior Lecturer (Associate Professor) in the Caledonian Academy, Glasgow Caledonian University. She studies how people learn at work and how they use digital technology to support their learning. Dr Margaryan has led over 20 research projects, her work having received financial support from the UK Economic and Social Sciences Research Council, Shell, BP, Energy Institute and the UK Higher Education Academy. She has over 100 publications in technology-enhanced professional learning. Her most recent book *Technology-Enhanced Professional Learning: Processes, Practices and Tools*, was published by Routledge in November 2013.

Dr Colin Milligan is a Research Fellow with the Caledonian Academy at Glasgow Caledonian University. He has undertaken a variety of educational development roles for 20 years, returning to a primarily research role in 2007. His research interests focus on knowledge workers and the personal learning networks they construct to support their own learning. At the Caledonian Academy, Colin has been involved in studies exploring knowledge workers' learning practices in knowledge-intensive organisations; examined learning in connectivist massive open online courses; supervised a PhD student exploring research student learning by examining their employability development; and undertaken some more 'blue sky thinking', specifying Charting tools to support knowledge worker learning. Further details and links to publications and project descriptions are available from www.gcu.ac.uk/academy/people/colin-milligan/.

Dr Ebba Ossiannilsson, works at Lund University, Sweden, where she was recently appointed to take the lead for the university to go towards open education and investigate strategic missions related to e-learning. She earned her PhD from Oulu University, Finland. Ossiannilsson works as a consultant and board member in international and national associations and projects on massive open online courses, open educational resources and open education. Her research focuses on international benchmarking and quality enhancement of e-learning in higher education, open learning cultures in innovative learning spaces and quality from rhizome perspectives. Ossiannilsson is active in social media and networks on innovation in open education.

Dr Sami Paavola is a University Lecturer at the Institute of Behavioural Sciences, University of Helsinki, Finland (see http://helsinki.academia.edu/SamiPaavola). The topic of his doctoral dissertation in philosophy (2006) was on abductive methodology on discovery. His other research projects have dealt with metaphors of learning (acquisition, participation, knowledge creation), and the trialogical approach to collaborative learning. The themes of his research have focused on models and theories on discovery, distributed cognition, and collaborative learning and knowledge work. He is currently working in a project on the use of building information modeling in construction projects.

Dr Marisa Ponti, is a post-doctoral researcher at the University of Gothenburg, Sweden, and visiting post-doctoral researcher at the University of Oslo, Norway. Her research focuses on the peer-to-peer learning environments and examines the challenges and opportunities offered by the use of open educational resources (OERs), crowdsourced evaluation, and Questions and Answers social networks. Other research interests include the use of digital technologies to support and inspire forms of peer production, such as citizen science initiatives and design of OERs.

Dr Yves Punie is senior scientist at the European Commission Institute for Prospective Technological Studies (IPTS) based in Seville. Currently, he is leading the IPTS research and policy activities on ICT for Learning and Inclusion. Before joining the IPTS in 2001, he was interim Assistant Professor at the Free University of Brussels (VUB) and senior researcher at SMIT (Studies on Media, Information and Telecommunications). He holds a PhD in Social Sciences from the VUB on the use and acceptance of ICT (information and communication technology) in everyday life, also termed 'domestication'. He is a regular speaker at conferences and publishes extensively on these issues, and in particular, during the last years, on the use and potential of ICT (including open educational resources) for innovating and modernising education and training, as well as addressing digital competence and twenty-first-century skills.

Dr Christine Redecker has been working at the European Commission's Institute for Prospective Technological Studies (IPTS) since 2008. During this time she was responsible for several research lines in the area of information and communication technology and learning, including a project on Learning 2.0 (2008–10) and a study on the Future of Learning (2009–11). She is currently leading IPTS research on open educational resources in Europe, focusing on a Foresight study on "Open Education 2030". Christine is a qualified secondary school teacher and holds a PhD in Philosophy. Before joining IPTS she worked for several years in education, as school teacher, teacher trainer and university lecturer.

Dr Katie Vale is Director of Academic Technology, Faculty of Arts and Sciences at Harvard University. She is course development manager for HarvardX and co-chair of the Harvard Teaching and Learning Consortium. Prior to Harvard, she was Assistant Director of the Office of Educational Innovation and Technology at Massachusetts Institute of Technology, where she worked on the Project Athena, OpenCourseWare, and iCampus initiatives; and at Brown University, where she was involved with the Intermedia hypertext program. She holds degrees from Brown and Boston universities, and was a 2012 Frye Fellow.

Dr Riina Vuorikari has actively worked in the field of education since 2000; her main interest is dealing with issues related to the adoption of new technologies in education. Currently she is a fellowship grant holder in the JRC-Institute for Prospective Technological Studies within the Information Society Unit. Dr Vuorikari holds degrees in education (MEd) and in hypermedia (DEA) and her PhD is from the Dutch research school for Information and Knowledge Systems.

1

INTRODUCTION

Reusing Open Resources for Learning

Allison Littlejohn and Chris Pegler

Opportunities for learning are opening up. Societal behaviours and attitudes towards open data have changed, fuelling a transformation in how, where and why online resources are created, shared, manipulated and reused for learning. Open resources provide a substrate that can be reused by anyone, anywhere to pursue their learning goals in education, at work and through everyday activities.

This book aims to extend the discussion and debate on the potential of open, online resources to support learning. The book follows on from *Reusing Online Resources: A sustainable approach to e-learning*, published in 2003 by Littlejohn, offering a vision of how learners and teachers might produce, reuse and repurpose resources for learning. At that time focus was on the creation, release and reuse of digital learning resources modelled on conventional educational materials. Questions were raised about how these resources support learning, how learning and teaching practices and learning environments might change and whether the models of resource production and sharing could be sustained.

Over the decade since that book was published our view of how online resources can impact on learning has transformed. The open release of resources and data is viewed as mainstream, rather than a specialist endeavour, changing societal expectations around resource access. The open access publishing movement has adopted the terms *gratis* and *libre* (Suber, 2008) to differentiate levels of openness. *Gratis* refers to items available free of charge to users, easily discoverable and openly accessible. *Libre* refers to openness to more extensive reuse, with freedom to build on and change resources based on permissions granted by the resource creator in the form of open licenses. As the cost of accessing resources or barriers to using them may be a significant deterrent to learning, *gratis* resources have the potential to open up access to previously excluded learners. In education there has been significant progress in opening access to (*gratis*) learning resources in the form of Open Courseware (OCW), Open Educational Resources (OERs) and Open Courses online, including Massive Open Online Courses (MOOCs). Some, but not all, of these allow *libre* openness in reuse, for example by using a Creative Commons (CC) licence (http://creativecommons.org/about) to alert users to additional freedoms beyond those offered in conventional copyright. The Open Education movement of the twenty-first century (Downes, 2011; Siemens 2010; Wiley, 2010) has moved beyond these initial steps, not only opening up education in terms of access by end-users to resources, but also in extending what they are permitted to do with these resources.

At the same time there has been wide recognition that access to resources alone is not sufficient for learning and expertise development (McGill et al., 2013). Learning requires the active agency of the learner. One form of reuse of resources is by 'remixing', or making something new from resources created by others (Lessig, 2008). This form of 'read-write' activity moves learners beyond passive, 'read-only' consumption of online resources. There have also been significant socio-technological advances since the publication of *Reusing Online Resources*, for example social network sites such as Facebook (started in 2004) and Twitter (began in 2006) and media sites such as YouTube (initiated in 2005) now provide spaces in which users can interact around resources, and do so openly. People use these networking sites for learning across a myriad of contexts, accessing and sharing personalised, online resources to mediate the dynamic flow of knowledge and social exchange. As they do so, they draw upon their own hardware and software tools—which increasingly are mobile, wearable, ambient—assembling bespoke, personalised, open learning environments. Learners plan their own personalised learning pathways, rather than necessarily relying on someone else (a teacher or expert) to structure their learning for them. In these situations where learners plan their own learning, the activity is often not recognised as *learning*. Thus, to open up learning, recognition of what constitutes learning needs to broaden so as to include activity outside formal education.

Even the most promising structured online resources do not encapsulate the knowledge needed to support learning and development (Francis, 2013; Falconer & Littlejohn, 2007). The knowledge that underpins practice has two qualities: *scientific knowledge* which has meaning in itself and may be codified and *instrumental knowledge* which involves solving specialist, practical problems (Boshuizen & van de Wiel, 2013). Learning scientific and instrumental knowledge requires open interactions, usually with other people (teachers, experts, peers) (Engeström, 1999) or sometimes with oneself, though inner, mental dialogue. Examples of learning interactions around online resources include collaborative knowledge construction (Paavola & Hakkarainen, 2005) or resource design (Ponti, 2013). Here, open, online resources serve as a focal point for the co-ordination of learning (either by a teacher or expert, or by learners themselves), rather than as 'learning materials' in the conventional sense. The ability to know who to turn to for learning support becomes critical (Edwards, 2010a). These online interactions around open, reusable resources form a basis for new open learning practices.

This reuse of digital learning resources to support learning is the central theme of this book. Sometimes digital learning resources are perceived narrowly as educational content or online courses 'delivered' via the web. This is not our intention here. While planning this book and identifying relevant areas and authors, we considered factors that impact on the reuse of open, online resources to support learning. We began by reviewing published and grey literature, identifying interconnected social and technological trends described in the next section.

Social and Technological Trends

Socio-technical factors that influence open, online learning extend beyond the conventional boundaries of education. These factors generally are associated with social cohesion, socio-economic inclusion as well as technological and economic growth in society.

Changing Societal Expectations Around Open Access to Learning Resources and Courses

The focus of open education movements historically has been on using technologies to extend learning support to students who could not easily have accessed university education otherwise. For example, UNESCO's Education for All initiative (UNESCO, 2014) has, for almost 25 years, been working towards providing 'quality, basic free-of-charge education for all', placing Open Educational Resources (OER) and open courses as central to achieving this ambition. Widening access to resources and courses or removing charges to ensure learning is free of charge (*gratis*) can be viewed as an extension of the open learning movement of the twentieth century (Lewis, 1993), during which very large open universities, or mega-universities, were established, initially in the UK and later in India, South Africa, China and elsewhere (Daniel, 1996). However, resources and learning opportunities were offered only to conventionally registered students of the 'open' institution. More recent models of open education include learners who are not registered students at a single institution, extending participation in education. For example, by sampling open courses from across several sources, learners can gain an OERUniversity degree (http://wikieducator.org/OERu/Home). Alternatively, learners can participate in stand-alone courses presented as a MOOC or learn by reusing OCW (www.ocwconsortium.org/).

Significant financial support has been channelled into extending open education by benefactors such as the William and Flora Hewlitt foundation, who provided $11 million of funding to help establish the Massachusetts Institute of Technology (MIT) OCW initiative (MIT, 2001; Vale & Long, 2003) and have continued to invest in OERs. The potential to translate resources into other languages, taking advantage of the *libre* nature of OERs, has resulted in translations of MIT OCW into 10 languages, including Spanish, Portuguese, Chinese, French, German, Vietnamese and Ukrainian; also support to teachers to help them adapt OERs to different cultural teaching contexts, for example the Teacher Education in sub-Saharan Africa (TESSA) and TESS-India projects (www.tess-india.edu.in/), have further increased the reuse of open resources available. There is an appreciation that resources for open learning may not resemble conventional educational resources, not only in form and use, but also in the level of unpredictability about how they will develop in the hands of others (McGill et al., 2013).

The high level of political and philanthropic support has given rise to expectations about what reuse of open resources can achieve in helping those who would otherwise be excluded from high-quality learning activity. Whether these expectations take fully into account all problems that learners may encounter when using open resources is a subject which several of the chapters in this book address.

What has been achieved is that institutions which would not formerly have been considered to be 'open' universities, including some of the most prestigious universities worldwide, are opening up courses as MOOCs or as OCW (www. ocwconsortium.org/). Other respected organisations are also releasing open resources, including some multinational companies, professional and government bodies as well as third sector organisations (McGill et al., 2013). Motivations to release resources range from providing professional development materials for members or employees to marketisation and reputation building (Falconer, Littlejohn, McGill, & Beetham, 2012).

Reliance on financial support from universities, governments or philanthropists means that the long-term sustainability of these models of production of open resources is unclear (Falconer et al., 2013). Potentially successful examples range from payment or 'freemium' models (where basic resources are free but learners pay for additional services) to diversification of who creates online learning resources and how these are released.

Diversification of How Online, Reusable Learning Resources Are Created and Released

Perhaps the most startling difference between open learning online and conventional education is that online resources are created not only by teachers or experts. Resources are as likely to be created or adapted by learners themselves (Falconer, McGill, Littlejohn, & Boursinou, 2013; Weller, 2010). In fact learners now routinely learn through creating, adapting and sharing their own open resources, often as user-generated resources across social networks (Beetham, McGill, & Littlejohn, 2009). There are many examples from everyday life, such as blogging or commenting on other people's blogs; uploading resources to social network sites such as Facebook; sharing media through social networks, for example videos in YouTube; micro-blogging through 'tweeting' or 'retweeting' in Twitter; filtering and sharing online resources via social bookmark sites like Delicious; using tools such as Scoop.it to source, discover, curate and share relevant resources. What we see is a less clear-cut distinction between teachers or experts and learners in terms of roles and division of labour, with a shift in agency from the teacher to the learner (Beetham, Littlejohn, & McGill, 2010). This has arisen at a time when publication for a global audience, whether through YouTube, SlideShare, Flickr or iTunes, has made it easier to share resources without attracting high costs. In fact, open sharing of resources has become an everyday activity.

Nevertheless, open sharing does not necessarily signify open, online learning. Another critical factor for open learning is the freedom and ability of learners to connect not just with resources, but also with other people to draw from their knowledge and support (Ponti, 2013). Other people are available online to support learners, or alternatively learners can support peers, providing sustainable models of online open learning (Ehlers, 2011; Littlejohn, Milligan, & Margaryan, 2012). This shift in the division of labour of learners and teachers calls for a reconceptualisation of learning–teaching roles (Candy, 2004; Fiedler, 2012). However, moving from conventional learning–teaching practice to new learning practices that extend beyond the boundaries of formal education has proved difficult (Blin & Munro, 2008). This problem is partly due to the deep-rooted values and cultures engrained in 'schooled societies' (Fiedler & Väljataga, 2011). However, attempts to 'democratise' learning through opening access to resources without (at the same time) making effort to enable learners to self-regulate their learning could be ineffectual (Francis, 2013).

The Escalation of Social Interaction Around Online, Reusable Learning Resources

As the information requirements for operating effectively in professional or personal life become more complex, we increasingly make use of a multifarious mix of distributed expertise and resources. Some of these resources (now almost inevitably digital) are used as mediating artefacts or 'social objects' (Engeström, 2005; Knorr-Cetina, 2001), linking people as they work and learn. For example, studies on medical workers' work and learning behaviours reveal that online patient records are critical mediating artefacts around which experts within different specialisms collaborate (Engeström, 2009). These resources create a basis for inter-professional learning within the medical professional, connecting doctors, nurses, social workers and ancillary medical professionals (Engeström, 2013). Health professionals relate to one another and exchange ideas using an online patient record as a mediating resource and a focal point for their learning. Other health professionals are a valuable resource to support learning. As learners interact with people with complementary knowledge, they have to have the ability to know who to turn to for learning support (Edwards, 2010a; Edwards, 2010b). This ability to know who to learn with is termed 'relational expertise'.

Science researchers have further opened up relational practices through the use of open data and 'open notebooks' as a focal point for collaborative work and learning (Bradley, 2007). Fears around well-resourced competitors 'running away with findings' have been unfounded (ibid). Rather, meta-level studies, which had previously been impossible, have now become a blossoming industry providing important evidence for work in areas as diverse as epidemiology, meteorology and astronomy. Thus, open datasets are online resources that are reused for learning. Progress in sharing open data has been slower in the social sciences, due partly to low interoperability of data, ethical concerns and a culture of individual working. Some social scientists are attempting to change this by opening up data, process and deliberations, for example within OER research, which presents particular problems because of the fluidity in access to and use of open resources by learners (McAndrew et al., 2012).

These examples illustrate that learning has moved from individual problem solving and *knowledge acquisition* (Schmidt, Norman, & Boshuizen, 1990) to *knowledge building* negotiated with others around tasks (Engeström & Middleton, 1996), sometimes by interpreting a common problem, then finding appropriate responses to those interpretations (Edwards, 2010a), to *knowledge creation* through social interactions around open resources (Paavola, Lipponen, & Hakkarainen, 2004).

Examples of learning through knowledge creation are also found in education contexts. In the Digital Storytelling course (ds106) at Mary Washington University in the USA, not only registered students but open learners following the course create and contribute images, text and sound files, collaboratively creating rich digital archives, with encouragement to actively remix and share the knowledge resources created. The course could be described as a hybrid of 'open' and restricted access; some learners in the course are campus-based students, while others, who are not formally registered students at the University, participate and contribute resources. These may be ds106 'alumni' who continue to actively engage, as learners and sometimes mentors, across different course presentations. Facilitating learning by registered students alongside non-registered learners has benefits for both (Levine, 2013).

In the PHONAR photography course at the University of Coventry in the UK, learners initiated their own open magazine as a way of extending their open sharing and making outputs from the course more visible (http://phonar.covmedia.co.uk/). This course has attracted 'professional mentors' from around the world who are experienced photographers wishing to contribute to the course. These are not faculty in the usual formal, contractual sense, although they could be seen as having parallels with visiting speakers at a campus-based course. There is evidence from studies in work contexts that experts are motivated by attaining stature and respect within a community and that experts themselves gain knowledge from novices through working with them (Margaryan et al., 2009a; Margaryan, Littlejohn, & Milligan, 2009b). Another common feature of these examples is that participants learn through the involvement of those outside their usual sphere of work and learning. Capitalising on access to potentially massive numbers of people to support online open learning by drawing on the social, online interactions requires a rethink of the social organisation of learning (Anderson, 2008).

New Social Organisation of Learning with Open Resources

Learning in social networks, with potential access to massive numbers of people, allows reconceptulisation of the social organisation of learning in terms of structure, composition, spatiotemporal cohesion, communication systems and leadership. One of the most visible recent attempts at a new social organisation of learning in education is MOOCs. Some MOOC designs are based on networks driven primarily from the bottom up (OBHE, 2013). These structures are anarchic and require learners to have well-developed digital literacies (Kop & Fournier, 2011; Kop, Fournier, & Mak, 2011) and self-regulation abilities (Milligan, Littlejohn, & Margaryan, 2013). These decentralised structures sit uncomfortably in the top-down hierarchies found in educational institutions (Dron & Anderson, 2010). Other MOOC designs are based on classroom-based courses (Vale, 2013). Conventional, online course designs are more familiar to learners and faculty and fit more easily within university organisational structures. However, some designs have been slated for missing opportunities for social participation and knowledge creation within the diverse range of participants (OBHE, 2013).

Empirical research around sensemaking and the 'collective' conscious demonstrated how social software provides an extra dimension to learning, in addition to conventional interactions between learners, teachers and knowledge resources (Dron, 2007). Learners co-operate within different constructs, such as groups, networks and with the collective (Dron & Anderson, 2010). Their co-operation is dependent on processes of discovery, synthesis and sharing of fragmented scientific and instrumental knowledge. As learners build knowledge openly, the knowledge changes and diversifies (Kaschig, Maier, Sandow, & Thalmann, 2010). The significance of this form of learning is that it brings together the individual with the collective in ways that are impossible with conventional (closed) learning approaches and systems (Littlejohn, Milligan, & Margaryan, 2012). Early attempts to inform and guide the formation and operation of social structures for learning have been through learning analytics to provide users with a level of organisation, empowerment and transparency (MacNeill, 2012). Systems and tools based on analytics provide an organising focus for learning, helping to connect each learner with the people and resources that are important for learning, thus developing a personal view of learning which (in turn) relates to other's learning (Littlejohn, Milligan, & Margaryan, 2012).

Concerns around analytics have been expressed chiefly in three ways. Firstly, the use of analytics is a form of surveillance which requires the learner to have a sophisticated understanding of how and when to manage online identity or identities (Dron, 2007). There are legitimate questions about how informed the acceptance of terms for engagement with open courses may be. Secondly, there is a perceived over-simplification of the application of analytics that tends to equate types of systems with users and stakeholders and a given (assumed) power relation (Berendt, Vuorikari, Littlejohn, & Margaryan, 2013). Typically, analytics systems display aggregates of learner behaviours in ways that primarily address teachers' needs for evaluating performance. Thirdly, learning involves human interactions with the environment mediated by expertise, extending beyond the rational decision making afforded by systems based on artificial intelligence (Edwards, 2010b). Therefore, systems cannot replace human expertise.

Removing Conventional Controls and Boundaries Around Learning Environments and Sites

Online, open learning through knowledge creation challenges conventional controls and boundaries (Paavola, Lipponen, & Hakkarainen, 2004). For example, in open education where learners work together to build knowledge in MOOCs, formal learning activity is transformed as a direct consequence of the activity of the learners themselves. It becomes less appropriate to talk about students within open education environments and more relevant to talk about open learners and open learning engaging with open resources from diverse sources. That there have been other movements, outside education, based on open online activity—open source; open science; open data; open innovation; open research—emphasises the role that open knowledge building plays in a wider shift in societal expectations and behaviours.

Open, online learning extends across parts of everyday life or work practice which learners may not regard as learning at all. For example the textile crafts site Ravelry (www.ravelry.com), with over 3.7 million users (by the end of 2013), is centred on a user-generated repository of patterns, projects and discussions within which users create and share information about projects, techniques and practices. Users can conduct research, solicit and offer advice on techniques or photographs of practice examples, sharing outcomes from what is often a solitary craft activity with a wider online community to obtain feedback and support; a learning model similar to open studio working (Brown & Adler, 2008).

As policymakers consider the mechanisms that have to be put in place for open learning to have sustained impact, there is a recognition that organisations that provide formal education have to radically open up through strategic commitments to reforming and developing new infrastructures (Redecker et al.,

2011). Therefore, rather than focusing on access to educational resources, in this book we adopt the Vygotskian (1978) idea of learning as a complex social interplay of mind, action and practice mediated by different types of resources. In this sense, open, online learning crosses conventional boundaries, drawing on resources and people within and across different contexts of education, work and everyday life.

Reusing Open Resources for Learning

Learners use and reuse open resources across the contexts of education, work and everyday life. These interrelated contexts provide a framework for the exploration of reusing open learning resources (Figure 1.1). For example, the use of resources in social networks (such as YouTube, Facebook, LinkedIn and Twitter) cuts across these contexts, transporting learning activity, resources and insights across life, work and education spaces. Resources shared can be discussions and comments, images and embedded media or links to blogs, wikis and so on. Use of these resources involves interactions with others across the networks. The cascade of boundary-crossing resources shared openly is largely determined by individual learners and is unpredictable, but often represents a visible and extensive reuse of open resources for learning.

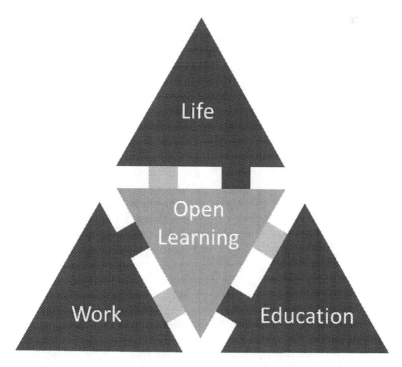

FIGURE 1.1 Open Learning Spanning Formal and Informal Contexts

In preparing this book, we assembled a group of distinguished experts whose work lends insight into the potential of open, online resources to support learning across these diverse contexts. These twenty-four contributors are distributed across nine different countries (Canada, Belgium, Estonia, Finland, Norway, Spain, Sweden, the United Kingdom and the United States of America). Their work spans *education, learning science, psychology, computer science* and *information science*. The authors contribute a range of thematic perspectives, ranging from *open learning; professional learning; technology-enhanced learning; lifelong learning policy; social organisation of learning; trust, privacy and disclosure; to socio-technical systems*. Their ideas are outlined in eleven chapters organised in three sections examining the reuse of open resources for lifelong learning, professional learning for work and learning in education.

The Sections of the Book

Section 1: Life

It is difficult to over-state the impact of open resources on the range and spread of learning opportunities beyond the traditional boundaries of educational institutions or workplaces. The four chapters in the section on *lifelong learning* particularly draw our attention to the tensions and opportunities that exist for open learners as a result of creating, sharing and adapting open online resources. These are changes which are predominantly connected to the effects of opening up the boundaries in learning, expanding the sources of resources, the types of learning and the motive and practice of learning. There is now a far wider pool of resources, learning experiences and activity online than would formerly have been associated with learning (Weller, 2011). These may not have been created intentionally as resources for learners or learning, but their openness to reuse increasingly allows this option. The ease of use and interconnectedness of network tools offered by services such as Google and others, the growing access to WiFi and increasing ownership of smart mobile and wearable devices make personal searching of the web in social contexts a familiar activity which supports learning in unfamiliar contexts and with new communities (Clow & Makriyannis, 2011).

Open resources may appear to have conventional equivalents, for example Wikipedia has some structural aspects similar to a proprietary encyclopaedia. However, the scale, open access, authorship and rate of change in entries are different (Messner & DiStaso, 2013). The open *libre* nature of the resource, the potential for users to engage directly in creating, editing, extending and commenting on the text, are the most startlingly different attributes of Wikipedia, which is based on user-generated input. This collaboratively generated open resource, produced outside the contexts of work or education, places demands on Wikipedia users in terms of the literacy required to reach informed decisions about the accuracy and appropriateness of using or contributing to a resource at a time when the quantity of this form of resource is relentlessly expanding: 'there has often been little or no charge for uploading user-generated content. As a result, the world's data centres are now replete with exabytes of user-generated content that, in addition to creating a corporate asset, may also contain data that can be regarded as a liability' (Wikipedia, 2013). Liabilities which are linked with use of open, online resources include concerns about rights status, accuracy, libel, racism, sexism and identity theft as well as concerns about spam and troll activity (advertising, false claims or abusive posts or comments). Social uses of the internet for learning, in lowering barriers to sharing online, also open up opportunities for posts by anonymous users which can include ill-judged online content. To share openly online is still novel, and new behaviour and the relationship of trust with others within social media can differ substantially, depending on context (Adams, 2000), with users often not aware who they are sharing with; for example, Facebook identified 68 million fake Facebook profiles (in July 2013). Issues of identity management have been recognised in online learning (Dron, 2003). The importance of learning context, intent and connection to other people are at the forefront in the four chapters within this section.

As the sources of open resources become more diverse there is a corresponding shift in the literacies that learners require so as to learn effectively and selectively. 'Digital literacies' are distinct from conventional forms of literacy, as these literacies can be expected to adapt and evolve rapidly throughout the learner's lifetime, in response to socio-technical changes (Littlejohn, Beetham, & McGill, 2012). Digital literacies extend to being able to learn and navigate within different social structures (Dron & Anderson, 2010), knowing not just what resource to connect with, but also who can support learning (Edwards, 2010a).

In Chapter 2, 'Agoraphobia and the modern learner', by Jon Dron and Terry Anderson, the choice of title suggests one of the dilemmas for learners who are seeking to navigate the pitfalls of open sharing within new styles of relationship with fellow learners. Anxiety when faced with the challenge and opportunities of learning within and across boundaryless, online, open environments is something that the 'modern learner' needs to conquer. The authors paint a vivid picture of how 'knowledge explodes through the network in ever-improving cycles of creation, consumption, transformation and change' as learners act as online authors, designers and creators in open learning environments. Dron and Anderson recognise that learner agency in open learning realises the potential outlined in the diverse learning approaches of constructionism, connectivism and distributed and social cognition. However, this also presents challenges for learners, particularly problems in terms of learner behaviour and confidence. This chapter raises issues about trust online relating to contributors or content—necessary concerns for social learning online in open systems which lack the usual safeguard within formal education of institutional checks and assurances. As the exposure to online, user-generated resources for learning grows, whether in formal or informal learning, these issues of trust are ones which several authors in this volume return to (for example, Littlejohn et al. in Chapter 8).

Dron and Anderson suggest a classification which differentiates between learners working within groups, nets, sets and collectives, where only one of these types (groups) is found in formal education. Through this typography they address what is happening as learners move beyond small, protected learning spaces with which they are familiar and to which access is restricted. As they point out: 'When learning moves into the open, parts of the safety net vanish.' Their groupings represent looser and less constrained memberships or connections with new demands on learners and in terms of social online literacies.

In Chapter 3, 'Open sourcing personal learning', Sebastian Fiedler presents a critical review of what he describes as a 'content fetish' around release of open educational resources through formal initiatives based in the developed world. This is, he suggests, too limiting an expectation. He points to the abundance of resources that already exist and the restrictive effect of adopting new styles of open resources without regard to changing the systems within which they are presented. While there is potential for open resources to support self-directed learners, he points to a history within formal education of using new tools to reinforce entrenched practices, drawing on personal learning environments (PLEs) as an example of how this has happened in the past: 'In an incredibly short time the whole contemporary discourse on PLEs became dominated by the search for technical solutions to the requirements allegedly dictated by the inner logic and demands of the overall system of "schooling"' (Fiedler & Väljataga, 2011). His chapter challenges us to not travel the same path with OERs, of emphasising the technology and the content while ignoring the potential to shift our conception of learning activity towards a 'new culture of learning'. Fiedler's use of the open learning model of 'hackers' as one classic example emphasises learners' agency in directing their own learning and creating their own learning environment. It acknowledges the necessarily evolutionary nature of online learning environments in the current climate of technological flux. While there are parallels between the Open Source Software (OSS) developer activity commented on by Milligan et al. (Chapter 6) and Ponti et al. (Chapter 9), Fiedler suggests that 'open sourcing' of personal learning is a particularly open approach to learning (beyond educational institutions or workplaces), drawing attention to the value that user-generated content in the form of 'networked accounts of personal learning' can bring: 'These accessible records of personal sense-making generally display a much deeper biographical and/or professional contextualisation than we could ever hope to gain from standard educational resources, regardless of whether they are delivered with an open licence or not.'

In Chapter 4 Allison Littlejohn, Isobel Falconer and Lou McGill offer a vision of open 'lifewide' learning, reminding us that learners can be at any stage of life and that their motivations for learning—and thus their requirements and contributions—will be diverse and subject to ongoing flux. It is hard for learners to be certain of what they will require over longer lifespans and with changes in the technologies and tools they use. This leads to the conclusion that the learner will increasingly need to control and personalise learning, as Fielder (Chapter 3) would suggest. This chapter also takes us further into consideration of issues of literacy and 'identity management'. In doing so it poses questions about how literacies, which are based on specific contexts such as discipline or sector, can be applied to open learning where boundaries are porous as open resources are migrated and reused. The chapter draws on Engeström's (1987) model of expansive learning to explore a future vision, anticipating disruptive changes in learning (culture, technologies, participants and motivations) and in the services that support and inform learning, from assessment to learning analytics. This chapter, as do many in this book, looks forward to how open learning may develop, but in taking a scenario-planning approach it is able to offer a bolder perspective on future open learning, while focusing on the aspirations of individual learners.

Any vision of open learning requires an insightful strategy. In Chapter 5, 'OER: A European policy perspective', members of the European Commission Institute for Prospective Technological Studies (IPTS) present recommendations for policy in relation to the Europe 2020 strategy to transform education and training across Europe (European Commission, 2013). Based on extensive, international workshops examining the role of open education, the chapter shares analysis of current trends in education, from schooling through to adult lifelong learning, exposing some of the challenges ('bottlenecks and barriers') identified in research and practice. For example, how can an appropriate international approach be driven forward when significant digital divides still exist, with some European countries exhibiting large differences in ICT infrastructure; for example, only 44 per cent internet penetration in Romania, as compared with 93 per cent in the Netherlands (2012 figures). This chapter offers several case examples of sustained and mainstreamed open education activity drawn from within Europe, but also directs attention to and makes comparisons with activity beyond, drawing on experience of systematic initiatives at scale in the USA (US Department of Labor, Employment and Training Administration, 2011) and Brazil (Rossini, 2010). In reviewing current, popular definitions of OERs, the authors identify people and content dimensions in these which reflect the blend of social/people and content/technical dimensions discussed in several other chapters in this book. The authors support the view that OERs play a part in making high-quality education available to large numbers at low cost, effectively breaking the hard links between quality, exclusivity and expense. Here the authors are concerned principally with the role of a public policy in ensuring that the fullest benefits of this next generation of open learning should be realised. Given the range of activity which is affected, they suggest that policymakers need to 'create framework conditions that allow all sorts of practices and business models, without artificial barriers to innovation'.

Section 2: Work

Many industries are founded on protection of patents and other intellectual property rights, which open access and open learning appear to challenge. Yet organisations, as well as many individuals working within them, increasingly use social networking technologies such as LinkedIn, YouTube, Twitter and large enterprise systems to support informal and formal learning. These systems may reach out to customers, clients, colleagues and even collaborations involving competitors. A frequently mentioned example of open resource exchange is that around open source software development, where engagement in the sharing of expertise online can be drawn on as examples of professional development and add credibility to a developer's work CV, even though this activity is directed at an open user base, rather than to a fixed organisation. The permeability of boundaries is even more complex where individuals work for several different organisations or are self-employed and have multiple networks connecting their work presences, as well as connecting their educational and social identities. Where a professional worker expects to move between organisations, maintaining a network on LinkedIn may be a more effective and robust way to establish a network to support their development and network activity than any enterprise system (Worthen, 2007), which they will usually be excluded from once they move employment.

A distinct shift in appreciation of the benefits of open access and open learning is increasingly articulated in publicly funded activity such as research or training (for example, US Department of Labor, 2011). This activity recognises that knowledge which had previously been closely controlled within the organisations which generated or created it could be of wider benefit to society if shared openly. This activity is often linked to initiatives such as open government, open data, open knowledge or open science which emphasise public involvement in publicly funded work. However as the chapters in this section show, the use of open networks within and across organisations can have direct benefits for workplace learning not only in sharing of explicit knowledge but in the sharing of and access to tacit knowledge.

In Chapter 6, 'Workplace Learning in Informal Networks', Colin Milligan, Allison Littlejohn and Anoush Margaryan focus their attention on informal learning within what they describe as 'knowledge intensive domains'—potentially the most demanding of learning contexts in terms of the quantity, type and instability of the learning required. It is worth reflecting on the informality of the most classic work-based learning example, the system of pairing novices with experienced mentors to support transfer of tacit knowledge through observation and interrogation. With informal online learning, and particularly open and online learning, the co-workers that the novice can draw on for support may not be co-located. They may employ online networks spanning the boundaries of the organisation, or the boundaries of their roles. These exchanges represent, using the typology of networks offered by Dron and Anderson in Chapter 2, interaction beyond the formality and safety of groups into more open and less controlled networks: sets, nets and collectives.

Drawing on their research into the practices of knowledge-intensive workers, Milligan et al. describe the individual's 'personal work and learning environment', one which blends the personal learning environment (PLE) with the work environment. This reflects a shift in workplace knowledge management away from reliance upon enterprise systems and towards a dynamic knowledge exchange through personal networks. Such connections can more effectively and responsively accommodate unplanned and unanticipated needs for advice and information. Milligan et al. recognise in this exchange the value of the knowledge-creation metaphor described in Chapter 7 by Sami Paavola as the basis for trialogical learning.

Milligan et al. emphasise social support via technical tools to enable effective informal learning. For example, the development of so-called 'charting tools' directed at helping users to expose and share goals in order to 'disrupt previously closed networks, freeing knowledge from internal silos'. The authors also note the potential usefulness of 'paradata', such as usage statistics and ratings, to understand the flow of learning interaction online. There are many links in this analysis to chapters throughout this volume, for example Chapter 11, by MacNeill et al. on 'Learning Analytics', Chapter 3, by Fiedler about 'Open Sourcing Personal Learning' and through use of the charting model, to Chapter 10 by Vale and Littlejohn on MOOCs and Chapter 8 by Littlejohn et al. on the tensions inherent in sharing open resources within closed communities. Such references expose connections in the concerns and interests underpinning informal learning across different contexts, whether in workplaces, educational institutions or lifelong learning settings.

Sami Paavola, in Chapter 7, 'Challenges of Collaborative Knowledge Creation—Work with Shared Objects', is also concerned with new approaches to knowledge practices relevant to engagement with networked technologies and learning. Paavola's approach to understanding 'newness' is set forward as trialogical learning design principles which emphasise the affordances that modern digital technologies offer. He values the potential for collaboration between learners, pointing out the differences between object-orientated collaborative activity and monologues and dialogues. In the first, learners collectively take responsibility for both the process and the product in their learning. Paavola refers to the challenge of organising work, considering informal work-based learning and formal educational contexts in his analysis. Observing that 'Human cognition is distributed in a fundamental sense', he refers to external (knowledge) artefacts and jointly developed practices. These could be seen, in some contexts, as having equivalents in some types of open educational resources and open education practices.

This chapter is valuable in drawing our attention to a widely applicable framework which recognises the existence and impact of uncertainty and the significance of object-orientation in online learning and particularly in 'knowledge work'. The framework is not yet fully mature, but offers some pointers to practice examples, drawing our attention to barriers to collaborative work, within short course contexts, which could have implications for the design of open courses, including MOOCs. Paavola also links ideas across other chapters in this book. For example, the challenge of newness in open educational research addressed by McAndrew in Chapter 12 and the knowledge work informal learning emphasis by Milligan et al in Chapter 6.

In Chapter 8, Open Networks and Bounded Communities: Tensions Inherent in Releasing Open Educational Resources', Allison Littlejohn, Lou McGill, Isobel Falconer and Helen Beetham review the networked and social online space in which learning as knowledge co-construction increasingly occurs. In doing so they identify a number of underlying tensions which policymakers and practitioners must navigate or address. This chapter is based on work in evaluating and analysing the outcomes of a large-scale programme of release of OERs. The analysis extended across eighty OER release projects based in over 100 universities and colleges in England and Wales.

These researchers use an activity system approach to analyse activity around the release of OERs in terms of their subjects, object, outcome and tools use, while also considering the implicit or explicit rules and influence of the social context or community. This approach allowed comparison of diverse projects while retaining a view of both the subjects (project teams) and the social context within which they were working. By coding and mapping data, points of tension, significant for a wider range of activities in other contexts, were identified. One example was the tension when academics wanted to restrict or control the way in which they shared content resources, sharing within familiar bounded communities rather than across open networks or applying limitations to the open license used (for example by adding non-commercial or no-derivatives qualifiers) (http://creativecommons.org/licenses). To share resources openly, without limits, is the ideal because this not only increases the prospect of reuse, and if necessary repurposing, but it also recognises the inherent unpredictability in reuse of open resources and the potential positive consequences. For example, disallowing derivatives would prevent translation into another language, an unanticipated but potentially positive derivative. There is an important tension between freedom to reuse (openness) and desire to maintain control of the resource, particularly when stepping beyond familiar communities with which trust has already been established. The chapter authors advise that change within communities may be an initial (although self-limiting) stage. They provide suggestions about how change in and of work-based communities could be approached, but also recognise that learners too have to change, as will social, economic and political systems and how they perceive 'learner agency and learner-teacher roles'.

Section 3: Education

The final section of this book focuses on open resources in *education*, gathering chapters which examine how open courses might be designed, how their use might be better understood using analytics and how the peculiar demands of open education research can be met through agile research methods. Each chapter looks at some aspect of using open resources, but no chapters focus on the creation and sharing of OERs as content. The provision of open resources as assets for learning, useful though this may be, is too narrow to illustrate the full potential of open resource reuse.

The previous sections indicated underlying the tensions of attempting to change teaching practices disruptively through reuse of OERs, indicating that, as with other workplaces and novel technologies, resistance is likely to occur without careful support and alignment of new practice with existing needs and motivations. As Pegler (2012) has pointed out, the alignment of technology, appropriate quality and the purpose for which reuse is proposed are significant interconnected factors in ensuring that reuse of online resources occurs.

Chapter 9, by Marisa Ponti, Magnus Bergquist and Ebba Ossiannilsson, touches directly on OER activity, in contrast to other chapters, which have explored openness as a connected but not focal activity. These authors write within the area of design across learning contexts, a test for reuse which, with open resource activity, may cross boundaries of discipline or geography. They identify matters of concern (Latour, 2005) related to open educational resource design, including some which address openness directly and intentionally, rather than peripherally or accidentally, a link to the problems of designing for uncertainty identified by Paavola in Chapter 7. Focus on the act of *designing*, rather than characteristics of the resource or designer, identifies differences between design of open source software (OSS) and the design of OERs. While the matters of concern for both activities may appear similar, there is an established culture in the OSS community, with motivation to collaborate on design, which OER providers lack. OSS participants operate within a similar disciplinary context (software development), while OER 'developers' can be drawn from any discipline and any level of knowledge, from primary to tertiary education and beyond. A valuable distinction is made here between the context of the original OER designs, which the authors describe as arising in 'project time' and the (usually) later period of use or reuse in 'user time'. The design approach of the OSS community fosters 'continuous participation and contribution' (Gasser, Scacchi, Penne, & Ripoche, 2003). Indeed, OSS provides an excellent example of informal learning by knowledge workers, explored in Chapter 6. For OER users and creators a considerable period may intervene between project and use time and there is often no clear path to maintaining resources once they have been published.

The authors emphasise that OER activity is 'intertwining' of design, learning and use, proposing a 'collaboratively organised world [in which] learners and educators can generate new ideas, learn from new concepts, build and test models, analyse solutions, and revise ideas'. This is a powerful picture of active, creative, emergent and disruptive 'read-write' activity involving learners and teachers with no sense of hierarchy or central control. The authors offer in this a networked and social view of open educational resource design activity. Indeed they stress that the design ideal is for users to be able to address unanticipated issues and to actively experiment and recontextualise open content even though they are not technical experts. Parallels can be identified with learning through knowledge creation by Paavola (in Chapter 7) and informal learning for work discussed in Milligan et al. (in Chapter 6), as well as some similarity in the consideration of responsive software development approaches in OER design with the 'agile' approach applied to OER research by McAndrew in Chapter 12.

From this broad view of design, in Chapter 10 Katie Vale and Allison Littlejohn focus on a specific instantiation of design, presenting insight into the design of MOOCs through a series of institutional case examples drawn from Harvard University in the USA. The authors move discussion from consideration of the individual learner and educator to institutional and governmental positions on 'open'. Drawing attention to the control exerted by government and society over 'cultural definitions of learning' and institutional reluctance to 'redraw business and workflow examples', they present and analyse examples from practice which push the boundaries of professional practice in conventional, campus-based educational institutions. Using five case studies from HarvardX MOOCs, they raise questions about future business and sustainability models for MOOCs that are still being considered and formulated. Concerns around inflexible organisational structures of universities and expectations of faculty and learners echo anxieties expressed by Fiedler (Chapter 3) that many focus on educational content, missing opportunities to empower learners to self-direct their own learning. However, self-direction could trigger a significant shift in the position of the academy in society, therefore universities are likely to exert influence on MOOC development. Also the uncertainty about what MOOC models may leave as legacy, or what they may develop into, is clear both in this chapter and in the earlier chapter on policy (Sabadie et al., Chapter 5 in this book).

Learning analytics offer, through deeper and richer mining of complex data, assistance to learners, teachers and researchers seeking to understand and interpret online learning activity or to put in place targeted interventions. In Chapter 11, 'Analytics for education', Sheila MacNeill, Lorna Campbell and Martin Hawksey examine the role that learning analytics may play in supporting, informing and understanding open education. The chapter provides a background to learning analytics, including consideration of their role in relation to commercial learning platforms and the rationale for their use to support teaching and learning management activity. For example, analytics can be used to offer information to individual learners about their own learning behaviours as well as the behaviours of their peers. However, analytics tends to focus on *education* activity, informing teaching activity, learning management (for example, marketing and recruitment of courses) and education administration, missing opportunities to inform *learning*. The potential of analytics to interpret and serve open learning activity from the perspective of the open learner in contexts beyond education is yet to be realised. Paradata, data about how a resource is used, by whom and in what context, offers some value, but only within limited teaching contexts, rather than the wider landscape of learning outside courses where metadata is used to describe 'content'.

In Chapter 12, 'Agile Research', Patrick McAndrew surfaces the peculiar uncertainties of researching OER activity, highlighting the problems that fully open systems (those systems without requirement to register to use) offer to tracking learner activity and the pressures that policymakers and funders put upon people who research OERs to address complex research questions within impossibly short timescales. McAndrew suggests an agile approach to research, using social media to disseminate findings, and encourages quick review and revision as further data becomes available and hypotheses are tested and rejected.

What We Hope You Will Gain from the Book

Our aim in assembling this book was to review and question the relationship between reusing resources and learning, signalling future directions the field may take. The chapter authors help us to explore what needs to happen for the potential of open resources to transform learning, for the promise to be realised. Given the significance of changes over the past decade since *Reusing Online Resources* (Littlejohn, 2003) was published, we can anticipate that many questions about the focus of open learning will be identified and addressed in the next decade. Several such areas of focus are emerging in these chapters. We hope you benefit from reading this book—as we have benefitted from editing the chapters—and will gain insight from the different perspectives they offer on reusing open resources in education, work and lifelong learning.

References

Adams, A. (2000). 'Multimedia information changes the whole privacy ballgame', *Proceedings of CFP'00*, Computers Freedom and Privacy: Challenging the Assumptions, Toronto, ACM Press, pp. 25–32.

Anderson, T. (2008). Towards a theory of online learning. Chapter 2 in *Theory and practice of online learning*, 45–74, 2nd Edition. Edmunton: AU Press.

Beetham, H., McGill, L., & Littlejohn, A. (2009). Thriving in the 21st century: Learning literacies for the digital age, LLiDA project Final Report, JISC. Available from: www.jisc.ac.uk/media/documents/projects/llidareportjune2009.pdf.

Beetham, H., Littlejohn, A., & McGill, L. (2010). Beyond competence: Digital literacies as knowledge practices, and implications for learner development, ESRC Seminar Series Literacies for the Digital University (LiDU), February 2010. Available from: http://kn.open.ac.uk/LiDU/Seminar2/Beetham_et_al_paper.doc.

Berendt, B., Vuorikari, R., Littlejohn, A., & Margaryan, A. (2013). Learning analytics. In A. Littlejohn, & A. Margaryan (2013) (Eds.), *Technology-enhanced professional learning: Processes, practices and tools.* London, UK: Routledge.

Blin, F., & Munro, M. (2008). Why hasn't technology disrupted academics' teaching practices? Understanding resistance to change through the lens of activity theory. *Computers & Education, 50*(2), 475490.

Boshuizen, H. P. A., & van de Wiel, M. W. J. (2013). Expertise development through schooling and work. In A. Littlejohn, & A. Margaryan (2013) (Eds.), *Technology-enhanced professional learning: Processes, practices and tools.* London, UK: Routledge.

Bradley, J. C. (2007). Open notebook science using blogs and wikis, *Nature Precedings.* Available from: http://precedings.nature.com/documents/39/version/1.

Brown, J. S., & Adler, R. P. (2008). Minds on fire: Open education, the long tail, and learning 2.0. *Educause Review, 43*(1), 16–20. https://net.educause.edu/ir/library/pdf/ERM0811.pdf.

Candy, P. (2004). Linking thinking: Self-directed learning in the digital age. Department of Education, Science and Training, Australian Government, Canberra. (http://www.voced.edu.au/content/ngv31516).

Clow, D., & Makriyannis, E. (2011). iSpot analysed: Participatory learning and reputation. In *Proceedings of the 1st International Conference on Learning Analytics and Knowledge*, Banff, Alberta, Canada, 28 February–1 March 2011, pp. 34–43.

Daniel, J. (1996). *Mega-universities and Knowledge Media: Technology Strategies for Higher Education.* London: Kogan Page.

Downes, S. (2011). The OER debate in full. Collection of WSIS forum posts on Half an Hour blog 08 May. Retrieved from http://halfanhour.blogspot.co.uk/2011/05/oer-debate-in-full.html.

Dron, J. (2003). The blog and the borg: A collective approach to e-learning. In *World Conference on E-Learning in Corporate, Government, Healthcare, and Higher Education* (Vol. 2003, No. 1, pp. 440–443). Phoenix, Arizona, USA.

Dron, J. (2007). *Control and constraint in e-learning: Choosing when to choose.* London: Ideas GroupPublishing.

Dron, J., & Anderson, T. (2010). How the crowd can teach. Chapter 1 in *Handbook of research on social software and developing community ontologies*, 1–17. Hatzipanagos, S., & Warburton, S. (Eds.). London: IGI Global, Ideas Group Publishing

Edwards, A. (2010a). Learning how to know who: Professional learning for expansive practice between organizations. In S. R. Ludvigsen., A. Lund., I. Rasmussen., & R. Säljö (Eds.), *Learning across sites: New tools, infrastructures and practices.* New York: Taylor & Francis.

Edwards, A. (2010b). *Being an expert professional practitioner: The relational turn in expertise.* Dordrecht, The Netherlands: Springer.

Ehlers, U. D. (2011). Extending the territory: From open educational resources to open educational practices. *Journal of Open, Flexible and Distance Learning, 15*(2), 1–10.

Engeström, R. (2013). New forms of transformative agency. In A. Littlejohn, & A. Margaryan (Eds.), *Technology-enhanced professional learning: Processes, practices and tools*, Chapter 6. London, UK: Routledge.

Engeström, R. (2009). Who is acting in an activity system. In A. Sannino, H. Daniels, & K. Gutiérrez (Eds.) *Learning and expanding with activity theory* (pp. 257–273). Cambridge, UK: Cambridge University Press.

Engeström, Y. (2005). *Developmental work research: Expanding activity theory in practice* (Vol. 12). Berlin: Lehmanns Media.

Engeström, Y. (1999). Activity theory and individual and social transformation. Chapter 1 in *Perspectives on activity theory*, 19–38. Engeström, Y., Miettinen, R., & Punamäki, R. L. (Eds.). Cambridge: Cambridge University Press.

Engeström, Y. (1987). *Learning by expanding. An activity-theoretical approach to developmental research*. Helsinki: Orienta-Konsultit.

Engeström, Y., & Middleton, D. (1996). Introduction: Studying work as mindful practice. Chapter 1 in *Cognition and communication at work*, 1–15. Engeström, Y., & Middleton, D. (Eds.) Cambridge: Cambridge University Press.

European Commission. (2013). Opening up education: Innovative teaching and learning for all through new Technologies and open educational resources, communication from the Commission to the European Parliament, the Council, the European Economic and Social Committee and the Committee of the Regions, 25 September COM(2013) 654. Available from: http://ec.europa.eu/education/news/doc/openingcom_en.pdf.

Falconer, I., & Littlejohn, A. (2007). Designing for blended learning, sharing and reuse. *Journal of Further and Higher Education, 31*(1), 41–52.

Falconer, I., Littlejohn, A., McGill, L., & Beetham, H. (2012). Motives and tensions in the release of Open Educational Resources. Available from:

Falconer, I., McGill, L., Littlejohn, A., & Boursinou, E. (2013). Overview and analysis of practices with open educational resources in adult education in Europe review, JRC Scientific and Policy Reports, C. Redecker, J. Castaño Muñoz, & Y. Punie (Eds.). European Commission. Available from: http://tinyurl.com/pk6nuvt.

Fiedler, S. (2012). Emancipating and developing learning activity: Systemic intervention and re-instrumentation in higher education. Unpublished doctoral dissertation, University of Turku, Finland. Available from: www.doria.fi/bitstream/handle/10024/77017/AnnalesB351Fiedler.pdf?sequence=1.

Fiedler, S. H., & Väljataga, T. (2011). Personal learning environments: Concept or technology? *International Journal of Virtual and Personal Learning Environments (IJVPLE), 2*(4), 1–11.

Francis, R. (2013). The agency of the learner in the networked university: An expansive approach. In G. Wells & A. Edwards (Eds.), *Pedagogy in Higher Education*, Cambridge: Cambridge University Press.

Gasser, L., Scacchi, W., Penne, B., & Ripoche, G. (2003). Understanding continuous design in F/LOSS projects. In *Proceedings of the 16th International Conference on Software & Systems Engineering and their Applications (ICSSEA-03)*, Paris, France.

Kaschig, A., Maier, R., Sandow, A., & Thalmann, S. (2010). Capturing practices of knowledge work for information systems design. ECIS Proceedings 7–9 June 2010, Pretoria, South Africa. Available from: http://aisel.aisnet.org/ecis2010/7/.

Knorr-Cetina, K. (2001). Objectual practice. In T.R. Schatzki., K. Knorr-Cetina., & E.V. Savigny (Eds.), *The practice turn in contemporary theory* (pp. 175–188). New York: Routledge. Available from: http://kops.ub.uni-konstanz.de/bitstream/handle/urn:nbn:de:bsz:352-opus-81918/kcobjectualpractice.pdf?sequence=1.

Kop, R., & Fournier, H. (2011). New dimensions to self-directed learning in an open networked learning environment. *International Journal of Self-Directed Learning, 7*(2), 1–18.

Kop, R., Fournier, H., & Mak, S. (2011). A pedagogy of abundance, or a pedagogy for human beings: Participant on Massive Open Online Courses. *The International Review of Research in Open and Distance Learning, 12*(7), 74–93.

Latour, B. (2005). *Reassembling the social: An introduction to actor-network-theory*. Oxford, UK: Oxford University Press.

Lessig, L. (2008). *Remix: Making art and commerce thrive in the hybrid economy*. London: Bloomsbury Academic.

Levine, A. (2013). ds106: Not a course, not like any MOOC, in *Educause Review Online* 28 January. Available from: www.educause.edu/ero/article/ds106-not-course-not-any-mooc.

Lewis, R. (1993). The progress of open learning. *Education and Training*, *35*(4), 3–8.

Littlejohn, A. (Ed.) (2003) *Reusing online resources: A sustainable approach to eLearning*. London, UK: Kogan Page Limited.

Littlejohn, A., Beetham, H., & McGill, L. (2012). Learning at the digital frontier: A review of digital literacies in theory and practice. *Journal of Computer Assisted Learning (JCAL)*, *24*(4), 333–347. Available from: http://onlinelibrary.wiley.com/journal/10.1111/(ISSN)1365-2729/earlyview.

Littlejohn, A. Milligan, C. & Margaryan, A. (2011). Collective learning in the workplace: Important knowledge sharing behaviours. *International Journal of Advanced Corporate Learning* (iJAC) *4*(4) Available from: http://online-journals.org/i-jac/article/viewArticle/1801.

MacNeill, S. (2012). Analytics: What is changing and why does it matter? *Cetis Analytics Series*, *1*(1). Available from: http://publications.cetis.ac.uk/2012/511.

Margaryan, A., Milligan, C., Littlejohn, A., Hendrix, D., & Graeb-Koenneker, S. (2009a). Self-regulated learning in the workplace: Enhancing knowledge flow between novices and experts. *4th International Conference on Organizational Learning, Knowledge and Capabilities (OLKC), Amsterdam, The Netherlands, 26–28 April, 2009*.

Margaryan, A., Littlejohn, A., & Milligan, C. (2009b). Self-regulated learning in the workplace: Enhancing knowledge flow between novices and experts. *13th European Conference for Research on Learning and Instruction, Amsterdam, The Netherlands, 25–29 August, 2009*.

McAndrew, P., Farrow, R., Law, P., & Elliott-Cirigottis, G. (2012). Learning the lessons of openness. In: *Cambridge 2012: Innovation and Impact—Openly Collaborating to Enhance Education, a joint meeting of OER12 and OpenCourseWare Consortium Global 2012, 16–18 April 2012, Cambridge, UK*. JIME Cambridge OER 2012 special issue Available from: http://jime.open.ac.uk/article/2012-10/pdf.

McGill, L., Falconer, I., Dempster, J. A., Littlejohn, A., & Beetham, H. (2013). Journeys to open educational practice: UKOER/SCORE review final report. Available from: https://oersynth.pbworks.com/w/page/60338879/HEFCE-OER-Review-Final-Report

Messner, M., & DiStaso, M. W. (2013). Wikipedia versus Encyclopedia Britannica: A longitudinal analysis to identify the impact of social media on the standards of knowledge, *Mass Communication and Society*, 16(4), pp. 465–486.

Milligan, C., Margaryan, A., & Littlejohn, A. (2013). Patterns of engagement in connectivist MOOCs. *MERLOT Journal of Online Learning and Teaching*, *9*(2), 1–11. Available from: http://jolt.merlot.org/vol9no2/milligan_0613.htm

MIT (2001). Mellon, Hewlett Foundations grant $11m to launch free MIT course materials on web. MIT News. 18 June. Retrieved from: http://web.mit.edu/newsoffice/2001/ocwfund.html.

OBHE (Observatory on Borderless Higher Education). (2013). BIS Research paper No.130, The Maturing of the MOOC, Observatory on Borderless Higher Education. Available from: www.obhe.ac.uk/documents/download?id=933.

Paavola, S., & Hakkarainen, K. (2005). The knowledge creation metaphor—An emergent epistemological approach to learning. *Science & Education*, *14*(6), 535–557.

Paavola, S., Lipponen, L., & Hakkarainen, K. (2004). Models of innovative knowledge communities and three metaphors of learning. *Review of Educational Research*, *74*(4), 557–576.

Pegler, C. (2012). Herzberg, hygiene and the motivation to reuse: Towards a three-factor theory to explain motivation to share and use OER, *Journal of Interactive Media in Education*, March. Available from: http://www-jime.open.ac.uk/jime/article/view/2012-04.

Ponti, M. (2014). Self-directed learning and guidance in non-formal open courses. *Learning, Media and Technology, 39*(2), 1–15. DOI: 10.1080/17439884.2013.799073.

Redecker, C., Leis, M., Leendertse, M., Punie, Y., Gijsbers, G., Kirschner,P., Stoyanov, S., & Hoogveld, B. (2011). The Future of Learning: Preparing for Change, IPTS Report (Eds. C. Redecker & Y. Punie). Available from: http://ipts.jrc.ec.europa.eu/publications/pub.cfm?id=4719.

Rossini, C. (2010). Green Paper: The state and challenges of OER in Brazil: From readers to writers? Open Society Institute. January. Available from: www.opensocietyfoundations.org/sites/default/files/OER-Brazil-100101.pdf.

Schmidt, H. G., Norman, G. R., & Boshuizen, H. P. (1990). A cognitive perspective on medical expertise: Theory and implication. *Academic Medicine, 65*(10), 611–621 [published erratum appears in *Academic Medicine 67*(4), 287].

Siemens, G. (2010). What's wrong with (M)OOCs? Available from: www.elearnspace.org/blog/2010/12/19/whats-wrong-with-moocs/elearnspace.

Suber, P. (2008) Gratis and Libre Open Access, SPARC Open Access Newsletter, August issue. Available at: www.sparc.arl.org/resource/gratis-and-libre-open-access.

UNESCO. (2014). History, Education for All website, UNESCO. Available from: www.unesco.org/new/en/education/themes/leading-the-international-agenda/education-for-all/the-efa-movement/.

US Department of Labor, Employment and Training Administration. (2011). *Notice of Availability of Funds and Solicitation for Grant Applications for Trade Adjustment Assistance Community College and Career Training Grants Program, Notice of Solicitation for Grant Applications (SGA).* Funding Opportunity Number: SGA/DFA PY 10-03, Catalog of Federal Domestic Assistance Number: 17.282, www.doleta.gov/grants/pdf/SGA-DFA-PY-10-03.pdf.

Vale, K. (2013). Educause MOOC Case Study 19. Available from: www.educause.edu/library/resources/case-study-19-cs50-harvard-most-rewarding-class-i-have-takenever.

Vale, K. L., & Long, P. D. (2003). Models for open learning. Chapter 6 in A. Littlejohn (Ed) *Reusing Online Resources*, pp. 60–77. Ed Littlejohn, A. London, UK: Kogan Page Limited.

Vygotsky, L. L. S. (1978). *Mind in society: The development of higher psychological processes.* Harvard, MA: Harvard University Press.

Weller, M. J. (2010). Big and little OER. Paper presented at *Open Ed 2010: Seventh Annual Open Education Conference, Barcelona, Spain, 2–4 November.* Available from: http://oro.open.ac.uk/24702/.

Weller, M. (2011). A pedagogy of abundance in the digital scholar: How technology is transforming scholarly practice. London: Bloomsbury Academic Press. Available from: www.bloomsburyacademic.com/view/DigitalScholar_9781849666275/acknowledgements-ba-9781849666275-0000023.xml.

Wikipedia. (2013). User-generated content, 10 May [online]. Available from: http://en.wikipedia.org/wiki/User-generated_content.

Wiley, D. A. (2010). Adoption as linking: A response to the Stephens. Blog post on Iterating towards openness blog, 28 October. Available from: http://opencontent.org/blog/archives/1696.

Worthen, J. (2007). User management—users who know too much and the CIOs who fear them, 15 February, CIO website, www.cio.com/article/28821/User_Management_Users_Who_Know_Too_Much_and_the_CIOs_Who_Fear_Them_ CIO.

SECTION 1

Life

2

AGORAPHOBIA AND THE MODERN LEARNER

Jon Dron and Terry Anderson

Until recently, the implicit focus of most research into open education resources has been on *teacher*-created content and its re-use in different learning contexts. But, as decades of research have shown, the learning value and outcomes achieved in the quality of what learners design, create and share with one another and with the outer world, are of at least equal and often greater value than the content provided by teachers (Jochen, Guzdial, Carroll, & Holloway-Attaway, 2002; Johnson & Johnson, 1994). This chapter focuses on learners as authors, designers and creators of content in an open learning environment.

The growth of social media and the read/write web since the mid-1990s has created many opportunities for new methods of distance and blended learning and teaching in formal, non-formal and informal settings (Pettenati, 2007). From online university courses to Massive Open Online Courses (MOOCs), from networks of bloggers to informal learning on Facebook and Twitter, the read/write web and, increasingly, mobile social (MoSo) apps have enabled and empowered learners to teach one another, to support one another's learning, to model practice and modes of thinking and to be privy to vast amounts of learner-generated information, constructive dialogue and connected knowledge. Many popular theoretical models emphasise the value to learners of creating things in a social context including constructionism (Papert & Harel, 1991), connectivism (Siemens, 2005) and distributed and social cognition (Saloman, 1993). While varying in detail, all point to the pedagogical benefits of sharing the artefacts that emerge from the learning process. In such models, the more openly that dialogue and artefacts are shared, the greater the benefits are to all concerned (Thorpe & Gordon, 2012). This can lead to a virtuous circle in which knowledge explodes through the network in ever-improving cycles of creation, consumption, transformation and change.

However, the benefits of openness and visibility come at a cost of individual and social vulnerability. Stepping outside the protective cave of closed systems exposes us to both opportunities and threats. Learning is, by definition, a leap into the unknown, and the unknown scares us. In addition, increased exposure to knowledge also means increased exposure to ignorance and, sometimes, malevolence. Furthermore, when our teachers are other learners that lack the assured reputability of certified or otherwise qualified educators, there are risks of the blind leading the blind, of incomplete, incorrect or poorly presented knowledge. Because of this, in formal teaching, we have evolved many spaces, behaviours, technologies and attitudes that help us to create safe environments. Safety is a prerequisite of survival. Learning, in particular, has flourished in the sheltered caves – homes and, more lately, campuses and schools. Pedagogically, private space creates an environment for reflection, dialogue and production. Within this space we enjoy permission to make mistakes, to stumble and fall without fear of serious injury, reasonably secure in the knowledge that teachers and students and the tools of the environment will support and nurture us until we have become confident in the subject at hand. These spaces are often guarded by access controls, whether these be physical classroom doors or password-protected learning management systems. When learning moves into the open, parts of the safety net vanish. Things that we publish in the open may reify our ignorance and error, display our insecurities and misconceptions, and reveal our weaknesses to those around us. Equally, others around us who are sharing openly may be as ignorant or wrong as we are and, as learners, we may not have the cognitive or moral tools to recognize and distinguish good from bad. In this chapter we will explore the nature of this problem through the lens of our typology of social forms, which characterizes the different ways of engagement for learning that are enabled through social media. We will suggest ways to mitigate the problem and end by briefly describing solutions that we have been working on to enable learners to benefit from open sharing while retaining the safety of the traditional learning classroom.

Social Learning

Social engagement is a prerequisite of many forms of meaningful learning, if only in providing the context in which learning is incubated and sustained. We are hard-wired to learn from others, at the very least by mimicry. When actions are performed by others, mirror neurons fire in our brains that would fire were we performing the actions ourselves, acting as a precursor for learning as well as helping us to understand the intentions of others (Gallese & Goldman, 1998). Beyond that, we have evolved as eusocial creatures, in which our behaviours have evolved not just to preserve our individual genes but also to preserve the groups to which we belong (Wilson, 2012). There is plentiful evidence that the size and complexity of our brains is primarily concerned and correlated with social behaviours (Dunbar, 1993). Language itself may have developed, at least in the first place, primarily to facilitate social coordination, and not as a tool for thinking and reasoning (Provine, 2004). Research on social cognition shows that we may think and process information as individuals, but that our knowledge is held not only in ourselves but in others (Pea, 1993; Sutton, Harris, Keil, & Barnier, 2010). The value of learning with others, from others, through others and supporting others in their learning is fundamental and hard to overstate. But there are many ways in which we learn with others, some formal, some not. The growth of the social read/write web has greatly extended our social reach and introduced forms of interaction that, though they resemble those familiar to our distant ancestors, add new or exaggerated flavours.

Groups, Nets, Sets and Collectives

Over the past few years we, the authors, have evolved a typology of social forms within which a collection of learners might participate, in order to help to make sense of the ways that social media can be used to support learning. We created this typology not because each of these forms is fully independent, nor to imply that they are static entities, but, rather, to help us to understand learners' behaviours in these aggregations and to help us create safe learning environments that meet varying pedagogical and social organization requirements and opportunities. We identify three basic forms, the *group*, the *net* and the *set*, each of which affords learning and teaching opportunities. We also identify a fourth concept, an emergent entity that is not a social form as such, but that derives from the combined behaviours of people in these social forms, which we call the *collective*. In the following subsections we describe each of these in turn.

Groups Defined

The group is the traditional social form found in most formal education. It is instantiated in organizations such as classes, tutorial groups, seminar groups, cohorts, clubs, committees, divisions, faculties, schools and institutions. Groups are intentionally convened collections of people that have leaders, hierarchies of control and formal or informal processes that define how they operate. Groups typically have an existence that is independent of the people in them. It is possible to intentionally create a group, to design its rules, processes and norms, to give it a name and to provide roles for its members, even if it initially has no members. In education, groups used for intentional learning (often called classes) tend to have fixed beginnings and ends, and often involve a temporal process such as might be defined by a curriculum, timetable or project plan. The size of the membership of a group varies considerably but is always a measurable number. Usually group members know or have the potential to know one another's names. Groups are defined at least as much by whom they exclude as by whom they include (Shirky, 2003). They define limits and boundaries. Generally there are rites of entry and rites of exit. It is not possible to be an unwitting member of a group—joining a group demands intention and commitment. There are often social and formal processes that make that commitment explicit. Groups tend to engage in collaborative ventures, working together to achieve some goal. The teaching/learning goal is typically to achieve an informal learning goal or to earn a formal learning accreditation (or both).

Nets Defined

Many authors have observed a different social form from that of the group that is usually described as the *network* (Castells, 1996; Downes, 2005; Rainie & Wellman, 2012; Siemens, 2005). Networks consist of and may be described by the connections between people. These are often mediated and structured by social objects such as blogs, community centres or social networking systems like Facebook, LinkedIn or Google+. Unlike groups, networks are not designed, have no devised processes, no independent existence, no explicit hierarchies, no explicit leaders, no explicit membership—they simply exist as an emergent entity that is the result of individual connections between people. One does not join a network like one joins a group; one forges or drops a direct or indirect connection with another person or other people, and thus the network evolves. Networks have shifting and indistinct boundaries. From the perspective of individuals, networks are the sum of people with whom they have a first-degree connection, who are themselves connected with others in the same way to form second-degree connections ('friends of friends'), and so on ad infinitum. In a meaningful sense, this makes everyone on the planet part of the same network, connected at varying degrees of distance but seldom much more than six links away from anyone else (Watts, 2004).

Topologically, networks can be differentiated into different sub-networks, described by the different social and organizational roles they perform in relation to a given individual. We might, for example participate in different sub-networks of friends, colleagues, fellow shoppers or people in a geographical community, which may overlap or may be joined only because we form a link between them. The network of any individual on the planet is different from the network of every other individual because, minimally, they are the centres of their own networks while, to others, they are attached to branches. People in networks sometimes collaborate and sometimes cooperate, their independent activities benefiting others in the network more as a side-effect than an intentional process. Networks have been associated most strongly with informal learning in communities of practice (Wenger, 1998), fan groups and amongst frequent attendees at sports or cultural events or community hangouts. Online networks evolve and flourish, covering interests as far ranging as from astronomy to gambling, and tools such as LinkedIn and Facebook have been created to support and nourish these networks. Networks form the basis of connectivist models of learning (Siemens, 2005), in which the connections, interactions and reified learning paths of those in a network structure and channel the content and process of learning. Networks are the typical social form that underpins informal learning, whether online or not (Chatti, Jarke, & Quix, 2010; Wenger, Trayner, & de Latt, 2011). The capacity of the internet to reify and extend networks is akin to the power of writing to reify and extend language, or the printing press to do the same for writing: The internet does not fundamentally alter the way people learn in networks, but it greatly enhances the power of networks to support learning in both scale and depth.

Sets Defined

Sets are simply collections of people and their creations that share a common attribute. From an individual's perspective, sets demand no social commitment of the sort found in groups and no social connection of the sort found in networks. It is possible to be a part of a set without knowing anyone else in it and, indeed, it is possible to participate in a set without being aware of doing so. Sets are formed by the act of categorization: One or more people choose attributes that are significant to them. The way that people help one another in sets tends to be cooperative and involves sharing rather than dialogue: Things that individuals do are of benefit to others but not done *with* others. Once dialogue emerges, with the exception of simple one-off questions and answers, it usually implies that the set has morphed into a network. Indeed, one of the benefits of sets is as a means of establishing network and, possibly, group connections. Among the more popular cyberspace applications that support sets are public wikis, notably Wikipedia, media-sharing sites such as YouTube, public Q&A sites like Yahoo Answers or StackOverflow, the use of hashtags in Twitter and similar tools, and social interest sites based on categorized content curation such as Pinterest and Learni.st.

Physically, libraries and museums function as places for sets of people to share and grow a set of interests. Set-oriented sites often support both network and group forms as well, but their predominant mode of engagement is through sharing of artefacts and processes by people who do not know one another. More often than not, such sharing is open. Indeed, for someone to be a member of a set, the attributes that are of interest and that make him or her a part of that set must be visible to others. Sets are thus the pre-eminent and often pre-cursory social form for open, just-in-time learning—affording the discovery of multiple answers to specific questions and potentially catalysing the formation of networked connections to people with relevant interests.

Collectives Defined

Beyond the social forms of sets, nets and groups is a class of entities that emerge from collective intelligence. Collective intelligence can occur when multiple

individual entities act together in ways that mean they are most usefully understood as a single super-organism. This is a field with a long heritage (e.g.,
Bloom, 2000; Grassé, 1959; Heylighen, 1999; Wells, 1937; Wheeler, 1911).
We describe these emergent agents as *collectives*. A collective is not a social form
in itself but is a consequence of the aggregated behaviours of people in sets, nets
or groups. The collective is a distinct actor, an agent that emerges as a result of
collecting and processing the actions of many actors, a manifestation of crowd
wisdom and, sometimes, of mob stupidity. In social software systems, software
is often used to aggregate crowd behaviours, though it is also commonplace for
the aggregation to be performed by the members of the crowd themselves and,
often, a collective results from a combination of the two. Sets are of particular
value in collectives, and are commonly mined for likenesses between behaviours, personal attributes and preferences, which are used to distinguish one
set from another. Networks are also often analysed to discover relationships
and connections between people, activities and things. For example, Google's
PageRank algorithm aggregates sets of implicit ratings in the form of links from
websites to other websites, each of which is itself similarly ranked, in order to
provide an aggregate quality ranking that is used in displaying search results
(Brin & Page, 2000). The algorithmically collected behaviours of individuals
lead to a recommendation that is often more useful than any one individual
could provide. In effect, the collective plays the part of a teacher or editor
who recommends useful learning resources. Similar principles underlie tag
clouds, recommender systems such as collaborative filters used by Amazon or
Netflix, reputation systems such as those used by eBay and citation-tracking
tools such as those used by Google Scholar (Segaran, 2007). Collectives do
not need machines for their algorithms, however: The spread of memes, for
example, relies on entirely human processing (Dawkins, 2006). Similarly, we
may observe and be influenced by, and thence influence, the behaviour of a
crowd, whether in our choice of shoes, our participation in a Mexican Wave
or our decision to carry an umbrella (Earls, 2009). In each case, the combined
and largely anonymous behaviours of many people are processed to extract
patterns that act to inform, influence or constrain behaviour of individuals. As
those individuals are typically part of the collective that is influencing or con-
straining, this deeply iterative process tends towards self-organization, recursive
augmentation and dynamic evolution. The collective-augmented tools Google
Search and Wikipedia are among the most well-used learning technologies on
the planet, but there are also more intentional uses of collectives to augment
learning, including collaborative filters to recommend learning content, people
and resources (Drachsler, Hummel, & Koper, 2008; Dron, Mitchell, Siviter,
& Boyne, 2000), social navigation systems that aggregate navigation behaviour
to help guide learning paths (Dron, 2004; Farzan & Brusilovsky, 2005; Koper,
2005; Kurhila, Miettinen, Nokelainen, & Tirri, 2002; Yu, 2009), as well as
combinations of different kinds of collective system to recommend learning

paths (Dron, 2005; Hummel et al., 2007). The lack of individual ownership tends to make collectives highly amenable to openness and sharing.

Blends and Degrees of Social Forms

The social forms we have identified overlap and blend: All groups can in some ways be viewed as both sets and nets, all nets as sets (the set of connections) and most sets as nets (networked by their shared attributes). As they merge into one another, other identifiable social structures emerge that combine elements of these forms in different proportions. Communities of practice, for example, tend to lack the rigid boundaries, hierarchies and rules of groups but have structure, persistence and purpose, distinguishing them from pure networks. Tribal affiliations can be purely set-like (crowds of supporters of sports teams, for instance) but similar tribal groups such as those who share the same religious beliefs may follow rules of behaviour, recognize leadership hierarchies and exclude non-members, much like groups. Even within a conventional classroom, different networks co-exist, intersect, overlap and merge, as do different sets—people who self-identify as members of races, religions or who just share an interest in drinking, for example. From each social form, collectives can emerge that play roles within them.

Trust, Safety and Social Forms

Each social form carries with it baggage that can affect willingness to disclose, to share, to make open. With that in mind, we turn to the opportunities and threats to openness in each of the social forms in turn.

The Safety of Groups

Traditionally, the 'safe' social space provided by formal learning is the group. The group is a safe structure where mistakes can be made, concepts can be explored and learners can work with others in ways that are defined and delimited by more or less formal rules of engagement, often determined, enforced or moderated by a teacher. Quality formal education addresses safety concerns by the creation of a context through activities, tools and structure that support learners' trajectories from non-competence to competence. The rule-bound, process-driven and boundaried nature of groups makes this a relatively simple matter to achieve. When work is submitted to a teacher, for instance, there is an expectation of professionalism and privacy. Even when it is submitted more openly to be revealed to, say, a class or tutorial group, there are limits on the ways other learners are expected to react to it, especially given the reciprocity that is implicit in the group's shared purpose. Formal or informal roles within groups can make feedback processes more useful and effective. The often tacit rules of engagement that attach to formal education mean that challenge or criticism is not so likely to be taken, nor meant, as a personal affront but as a means to foster improvement. There is a flipside to this feeling of safety: That students are often unwilling to be overly critical of their fellows and even more so of the teacher. We and others have observed a pathological politeness in groups that can, on occasion, be crippling to intellectual stimulation and growth (Archer, 2003). This politeness to other group members (especially during group formation) often develops in cultures within which a personal challenge may be perceived as anything from an insult to a compliment, with the necessity of making oneself visible being the price to find out which.

One of the main disadvantages of sharing that educational groups engender is that any knowledge generated or artefacts created seldom go far beyond the group and, if they do, this is usually through regulated channels, such as the publication of graduate theses or prize-winning work. While, increasingly, teachers send students out into the wider world, for example to create or modify Wikipedia pages or to engage in virtual field trips on social media sites, such adventures into the wild and open spaces of the internet are often pre-scouted by teachers, and students are warned of challenges and of ways to maintain safety. Nonetheless, these voyages can actively discourage those who do not feel sufficiently confident to share what they know, whether or not such feelings are justified.

The implicit and explicit rules of the group ensure a well-understood set of norms and activities that easily create safe contexts for teaching and learning. However, this safety comes at a pedagogical cost of isolation, group-think, potential domination by teachers, a tendency for learners to delegate their learning and their safety to others. The tendency of groups is therefore to reinforce attitudes that counter openness, to create hidden curriculums (Ahola, 2000) and to keep learner-created resources to themselves. Their one significant benefit to openness is that work that does escape their gravitational pull tends to be carefully vetted and of potentially high value to others.

Safety and Value in Networks

Networks are built of people whom we know, though that knowing may not be reciprocated. Within them, ties may be weaker or stronger (Granovetter, 1973). The notion of weak and strong ties is, however, a simplification of the rich and complex relationships that we have with one another. There is a broad spectrum of ways in which we relate to people in our networks that vary according to context and purpose. This is particularly relevant to sharing, and subsequently to teaching/learning. The popular press abounds with examples of the problems that occur when photos or comments relating to personal networks are revealed to networks of people whom we work or worship with. People have been hired or not hired, and fired, on the basis of information revealed in a work context that was intended to remain private to a personal context. Because networks do not have the defined norms and rules of groups, our perception of what is personal or private may differ from that of others in our networks, especially among those with whom we have weaker ties. We have found in our own teaching using networked tools that fear of such disclosure can become a major impediment to sharing within a network.

Willingness to share is not simply related to the strength of network ties. Sometimes it feels safer to share with people whom we do not know so well than with those closer to us. For example, as a musician, I (first author) find it considerably more intimidating to play to a small circle of friends and family with whom I share strong connections than to a crowd of thousands of people, with whom I may share little or no connection at all. For similar reasons, conflicts of interest need to be declared in peer reviews of academic papers because those who know us well may give biased appraisals of our work, for better or worse, while those that don't can often be better relied upon to provide dispassionate and therefore (often) more useful feedback from which we can learn and improve our work more effectively. Learners themselves typically know with whom they feel comfortable sharing, to whom they can turn to for different kinds of help, who would be supportive in a given context and who would not.

Networks expose linkages outside of our formal group learning contexts, which can be a powerful learning catalyst. As Ronald Burt quipped 'People who live in the intersection of social worlds are at higher risk of having good ideas' (Burt, 2005). Extended networks are usually larger than groups; thus the peda-gogical benefits of being exposed, contradicted or informed by a novel solution or application during our learning increases accordingly, albeit at the cost of decreased safety. Learners (and teachers) need to develop network literacy and efficacy in order to know how much to share, to be confident in sharing and to comprehend the dimensions of the networks to which they contribute. Nefarious trolls inhabit network perimeters, looking for the vulnerable, and thus learners must be on their guard, yet also willing to make judicious commitments to their network, in order to reap its rewards.

We cannot end this discussion of networks without highlighting the personal esteem and gains that networks can provide for learners and teachers. Humans are attuned to the attention and praise of others. Recognition for one's contributions to a learning network can be very motivating and also results in increases in per-sonal social capital. This capital can be used to acquire services, goods or assistance immediately or in the future to enable and support individual, group or network learning goals (Daniel, Schwier, & McCalla, 2003). Successful learning in networks can be very successful indeed, and, the more openly learning is shared, the greater the accrual of social capital. Networks motivate the open spread of knowledge at least partly because of the social capital that some attain in large amounts.

Security through Anonymity in Sets

Because sets are concerned with topics and interests rather than people, in topic- or interest-focused public sites it is far more common to find user names that obfuscate the identities of the individuals involved than it is in more networked environments. For sites that are concerned with sensitive information, such as those supporting people with certain medical conditions, this provides obvious benefits, enabling open sharing, but the value carries over to other contexts too. Even where registration is encouraged and groups and networks abound, some people on public sites choose to remain anonymous. Anonymity can be beneficial in enabling a greater sense of privacy and non-disclosure. It may often be easier for a learner to ask a stupid question on an anonymous special interest site than on one where people are part of the learner's network or groups. Whether people choose anonymity or not, many appear to contribute and help others for altruistic reasons or, as often as not, out of simple passion for a topic. Of sixty-seven individuals identified as the top Wikipedia contributors, an internal Wikipedia study surprisingly revealed that five chose to remain anonymous (IP address only), though their edits were highly respected and their contributions were among the most prolific (Various, 2005).

Currently, among the more visible examples of set-based sites explicitly intended for teaching and learning is the curation site Learni.st. Not unlike Pinterest, on which it is modelled, Learni.st curators create 'Learn boards' that they then populate with a variety of digital content that they believe will be of value to other members of the set of people interested in that topic. Typically, the board will be browsed only by those with an interest, though some may make comments or re-pin content to their own boards. This spread of ideas mediated through shared objects is typical of set interactions. The Khan Academy provides a slightly more top-down approach to set creation but similarly encourages engagement: Each lesson is accompanied by a mostly anonymous discussion board. Some of the larger MOOC providers such as Udacity and Coursera operate a similar approach.

One notable downside of the relative anonymity of sets is that it is not uncommon for people to feel emboldened to flame and to act as trolls. The impersonality of engagement in sets can lead to comments and exchanges that are highly disheartening and demotivating for those who are, or feel they are, attacked. These same ideas would perhaps not be expressed so hurtfully within a group or a network, at least in part because of the inherent accountability for one's known actions.

Exposure of one's membership in a set may in itself be a violation of one's privacy. It really is no one's business if I belong to the set of Sherlock Holmes fans, but this knowledge may be of interest to book sellers. This is one reason for the prevalence of anonymity in sets, although the powerful data-mining tools that are now available render this a weaker defence. The potential loss of privacy and safety provides a compelling argument against making use of set-based and social networking systems within a traditional, group-oriented class of students where group trust remains important. The internet is a wilderness in which diverse ethical standards co-exist uncomfortably but often invisibly, and learners are particularly vulnerable. A solution is to supervise such engagement but there is a fine line between caring and becoming a helicopter teacher, hovering noisily and intrusively in ways that can be as pedagogically harmful as ignoring the problem altogether.

Another major problem in set-based learning is that (as the famous *New Yorker* cartoon has it) 'on the Internet, no one knows you are a dog'. Without the known roles in groups, or the assurance of knowing people in networks, the chances of getting poor or wrong feedback in set-based social forms are greatly increased. One of the most effective ways of dealing with that problem is to rely on collectives, which, happily, are most easily formed in response to the activities of people in sets.

Collectives as Teachers and Editors

Collectives, though comprised of the behaviours of many, are singular agents that are both human and impersonal. The crowd that pushes a page to the top of Google Search results, or whose aggregated rankings of books contribute to rec-ommendations of what we may or may not like, consists of an unknown number of unknown individuals, few of whom intentionally contribute to the collective, and those that do often have selfish or pecuniary motives: The collective is a by-product of other activities. Equally anonymously but more intentionally, Learni. st users (for instance) may rate or endorse individual items. Algorithms may then be used to search and sort sets and items in the set based on popularity, views or endorsements. This can be beneficial in providing meaningful feedback without the risks of pathological politeness, on the one hand, or flaming, on the other. While it might sometimes feel worse to be judged or ignored by many people rather than one, the objectivity of the many is potentially greater than that of people we know, and more reliable than that of individuals we do not know. Collectives are put to great use in a number of set-based sites such as Reddit and Digg, but are exemplified best of all by SlashDot, which employs a wide range of collective technologies to allow controllable collectives to emerge, includ-ing an ingenious means of self-organizing reputation through karma points, multi-dimensional tagging and nuanced categorized ratings. Collectives, when well designed, restore to sets and, to a lesser extent, networks at least some of the assurance we feel when receiving advice from a teacher in a group. One individual can be wrong, but many, at least when acting independently of one another, even (and sometimes *especially*) when not themselves experts, can, under the right circumstances, be more reliable than the best experts (Page, 2008). Of course, much depends on the algorithms that power the collective, the nature of the problem and, to a lesser extent, the nature of the crowd. There are risks that a naively designed collective algorithm can magnify the influence of the people whose actions are first captured, thereby making the crowd no smarter than the first person to act (Knight & Schiff, 2007; Surowiecki, 2004). Most col-lective systems that are used for learning are not designed with learners in mind. Also, the crowd must have at least some knowledge: A totally ignorant crowd aggregated into a collective remains totally ignorant. Collectives can and do exist within closed groups and proprietary networks, but the fact that they gain value when generated by larger numbers of individuals means that they tend towards openness. It is hard for any individual to assert ownership of the knowledge that collectives create, it being generated by everyone, and no one in particular, even though individuals and companies may own the systems that host them.

Controllable Disclosure

Skilful learners know when and how much to share and to disclose and in which of our social contexts this is both effective and safe. Just as physical spaces afford different amounts of security (from the home to city streets late at night), different network contexts and social aggregations share different possibilities and safety channels. Through training, reflective experience and exposure, students can learn to achieve the benefits of openness, while minimizing the risks. In part, it is a question of nurturing confidence. One of the marks of a successful networked learner (and indeed any learner) is the ability to be unafraid and unashamed to be wrong. Unfortunately, one of the problems of being in an educational process where judgement is the norm is that the rewards and punishments that drive the system are almost inevitably demotivating, for both winners and losers (Kohn, 1999). Traditional group processes, without careful design and management, can amplify this problem by encouraging comparison with others. Moving outside such a system, into the networked world, brings new reasons for fear: Loss of social capital, the fear of ridicule and uncertainty of what personal information may spread further into the network. The broader world of sets carries different risks: of being a potential victim of trolls, of having privacy compromised and of uncertainty in ascertaining the validity of feedback and help. One of the most important lessons to learn is therefore to recognize and deal with it. Another is to understand the potential for damage. Once genuine risks have been identified, there are numerous ways to reduce them. We have already mentioned the importance of gaining network literacy, and to be aware of ways in which private and personal disclosures can be compromised. Awareness of the kind of disclosures we make, and to whom they may be made, is vital. However, there are also technological solutions to the problem. We head towards a conclusion to this chapter by describing part of our own approach to dealing with the issue, which illustrates some of the value of recognizing the distinctive nature of different social forms.

The authors' institution, Athabasca University, provides self-paced undergraduate courses that are normally more set-like than group-like in nature. Students can join courses at any time of year and choose their own pace and time to work through the course process. There are thus fewer opportunities for the application of typical processes and norms that form in groups of learners following a paced course of study. A traditional solution to this problem has been not to engage at all and many learners take the word 'independent' in 'independent study' very seriously. For those that do engage with others through the institutional Learning Management System (LMS), while some safety is guaranteed by the explicit terms of contract which the university requires before system access is granted, this makes social engagement a pedagogically riskier affair for our students. The crowd is unknown, a set of people with shared purposes, some shared rules of behaviour, but seldom any explicit group processes and no innate networks. Some students do, nonetheless, form networks of colleagues and friends, and some go so far as to form study groups, which contribute greatly to motivation and the chances of success, not to mention the usual social benefits of learning with others (Paulsen, 2008). It is thus useful to embed the flexibility in our systems to facilitate and encourage the formation of these social forms and, through collectives, to make it easier for people to find others with shared interests or behaviours. To support this, we have created Athabasca Landing, an Elgg-based social site built to provide explicit support for groups, social networks and interest-oriented sets, and to utilize collectives. The Landing is a walled garden with windows: Anyone can choose to share anything with as few or as many people as they like, including the whole world, but site membership is limited to verified users and a few invited guests. This immediately creates a greater atmosphere of trust than might be found within public social tools and systems. This trust is further refined by the use of groups that are often used to support courses, as well as the ability for students to form social networks of those whom they trust, and to subdivide them into different sub-networks (or 'circles') that may be used to disclose selectively to different clusters of people with whom they are connected. The Landing's use of Elgg, a site-building framework that enables controllable disclosure, by default enables fine-grained permissions to be set on every item published. We have taken this considerably further, by allowing learners to create distinct tabbed pages for different audiences, including their groups, networks, sub-networks and sets of interest, each with the usual range of permissions available. Thus not only can they choose to filter the content, but pages intended for different audiences may have a totally different look and feel. They thus control not only what they disclose but how it is disclosed and to whom.

The Landing is far from perfect. It is all too easy for posts relating to one context to appear in or near to another. This can be problematic. For example, when students of a course in database management are confronted with posts from students studying radical gender politics, misunderstandings can ensue, and have done so, that make both parties feel discomfort and uncertainty—just the things we have taken pains to try to avoid. Of course, there are at least as many benefits to learners from serendipitous discovery of knowledge and people that would not accrue in a closed group LMS, but the balance between openness and safety is delicate and ever shifting.

Conclusion

Openness and disclosure is a two-edged sword for the learner. On the one hand, it brings the potential for engagement, knowledge sharing and co-construction, and the valuable feedback of others. On the other hand, it can be discomforting and sometimes dangerous, and what is shared may be useless or worse for other learners making use of it. There are few simple solutions to the problem, beyond learning to deal with it. Though some of the technological approaches suggested in this chapter begin to point towards ways of building systems to support learners in dealing with different social contexts and forms, technologies of this sort are always cyborgs, part human, part machine. It is vital that we, the human parts, learn ways of being, ways of understanding different forms of social engagement and of recognizing both the value and the risks of sharing with others if we are to gain the full benefit of engagement in social media for learning.

Note

1 The ideas in the chapter have been expanded in the book Dron, J., & Anderson, T. (in press) *Teaching crowds: The role of social media in distance learning*. Edmonton: Athabasca University Press.

References

Ahola, S. (2000, August). *Hidden curriculum in higher education: Something to fear for or comply to?* Paper presented at the Innovations in Higher Education, Helsinki, Finland.

Archer, W. (2003). Cited in D. R. Garrison & T. Anderson (Eds.), *E-Learning in the 21st century: A framework for research and practice*. London: Routledge/Falmer.

Bloom, H. (2000). *Global brain: The evolution of mass mind*. Toronto, Canada: Wiley.

Brin, S., & Page, L. (2000). The anatomy of a large-scale hypertextual web search engine. Retrieved from http://www–db.stanford.edu/pub/papers/google.pdf.

Burt, R. (2005). *Brokerage and closure: An introduction to social capital*. Oxford, England: Oxford University Press.

Castells, M. (1996). *The information age: Economy, society and culture: The rise of the networked society* (Vol. 1). Oxford, England: Blackwell.

Chatti, M. A., Jarke, M., & Quix, C. (2010). Connectivism: The network metaphor of learning. *International Journal of Learning Technology, 5*(1), 80–99.

Daniel, B., Schwier, R., & McCalla, G. (2003). Social capital in virtual learning communities and distributed communities of practice. *Canadian Journal of Learning and Technology, 29*(3), http:/cjlt.csj.ualberta.ca/index.php/cjlt/article/view/85/7.

Dawkins, R. (2006). *The selfish gene* (30th anniversary ed.). Oxford, England: Oxford University Press.

Downes, S. (2005). E-Learning 2.0. *ELearn Magazine,* http://elearnmag.acm.org/featured.cfm?aid=1104968.

Drachsler, H., Hummel, H. G. K., & Koper, R. (2008). Personal recommender systems for learners in lifelong learning networks: The requirements, techniques and model. *International Journal of Learning Technology, 3*(4), 404–423.

Dron, J. (2004, June). *Termites in the schoolhouse: Stigmergy and transactional distance in an e-learning environment*. Paper presented at the Ed-Media, Lugano, Switzerland.

Dron, J. (2005, October). *A succession of eyes: Building an e-learning city.* Paper presented at the E-Learn, Vancouver.

Dron, J., Mitchell, R., Siviter, P., & Boyne, C. (2000). CoFIND- an experiment in n-dimensional collaborative filtering. *Journal of Network and Computer Applications, 23,* 131–142.

Dunbar, R. I. M. (1993). Coevolution of neocortical size, group size and language in humans. *Behavioral and Brain Sciences, 16*(4), 681–693.

Earls, M. (2009). *Herd: How to change mass behaviour by harnessing our true nature* [Kindle]. Wiley. Retrieved from www.amazon.com/Herd-Change-Behaviour-Harnessing-ebook/dp/ B002M0HH84/ref=tmm_kin_title_0.

Farzan, R., & Brusilovsky, P. (2005, July). *Social navigation support through annotation-based group modeling.* Paper presented at the UM (User Modelling) 2005, Edinburgh, Scotland.

Gallese, V., & Goldman, A. (1998). Mirror neurons and the simulation theory of mind-reading. *Trends in Cognitive Sciences, 2*(12), 493–501. doi:http://dx.doi.org/10.1016/ S1364-6613(98)01262-5.

Granovetter, M. (1973). The strength of weak ties: A network theory revisited. *American Journal of Sociology, 78,* 1360–1380.

Grassé, P. P. (1959). La reconstruction du nid et les coordinations inter-individuelles chez Bellicoitermes natalenis et Cubitermes sp. La theorie de la stigmergie: Essai d'interpretation des termites constructeurs. *Insect Societies, 6,* 41–83.

Heylighen, F. (1999). Collective intelligence and its implementation on the web: Algorithms to develop a collective mental map. *Computational and Mathematical Theory of Organizations, 5*(3), 253–280.

Hummel, H. G. K., Van Den Berg, B., Berlanga, A. J., Drachsler, H., Janssen, J., Nadolski, R., & Koper, R. (2007). Combining social-based and information-based approaches for personalised recommendation on sequencing learning activities. *International Journal of Learning Technology, 3*(2), 152–168.

Jochen, R., Guzdial, M., Carroll, K., & Holloway-Attaway, L. (2002). Collaborative learning at low cost: CoWeb use in English composition. In *Proceedings of the CSCL 2002* (pp. 435–442). ISLS.

Johnson, D., & Johnson, T. (1994). *Learning together and alone: Cooperative, competitive, and individualistic learning.* Toronto, Canada: Allyn and Bacon.

Knight, B. G., & Schiff, N. (2007). Momentum and Social Learning in Presidential Primaries. Brown University/National Bureau of Economic Research.

Kohn, A. (1999). *Punished by rewards: The trouble with gold stars, incentive plans, A's, praise, and other bribes* [Kindle version]. Retrieved from www.amazon.com/ Punished-Rewards-Trouble-Incentive-ebook/dp/B004MYFLDG/.

Koper, R. (2005). Increasing learner retention in a simulated learning network using indirect social interaction. *Journal of Artificial Societies and Social Simulation, 8*(2), http://jasss. soc.surrey.ac.uk/8/2/5.html.

Kurhila, J., Miettinen, M., Nokelainen, P., & Tirri, H. (2002, October). *Use of social navigation features in collaborative E-Learning.* Paper presented at the E-Learn, Montreal, Canada.

Page, S. E. (2008). *The difference: How the power of diversity creates better groups, firms, schools, and societies (New Edition)* [Kindle version]. Retrieved from www.amazon.com/ The-Difference-Diversity-Societies-ebook/dp/B003TFELFI/.

Papert, S., & Harel, I. (1991). Situating constructionism. In S. Papert & I. Harel (Eds.), *Constructionism.* Wesport, CT: Ablex Publishing Corporation.

Paulsen, M. F. (2008). Cooperative online education. *SeminarNet, 4*(2), http://seminar.net/index. php/volume-4-issue-2-2008-previousissuesmeny-124/100-cooperative-online-education.

Pea, R. (1993). Practices of distributed intelligence and designs for education. In G. Saloman (Ed.), *Distributed cognitions: Psychological and educational considerations* (pp. 47–87). Cambridge, England: Cambridge University Press.

Pettenati, M. (2007). Social networking theories and tools to support connectivist learning activities. *International Journal of Web-Based Learning and Technologies, 2*(3), 42–60.

Provine, R. R. (2004). Walkie-talkie evolution: Bipedalism and vocal production. *Behavioral and brain sciences, 27*(4), 520–521. doi:10.1017/S0140525X04410115.

Rainie, L., & Wellman, B. (2012). *Networked* [Kindle version]. Retrieved from www.amazon.com/Networked-ebook/dp/B007Z6GW0Y/.

Saloman, G. (1993). *Distributed cognitions: Psychological and educational considerations.* Cambridge, England: Cambridge University Press.

Segaran, T. (2007). *Programming collective intelligence* [Kindle version]. Retrieved from http://shop.oreilly.com/product/9780596529321.do.

Shirky, C. (2003). A group is its own worst enemy. Retrieved from www.shirky.com/writings/group_enemy.html.

Siemens, G. (2005). Connectivism: A learning theory for the digital age. *International Journal of Instructional Technology and Distance Learning, 2*(1), 3–10.

Surowiecki, J. (2004). *The wisdom of crowds.* London, England: Little, Brown.

Sutton, J., Harris, C., Keil, P., & Barnier, A. (2010). The psychology of memory, extended cognition, and socially distributed remembering. *Phenomenology and the Cognitive Sciences, 9*(4), 521–560. doi: 10.1007/s11097-010-9182-y.

Thorpe, M., & Gordon, J. (2012). Online learning in the workplace: A hybrid model of participation in networked, professional learning. *Australasian Journal of Educational Technology, 28*(8), 1267–1282.

Various. (2005). What do Wikipedians do all day? Retrieved from http://en.wikipedia.org/wiki/User:Statistics—Case_1:_Anon_Surprise.21.

Watts, D. (2004). *Six degrees: The science of a connected age.* Norton: New York.

Wells, H. G. (1937). World brain: The idea of a permanent world encyclopaedia. Retrieved 3 January 2006 from http://sherlock.berkeley.edu/wells/world_brain.html.

Wenger, E. (1998). *Communities of practice: Learning, meaning and identity.* New York: Cambridge University Press.

Wenger, E., Trayner, B., & de Latt, M. (2011). Promoting and assessing value creation in communities and networks: A conceptual framework. *Ruud de Moor Centru, Open Universiat, Netherlands, 18.*

Wheeler, W. M. (1911). The ant-colony as an organism. *Journal of Morphology, 22*(2), 307–325. doi: 10.1002/jmor.1050220206.

Wilson, E. O. (2012). *The social conquest of earth* [Kindle DX].

Yu, Z. (2009). *Wiki-enabled emergent knowledge processes through acceleration of stigmergic collaboration.* Unpublished master's thesis, City University of Hong Kong, Hong Kong.

3

'OPEN-SOURCING' PERSONAL LEARNING

Sebastian H.D. Fiedler

Introduction

While I have always found myself close to the core ideas promoted by the 'free and open culture' movement in general, I have never felt really at ease with all the attempts to promote and celebrate open educational resources (OER) as a major development with truly transformative potential. I have never managed to get as excited as, for example, Iiyoshi and Kumar (2008) when they announced that 'tens of thousands of course Web sites and other educational materials are now freely available from hundreds of institutions, organizations, and projects from thousands of educators around the world, representing an unprecedented upsurge in access to educational resources' (p. 2–3).

Annunciations like this have always left me rather unimpressed. The main reason for this has always been and continues to be that I have hardly found myself in situations where my personal learning, or teaching for that matter, was severely impaired by the lack of access to 'educational resources' of acceptable quality. Regardless of my particular learning intentions, I tend to find myself in a situation of abundance, not scarcity. Access is very rarely an issue. And I would like to argue that this is a pretty common experience for anyone who has grown up and continues to live in parts of the so-called first world, or 'developed' societies. Even in pre-digital times a myriad of learning intentions could be met within a rich landscape of free or very affordable offers from city libraries, community colleges, book stores, public TV, free public universities and their libraries, and so forth. Digitisation and networking only continues to re-mediate and dramatically simplify the access to an ever-expanding pool of cultural artefacts and potential resources for learning. That parts of some Western societies are presently getting so thrilled about 'open educational' offers such as open online courses only reflects the gradual cultural loss of core ideas of common goods and services in recent decades. It doesn't really surprise that the discourse on OER is presently dominated by scholars from the US and the UK, where the access to higher education is increasingly built on the concept of personal or familial financial indebtedness.

The majority of our present, global society, however, does not live in environments that are as materially privileged as I have sketched it above. From a perspective of difficult or uneven access the OER movement might offer a first-line solution. Some authors, such as Oblinger and Lombardi (2008), thus suggest that the term 'open educational resources', first heard at a 2002 UNESCO forum, is commonly used to describe a strategy for sharing timely teaching materials (content modules, courseware, learning objects, online learning communities) that would otherwise not be available to instructors in less-developed countries (p. 369). The OER movement seems certainly broader than this particular interpretation suggests, and naturally offers a variety of terminological boundaries.

Be that as it may, I would like to point my reflection back to the implicit, or explicit, standard notion within the OER movement that quality content, or rather its lack, is the main educational challenge of our times. With their focus on open and reusable content, modules, course packages and entire curricula, OER initiatives tend to remain within the boundaries of the established activity systems of 'schooling' that are formed around the seemingly incontrovertible claim that all serious learning activity has to be closely coupled to a corresponding teaching activity (executed by either a human actor or a technical system) and its instrumentation. By limiting their efforts to issues of 'quality content', its design and production, licensing, distribution and so forth, many proponents of OER fail to run a broader analysis of the cultural-historical development of learning activity to date and its potential (or already emergent) further development in the light of the unfolding digital transformation of our societies. A good part of the present OER movement seems to be driven by the same old 'content fetish' that Gee (2004) identified as a principal barrier to transformative change in formal education.

In the face of this continuously re-enacted and reproduced 'content fetish' in our formal educational systems, even proponents of OER seem to have their second thoughts. Iiyoshi and Kumar (2008), for example, remind their audience that 'despite the increasing interest in open education and the availability of these growing collections of educational tools and resources, we risk missing the transformative and innovative opportunities' (p. 3). I wholeheartedly agree. And, as I have tried to suggest above, I am not at all convinced that the provision of open, digital educational resources as such constitutes a major transformative opportunity at this present stage of development. At least not in 'first world' societies already experiencing material abundance and an accelerated expansion of cultural production in the digital realm.

To be clear, there are some indisputable advantages and benefits if practices such as the use of open licences are promoted and established within formal education and other societal activity systems. However, I would argue that 'transformative opportunities' could rather be realised around learning activity and its further development. From this perspective it seems useful to first conceptualise and examine learning activity (German: Lerntätigkeit) as a product of cultural-historical development (see for example Roth & Lee, 2007).

Learning Activity as a Product of Cultural-Historical Development

From a cultural-historical perspective it is important to distinguish between learning as a process embedded *in* activity and learning *as* activity. Fundamental processes of learning are undoubtedly part of the biological make-up of human beings, allowing for a flexible adaptation to the environment through the modification of behaviour. Through cultural-historical development, however, humans have increasingly shaped and changed their environment and society and objectified their collective accomplishments through the production of a great variety of artefacts and cultural instruments. While learning (as a process) was historically embedded in collective (work) activity, it emerged as a specific activity only slowly over time. Lompscher and Hedegaard (1999), for example, describe contemporary learning activity in the following words: 'It is a special kind of activity directed towards the acquisition of societal knowledge and skills through their individual re-production by means of special learning actions upon learning objects (subject matter methods and knowledge)' (p. 12). Erdmann and Rückriem (2010) rightfully emphasise that this development of 'learning activity' as a specific activity was closely tied to the emergence and dissemination of a new media-historical form of knowledge within the 'print and book culture' (see also Giesecke, 2002) and its accompanying societal challenges and demands. Before the book (printed text) emerged as the new leading medium, learning was pre-dominantly contextualised and experience based. It was coupled to the body and (mostly local) social practice. Observation, co-ordinated action, apprenticeship and so forth characterise this form of learning. Only in the print and book culture de-contextualised, systematically instructed learning becomes the dominant format and gets institutionalised in 'school'. Over time the development of public, compulsory schooling ensured that learning activity (for a historic reconstruction see for example Fichtner, 1996) became the dominant form of cultural appropriation through learning.

While earlier forms of learning have never been replaced entirely, they certainly became more and more marginalised within so-called developed societies. The ensuing societal monopoly of teaching- or instruction-dependent learning activity resulted in the gradual expansion and differentiation of activity systems of 'schooling' stretching over ever-wider parts of a human lifespan. Over time, this ever-growing monopoly of 'schooling' over societally accredited and organised human change through learning has been challenged and tested regularly on educational, psychological, economical and philosophical grounds. A well-known and particularly outspoken critique was formulated by Illich (1971), who called for nothing less than the comprehensive 'deschooling of society'. In adult education some scholars tried—albeit with limited success—to emphasise the necessity to foster self-direction in learning and the importance of adult learning projects outside out formal educational environments (see for example Brookfield, 1986; Knowles, 1975, 1984; Tough, 1971). At large, however, it seems fair to attest that many of these attempts to systematically emancipate learning activity from teaching and from being 'other-organised' (Harri-Augstein & Thomas, 1991; Thomas & Harri-Augstein, 1985) were undermined or assimilated by the overall activity system of 'schooling' and its numerous disciples and avid defendants within the various professions.

The academic body of literature on self-direction in learning itself might serve as a good example for this tendency in educational practice and research. In his comprehensive literature review Candy (1991) attested that in parallel to the professionalisation and formalisation of education 'the debate about self-direction in learning has largely shifted from a concentration on the independent pursuit of learning opportunities (autodidaxy) to methodological and other issues surrounding the involvement of learners in determining the form and focus of instruction (learner control)' (p. 30). Candy also demonstrated in his analysis that only a fraction of the literature on self-direction in learning actually deals with independent, informal, adult learning projects of any kind, for which Candy suggested to reserve the label 'autodidaxy'.

Candy (1991) had carried out his literature review at a time when digitisation and networking within our society was in its infancy. Thirteen years later, he still felt the need to comment on the ongoing marginalisation of 'self-directed learning' on the one hand, while offering a rather optimistic outlook for its increasing importance within the unfolding digital transformation:

> Self-directed learning is often portrayed somewhat unfairly as a dilettante activity, an adornment to the real business of learning that occurs in schools, colleges, universities and training centres. While this was probably never a fair characterisation, it is even less true today, when the sheer volume of information combined with the rapidity of change has catapulted us into an era of continuous learning, most of which is self-directed. Far from being a marginal activity, self-directed learning is now a major way in which people cope with the turbulent and unpredictable worlds in which they find themselves both personally and professionally. If the move of self-directed learning from the periphery to the core is notable, so too is the move of technology within self-directed learning from the periphery to the core.
>
> (Candy, 2004, pp. 281–282)

One would expect that in the light of the accelerated expansion of digitisation and networking into more and more areas of practice this projected move of self-education from the periphery to the core of society and the educational profession should be a sure thing. However, that is apparently not quite the case. To the contrary, the activity systems of 'schooling' have remained incredibly resilient and relatively resistant to any fundamental challenge to their underlying core patterns and dogmas. In some ways, the digital transformation was even used to expand the reach of 'schooling' into realms of higher education that had partially preserved alternative patterns of responsibility, division of labour, evaluation, and so forth. Almost in parallel to Candy's hopeful statement regarding a possible renaissance of independent pursuits of learning, Himanen (2001) shared the following observation: 'The irony is that currently the academy tends to model its learning structure on the monastic sender-receiver model. The irony is usually only amplified when the academy starts to build a "virtual university: the result is a computerized monastery school"' (p. 76). The gift-wrapping approach in which digital instruments are 'merely wrapped around old frameworks for education' (Fischer & Scharff, 1998, p. 6) is very well and alive in contemporary higher education and beyond. Noble (1998) even warned that from his perspective the dominating form of digital (re-)instrumentation in higher education is 'not a progressive trend towards a new era at all, but a regressive trend, towards the rather old era of mass production, standardization and purely commercial interests' (p. 1).

As a continuous observer and regular collaborator in the field that trades under the somewhat unfortunate label of 'technology enhanced learning', I cannot help but confirm that these critical remarks are still very much on the spot. Even the progressively expanding instrumentation options in the digital realm are regularly stripped of their emancipatory potential for independent, individual and collective learning activity as soon as the various professions that have started to colonise the field of education get a hold of it and put it into place within the activity system of 'schooling'.

A recent incarnation of the overall tendency to assimilate and somewhat neutralise ideas of freedom, self-organisation or self-direction in learning can be found in the contemporary discourse on personal learning environments (PLEs). While the notion of PLEs emerged as a counter-concept to the dominating digital instrumentation of formal teaching and learning activity, it quickly was reinterpreted by the 'engineering crowd' of the wider activity system of schooling as a predominantly computational challenge that would allow the integration of distributed digital tools and services in an institutional landscape, while maintaining the integrity of the system's core functions of control, assessment, guidance and so forth. What started out as a notion of individual instrumentation of 'personal learning' in many cases was quickly turned into the provision of 'personalised' interfaces to institutionally sanctioned sets of tools and content—of course, always with the promise to make things more efficient and convenient for anyone. In an incredibly short time the whole contemporary discourse on

PLEs became dominated by the search for technical solutions to the requirements allegedly dictated by the inner logic and demands of the overall system of 'schooling' (Fiedler & Väljataga, 2011). It wasn't any longer about the development, maintenance and digital instrumentation of individual and idiosyncratic environments for personal learning as an object of inquiry and change. All attention shifted to the institutional landscapes of tools and services and how they could be re-engineered in order to make a better fit with a range of practices that people had allegedly adopted in the context of social software and the so-called read-and-write Web (Fiedler & Väljataga, 2013). It is more than likely that one main outcome of these efforts will be the preservation of the core patterns that drive the rationale of teaching-dependent learning activity.

Though I have presented these short sketches of how the discourse on self-direction in learning and around the more recent notion of personal learning environments has successfully been twisted and tweaked by the proponents of 'schooling' as the primary form of systematic human change through learning across the lifespan, I don't want to imply that de-contextualised, instructed learning has no contenders or competitors and cannot be challenged successfully under the present cultural-historical conditions. To the contrary, I want to suggest that the digital transformation offers the chance not only for the renaissance and further development of older, formerly marginalised, forms of learning activity. Altogether, it also seems to catalyse the development of historically new forms of learning activity.

Emergence of New Forms of Emancipated Learning Activity

The progressive manifestation of global digitisation and networking as the new leading medium of our time seems to 'provide totally new and rather inexhaustible potentials to human practice' (Rückriem, 2009, p. 89), on the one hand, while posing formidable developmental challenges for individuals and a wide range (if not all) societal activity systems, on the other. We seem to be living through a cultural transition phase characterised by mounting tensions and some outright contradictions within existing systems of human activity and social practice. Human needs, dispositions and activities seemingly co-evolve and shape the further development of the leading medium, just as much as they are shaped by the leading medium and its evolving range of instrumentation options. Since the speed and visibility of this transformational, co-evolutionary drift has been particularly high within societal systems of work and production, it comes with little surprise that the changing nature of work has become dominating in the discourse on and theorising about human dispositions and their systematic development through 'learning' (see, for example, Hakkarainen, Palonen, Paavola, & Lehtinen, 2004). This tendency has resulted in mounting societal pressure on all levels of institutionalised systems of formal education, and the repeated cry for their radical reform and better alignment to the perceived needs, demands and requirements of the various, inter-linked systems of work and their ongoing transformation.

One recent response to these continuous reformational calls is the attempt to outline and project a 'new culture of learning' (see, for example, Erdmann & Rückriem, 2010; Giest, 2010; Giest & Lompscher, 2004; Heyse, Erpenbeck, & Michel, 2002; Jünger, 2004; Thomas & Seely Brown, 2011). Though I tend to agree with Erdmann and Rückriem (2010), who attest that at this point in time the term is mostly used as a 'container' for a wide and disparate range of observations and deliberations, the notion of a 'new culture of learning' seems to be somewhat instrumental for widening again the scope of analytical and empirical inquiry into new forms of individual and collective learning activity beyond the monopolistic, teaching-based approach to education (see, for example, Thomas & Seely Brown, 2011).

Regardless of whether scholars make an explicit use of this container term, we are seeing an increasing amount of descriptive, empirical work focusing on particular (sub-)cultures of learning that are seemingly co-evolving together with the ongoing development of the new leading medium and the instrumentation and mediation options it provides. While this is certainly not the place for a comprehensive overview of such descriptive and analytical efforts, some selected examples might help to illustrate the type of contributions that I have in mind here.

The Open Learning Model of Hackers

In the context of his work on the culture and ethics of hackers, Himanen (2001) also described 'the hacker learner model' that he sees closely related to the open academic model ideally guiding all free, scientific research. For Himanen,

> hackers' learning is modelled the same way as their development of new software (which can actually be seen as the frontier of their collective learning). Thus, their learning model has the same strengths as the development model. A typical hacker's learning process starts out with setting up an interesting problem, working toward a solution by using various sources, then submitting the solution to extensive testing. Learning more about a subject becomes the hacker's passion.
>
> (p. 73)

Another strength of this learning model is apparently the fact that 'it is a continuously evolving learning environment created by the learners themselves. The learning model adopted by hackers has many advantages. In the hacker world, the teachers or assemblers of information sources are often those who have just learned something' (p. 75). It seems important to note here that the provision of open 'content' in the sense of specifically designed instructional materials or artefacts allegedly plays no significant role whatsoever. Himanen finally summarises his reflections on the learning of hackers in the following words:

after the hackers' reminder of the full significance of the academic model, it would be odd to continue our current practice of providing learners mainly with results, without making them learn much more deeply the academic model itself, which is based on a collective process of posing of problems, the questioning of them, and the development of solutions—a process driven by passion and recognition for socially valuable contributions.

(p. 79)

Altogether, Himanen's descriptions deliver a form of collective, emancipated learning activity that seems to be organised around problems, questions and prototypical solutions that get scrutinised and tested, rather than specifically designed educational content of any kind.

Open Learning around Affinity Spaces

Another descriptive, analytical contribution is offered by Gee (2004), who, in the context of his research on computer gaming and learning, has come up with the description of 'affinity spaces' as 'another important social configuration in which people participate and learn' (p. 70). Gee further emphasises that 'modern technologies allow the creation of more and more spaces where people can enter and interact with others (and with objects and tools) at a distance. So when I talk about "spaces" I don't mean just physical spaces' (p. 71–72). He argues that affinity spaces are an important contemporary form of social affiliation. Oblinger and Lombardi (2008) suggest that, for example, 'social networking Web sites, fan-fiction communities, multiuser online gaming environments, and other immersive online experiences where sociability is placed in service of a common creative enterprise' (p. 392) can be described as such self-organising affinity spaces. Oblinger and Lombardi (2008) also hold the view that these affinity spaces 'capture key aspects of active learning environments, including abundant cooperation, self-expression, and collaborative problem solving' (p. 392). Gee (2004) makes clear that 'what people have an affinity with (or for) in an affinity space is not first and foremost the other people using the space, but the endeavor or interest around which the space is organized' (p. 77). Gee and others are able to describe elaborate forms of learning activity around these digitally enabled affinity spaces that show no sign of teaching activity or explicit educational content provision in a traditional sense.

Sense-Constituting Learning in a Global, Networked Society

While many of the attempts to describe emerging forms of learning activity within the digital transformation focus on collectives as their preferred unit of analysis, Erdmann and Rückriem (2010) take a decidedly different perspective. In the context of their media-historical analysis of learning, these scholars describe a new type of learning activity that emerges in the wake of the global, digital transformation. They label this new media-historical type as 're-contextualised, sense-constituting, reflexive learning' (German: rekontextualisiertes sinnkonsti-tuierendes reflexives Lernen). What gets on centre-stage is the learning of sense-constituting or sense-making. Erdmann and Rückriem acknowledge that the former (media-)historical types of learning were also 'sense-based', of course. However, sense was either coupled with the actual contextualised personal (and social) experience, or the de-contextualised (book-)knowledge. What the authors see emerging is the de-coupling of knowledge (generating) systems and mean-ing (generating/constituting) systems in the information society. Since sense-orientating traditions, social norms and commonly shared cultural values are under permanent development within an increasingly networked global society, we find ourselves in a permanent crisis of collective meaning and personal sense. Learning how to find or constitute sense becomes thus an important individual and societal task. Erdmann and Rückriem (2010) furthermore propose that the histori-cal types of learning they have identified in their analysis have emerged and devel-oped in a successive, irreversible manner. However, these learning types co-exist largely unconnected in this early stage of the unfolding cultural transformation.

Beyond the 'Master Explanator'

Together, the rising number of analytical descriptions that capture various emer-gent forms of digitally mediated learning activity deliver mounting evidence that it is time to move beyond the 'content fetish' and the obsession with instruction-dependent learning activity in educational research and practice. I have my doubts that the open education and OER movement is actually prepared for such a shift of perspective. Many proponents of OER seem to be happily remaining within the conceptual boundaries of the activity system of 'schooling' and its insistence on de-contextualised, instruction-dependent learning activity. While they are promoting 'open educational practices' of various kinds, they seem to have a hard time imagining practices of free, autodidactic, self-education in a digital and net-worked world, without relying on any 'master explicator' as Ranciere (1991) has put it. Ranciere (1991) said about autodidactic self-education, which he oddly calls 'universal teaching', that

> this method is practiced of necessity by everyone, but no one wants to rec-ognize it, no one wants to cope with the intellectual revolution it signifies. The social circle, the order of things, prevents it from being recognized for what it is: the true method by which everyone learns and by which everyone can take the measure of his capacity. One must dare to recognize it and pursue the open verification of its power—otherwise, the method of powerlessness, the Old Master, will last as long as the order of things.

(p. 16)

Fundamentally, there is good reason to believe that the mainstream OER movement either intentionally or unintentionally tends to serve the Old Master.

Personal Learning as Open and Networked Autodidaxy

A lot of descriptive research that tries to portray emerging modes of learning activity in the context of the digital transformation of society seems to focus on collectives of various kinds as their primary unit of analysis (activity systems, networks, communities, spaces and so forth). While this certainly produces important insights, I would like to suggest that we could equally gain from carrying out systematic inquiry on individual autodidaxy as the personal and independent pursuit of learning under the emerging conditions of expanding networking and digitisation.

In parallel with the ongoing efforts for the digital re-instrumentation of formal education, the last decade has actually seen a steady increase in accessible and affordable digital instrumentation options for all kinds of individual and collective learning activity, fully de-coupled from teaching and instruction. Individuals are actually managing to form, shape, and maintain their personal learning environments and networks by experimentally combining digital and non-digital instruments and resources around their own interests and projects. They partially externalise their learning activity through published, addressable, digital records of (communicative, productive, explorative) action, items of experience and reflection and items of intention and chance-seeking (Bardone, 2011), mediated by an array of loosely coupled, networked instruments. This partial 'open-sourcing' of efforts of personal learning affords the emergence of a wide range of networked learning practices that range from turning one's own digital traces into a potential open resource for others to the development of inter-personal, collective learning activity with other networked subjects.

The digital traces of such semi-open endeavours of self-education display qualities that are radically different from the standard items of purpose-designed, de-contextualised knowledge that tend to be used in the context of instruction-dependent learning activity. In fact, what one can regularly find are elements of networked narrative; biographical contextualisation of various kinds; and the description of problems, distractions, deviations, chance encounters, moments of serendipity and so forth. Not a surprise really, since earlier research on autodidaxy had regularly recorded that

> Accident or serendipity plays an important role in determining the direction that many learning projects take. Chance meetings, offhand comments, resources accidentally discovered or mentioned in conversation, and changing life circumstances all contribute to the form and extent of individual learning projects, and few if any of these features could be anticipated or predicted at the beginning. Linked to this is the nonlinear nature

of such learning efforts, which often zigzag from one 'organizing circum-
stance' to the next in an apparently random way.

(Candy, 1991, p. 199)

What is still relatively new, however, is the ease of creation of publicly accessible
and addressable records of these personal trajectories of learning on the global
network.

Around ten years ago I tried to interpret and describe the emerging personal web-publishing practices (weblogs, webfeeds and so forth) as a 'reflective conversational tool for self-organized learning' (Fiedler, 2003). A decade
later these practices still represent some core instruments for mediating many
open manifestations of networked autodidaxy. However, the scope and availability of web-publishing tools and services and mobile devices that can be
combined for the recording, creative expression and narration of learning
actions has grown tremendously. This potentially enriches our capability to
mediate learning conversations with ourselves and with others. And the range
of digital artefacts that we can draw into our networked conversations is still
expanding steadily.

What seems remarkable to me here is the fact that these networked accounts
of personal learning start to form a whole new, and very interesting, class of open
resources for learning, regardless of the fact that they hardly ever comply with the
criteria of quality (such as structure, clarity in exposition, transparency of goals
and so forth) that are promoted for purpose-designed educational resources. In
a situation of abundance of information artefacts on just about every topic, the
actual acquisition of primary material of adequate quality becomes a marginal
issue. It becomes an occasional nuisance, rather than a fundamental barrier to following a particular learning intention. And this is exactly why it might become
increasingly interesting and important to be able to trace the very personal, highly
idiosyncratic trajectories of intentional learning of others within the global network. These accessible records of personal sense-making generally display a much
deeper biographical and/or professional contextualisation than we could ever
hope to gain from standard educational resources, regardless of whether they are
delivered with an open licence or not. Engaging with and inquiring into this type
of record might become equally important as collecting resources that have been
sanitised for 'educational' consumption.

If Erdmann and Rückriem (2010) are not completely wrong with their
analytical projection of a new media-historical type of 'contextualised, sense-
constituting, reflexive learning' emerging within the global networked society,
then we need to think about how we can achieve the partial reification—
metaphorically speaking, the 'open-sourcing'—of personal sense-making. Only
then we could hope to turn it into an object of inquiry and potential improvement over time (Fiedler, 2012). It seems to me that contemporary expressions
of networked autodidaxy on the network could be interpreted as rudimentary

'proto-types' of the kind of open resources that might support the further development of historically new forms of learning activity.

Recently, Seely Brown (2010) has reminded us that

> although learning about and learning to be worked well in a relative stable world, in a world of constant flux, we need to embrace a theory of *learning to become*. Where most theories of learning see becoming as a transitional state toward becoming something, the twenty-first century requires us to think of learning as a practice of becoming over and over again. In order to understand what that means and how it might be achieved, we need to examine some of the new modes of learning that have emerged.
>
> (p. xi–xii)

Networked autodidaxy and the open-sourcing of personal learning might just be one of these.

Coda

From my perspective the types of 'problem descriptions' that the OER movement promotes and claims to address remain largely within the boundaries of the activity system of 'schooling' and its specific needs, requirements and overall rationale. It has thus inherited the very same 'content fetish' that is driving much of formal education as the hegemonic form of systematic, intentional human change through learning in all societies that are heavily invested in the book and print culture. As long as OERs and practices are always treated as simply another element in this larger fabric of de-contextualised, instructed 'learning', it seems difficult to imagine that we can engage in a truly co-evolutionary drift with the unfolding digital transformation. The abundance of (potentially networked) human artefacts and the diversity of knowledge claims that this transformation apparently produces cannot be met by an accelerated production and consumption of 'quality content' alone—regardless of whether such content carries open licences or not. It calls, rather, for a collective shift of focus towards the further development of historically new forms of learning activity in an increasingly networked, global society. If we dare to look beyond the boundaries of contemporary formal education we might be able to describe some embryonic forms of such emerging learning activity and reformulate our ideas on the role of open resources and open practices accordingly.

More than anything, we need to scrutinise our problem descriptions within the unfolding digital transformation and expose our present 'boundary judgements' (see, for example, Midgley, 2000)—of what currently is and what should be—to review and critique. Only then we will be able to evaluate if 'open resources' and 'open practices' can actually play a transformative role for (self-)education.

References

Bardone, E. (2011). *Seeking chances: From biased rationality to distributed cognition*. Berlin: Springer.

Brookfield, S. D. (1986). *Understanding and facilitating adult learning*. San Francisco, CA: Jossey-Bass.

Candy, P. (1991). *Self-direction for lifelong learning: A comprehensive guide to theory and practice*. San Francisco, CA: Josey-Bass Inc.

Candy, P. (2004). Linking thinking: Self-directed learning in the digital age. Retrieved 23 October 2005 from www.dest.gov.au/sectors/training_skills/publications_resources/profiles/documents/report_x7_pdf.htm.

Erdmann, J. W., & Rückriem, G. (2010). Lernkultur oder Lernkulturen—was ist neu an der, Kultur des Lernens? In G. Rückriem & H. Giest (Eds.), *Tätigtkeitsteorie und (Wissens-)Gesellschaft* (pp. 15–52). Berlin: Lehmans Media.

Fichtner, B. (1996). *Lernen und Lerntätigkei. Ontogenetische, phylogenetische und epistemologische Studien*. Marburg: BdWi.

Fiedler, S. (2003). Personal webpublishing as a reflective conversational tool for self-organized learning. In T. N. Burg (Ed.), *BlogTalks: European Conference on Weblogs* (pp. 190–216). Wien: Cultural Research—Zentrum für wissenschaftliche Forschung und Dienstleistung.

Fiedler, S. H. D. (2012). *Emancipating and developing learning activity: Systemic intervention and re-instrumentation in higher education*. Turku: Painosalama.

Fiedler, S. H. D., & Väljataga, T. (2011). Personal learning environments: Concept or technology? *International Journal of Virtual and Personal Learning Environments, 2*(4), 1–11.

Fiedler, S. H. D., & Väljataga, T. (2013). Personal Learning Environments: A conceptual landscape revisited. *eLearning Papers* (35), 1–16.

Fischer, G., & Scharff, E. (1998). Learning technologies in support of self-directed learning. *Journal of Interactive Media in Education, 98(4)*. Retrieved 16June, 2004 from http://www-jime.open.ac.uk/98/4/.

Gee, J. P. (2004). *Situated language and learning: A critque of traditional schooling*. New York and London: Routledge.

Giesecke, M. (2002). *Von den Mythen der Buchkultur zu den Visionen der Informationsgesellschaft: Trendforschung zur aktuellen Medienökologie*. Frankfurt a. M: Suhrkamp.

Giest, H. (2010). Was bedeutet neue Lernkultur für den Unterricht? In H. Giest & G. Rückriem (Eds.), *Tätigkeitstheorie und (Wissens-)Gesellschaft* (Vol. 32). Berlin: Lehmanns Media.

Giest, H., & Lompscher, J. (2004). Tätigkeitstheoretische Überlegungen zu einer neuen Lernkultur. In B. Friedrich (Ed.), *Bildung heute—Gefährdungen und Möglichkeiten* (pp. 101–124). Berlin: Trafo.

Hakkarainen, K., Palonen, T., Paavola, S., & Lehtinen, E. (2004). *Communities of networked expertise*. Amsterdam: Elsevier.

Harri-Augstein, S., & Thomas, L. (1991). *Learning conversations: The self-organised way to personal and organisational growth*. London: Routledge.

Heyse, V., Erpenbeck, J., & Michel, L. (2002). *Lernkulturen der Zukunft. Kompetenzbedarf und Kompetenzentwicklung in Zukunftsbranchen* (No. 74). Berlin: Arbeitsgemeinschaft Betriebliche Weiterbildungsforschung, e.V.

Himanen, P. (2001). *The hacker ethic: And the spirit of the information age*. New York: Random House.

Iiyoshi, T., & Kumar, M. S. V. (2008). Introduction: An invitation to open up the future of education. In T. Iiyoshi & M. S. V. Kumar (Eds.), *Opening up education. The collective advancement of education through open technology, open content, and open knowledge* (pp. 1–10). Cambridge, MA: MIT Press.

Illich, I. (1971). *Deschooling society*. New York: Harper & Row.

Jünger, S. (2004). *Selbstorganisation, Lernkultur und Kompetenzentwicklung*. Wiesbaden: Deutscher Universitätsverlag.

Knowles, M. S. (1975). *Self-directed learning. A guide for learners and teachers*. Englewood Cliffs, NJ: Prentice Hall.

Knowles, M. S. (1984). *Andragogy in action: Applying modern principles of adult learning*. San Francisco, CA: Jossey Bass.

Lompscher, J., & Hedegaard, M. (1999). Learning activity and development: Introduction. In M. Hedegaard & J. Lompscher (Eds.), *Learning activity and development* (pp. 10–21). Aarhus: Aarhus University Press.

Midgley, G. (2000). *Systemic intervention: Philosophy, methodology, and practice*. New York: Kluwer Academic/Plenum Publishers.

Noble, D. F. (1998). Digital diploma mills: The automation of higher education. *First Monday, 3*(1), 1–8.

Oblinger, D. G., & Lombardi, M. M. (2008). Common knowledge: Openness in higher education. In T. Iiyoshi & M. S. V. Kumar (Eds.), *Opening up education. The collective advancement of education through open technology, open content, and open knowledge* (pp. 389–400). Cambridge, MA: MIT Press.

Ranciere, J. (1991). *The ignorant schoolmaster. Five lessons in intellectual emancipation*. Stanford, CA: Stanford University Press.

Roth, W.M., & Lee, Y. J. (2007). 'Vygotsky's neglected legacy': Cultural-historical activity theory. *Review of Educational Research, 77*(2), 186–232.

Rückriem, G. (2009). Digital technology and mediation: A challenge to activity theory. In A. Sannino, H. Daniels & K. D. Gutierrez (Eds.), *Learning and expanding with activity theory* (pp. 88–111). Cambridge: Cambridge University Press.

Seely Brown, J. (2010). Foreword: Education in the creative economy. In D. Araya & M. A. Peters (Eds.), *Education in the creative economy: Knowledge and learning in the age of innovation* (pp. ix–xii). New York: Peter Lang.

Thomas, D., & Seely Brown, J. (2011). *A new culture of learning*. Charleston, SC: Createspace.

Thomas, L., & Harri-Augstein, S. (1985). *Self-organised learning: Foundations of a conversational science for psychology*. London: Routledge.

Tough, A. (1971). *The adult's learning projects: A fresh approach to theory and practice in adult learning*. Ontario: The Ontario Institute for Studies in Education.

4

OPEN NETWORKS AND BOUNDED COMMUNITIES

Tensions Inherent In Releasing Open Educational Resources

Allison Littlejohn, Isobel Falconer,
Lou McGill and Helen Beetham

The Tension: Open Release within Bounded Communities

The ubiquity of networked and social technologies provides an environment within which new approaches to knowledge sharing and co-construction have flourished. This trend in knowledge co-construction is taking place within a society that increasingly is open.

One of the most visible manifestations of emerging approaches to knowledge sharing within the formal education domain is the discourse around Open Educational Resources (OERs). OERs have been defined as 'digitised materials offered freely and openly for educators, students and self-learners to use and reuse for teaching, learning and research' (OECD, 2007).

Ideas around OER originated around 2002 through the Education Program strategic plan of the Hewlett Foundation on *Using Information Technology to Increase Access to High-Quality Educational Content* (Atkins, Brown, & Hammond, 2007) and the MIT Open CourseWare initiative (see the Chapter 10 in this volume). OERs have been informed by concepts around open and distance learning, open access to knowledge, free sharing and peer collaboration. Activity around OER has been prolific since 2004: a Google search on open educational resources now produces over 163 million results.

The origins have focused OER activity around content production, release and use in education, rather than the wider use and benefits of OER for learning in general. While potential benefits of OER have been recognised (McGill, Beetham, Falconer, & Littlejohn, 2010; OECD, 2007; Yuan, MacNeil, & Kraan, 2008), OER release and use are not widespread professional practices, even within the education sector, and understanding of the impact on teaching and learning is limited. While it is recognised that the release of OER in itself does not automatically lead to use by others (Lane & McAndrew, 2010; McGill et al., 2010), the contexts within which OERs can impact on the learning practice and/or the professional practice of academics are unknown.

On the surface, educational communities of practice such as subject communities seem ideal settings to encourage and support the release and sharing of OERs. However, earlier studies have flagged inherent difficulties in the community release of online resources—for example, to create economies of scale (Margaryan & Littlejohn, 2008). Firstly, academics dealing with day-to-day, immediate work issues tend to focus on short-term goals, missing potential longer-term gains associated with releasing resources that can be used by (unidentified) others (ibid.). Secondly, academics place importance on contextual factors that conflict with the idea of open reuse of resources across a range of contexts (ibid.). Thirdly, although communities provide a trusted environment for changing professional practice, in the long term these communities can become inward facing, inhibiting potential growth, creativity and innovation (Littlejohn, Beetham, & McGill, 2012). These underlying tensions inherent in the enterprise of OER release and the role of communities may undermine successful implementation of OER initiatives, yet are often overlooked by policy makers and practitioners (Littlejohn & Margaryan, 2010).

The characteristics of bounded communities, where people have tight links with colleagues and learners, are at odds with the diverse needs of a wider group of (often unknown) users in open networks (Margaryan & Littlejohn, 2008). Bounded communities—for example, groups of academics working within a single subject discipline—tend to be more tightly knit than dispersed groups, such as industry subject experts who are seeking resources to teach a specific concept. Academics, particularly those who are used to teaching within conventional 'closed' courses, often fail to consider the wider groups of people who may benefit from the resources released.

Dimensions affecting communities include the purpose (shared goal and interests), interaction (modes of participation and communication), roles and responsibilities, coherence (whether the community is close knit or loosely confederated and transient), context (the broader ecology within which the community exists), rules (implicit and explicit rules that govern the functioning of the community) and practices (predominant approaches used in the community) (Margaryan & Littlejohn, 2008). These characteristics vary across different user communities, which may cause problems if OERs are designed for a specific group of users, making them less adaptable by individuals and groups across a range of diverse communities.

The aim of this chapter is to surface intrinsic problems in the release of OERs within communities bounded by common expectations, practices or other parameters. We focus on emerging rules and roles relating to new professional practices. These were identified within the context of the UK

Higher Education Academy and Joint Information Systems Committee's (JISC) UKOER pilot programme.

The Context of Study: the UK Open Educational Resources Programme (UKOER)

This study was conducted within the UK Open Educational Resources Programme (UKOER), a large-scale programme of projects supporting the release of OERs. This £15 million programme was funded from 2009 to 2012 by the UK government through the Higher Education Funding Council for England (HEFCE) and the UK Higher Education Academy (HEA). Over eighty projects based at universities, colleges and national subject centres distributed across England and Wales released thousands of resources under Creative Commons licences. Programme goals were firstly to make a wide range of digital learning resources freely available and easily discoverable by educators and learners and secondly to create long-term, sustained change in professional practice towards open educational practices. These goals were underpinned by two underlying assumptions: (1) that widespread involvement of faculty and support staff within the programme would bring about a sustainable change in culture from focusing on content ownership, to focusing on open sharing; and (2) that building a critical mass of OER would bring about sustainable change in practices of reuse and repurposing.

Communities of practice provide a positive environment for changing professional practice. However, there are inherent differences and even conflict between the practices of bounded communities and the more open practices of networks, including knowledge sharing, the co-construction of knowledge and other open educational practices (McGill et al., 2013). The UKOER programme provided a context to explore these tensions and to highlight the benefits and limitations of communities in supporting change in professional practice. We acknowledge the potential influence of project funding within the UKOER programme and the limitations of viewing a time-bound and funded initiative as a community of practice. However, since the programme funding ceased, the community has remained active within social media channels, such as Twitter (see #UKOER). This analysis is part of a larger study of the UKOER programme (available from http://tinyurl.com/pd8sbgb).

Data were collected using a mixed method approach. Data were gathered through two primary sources: project reports from all the UKOER projects during Phase 1 of the programme (2009–10) and focus group discussions. Data were coded and synthesised within an OER Evaluation Framework (https://oersynth.pbworks.com/w/page/29860952/Pilot-Phase-Synthesis-Framework) comprising key focus areas that emerged from the data (McGill et al., 2010). We acknowledge a limitation in using project data reported to funders as evidence, in that these sources may attribute any problems to others, skewing responsibility away from the project team. However, the data provide a baseline for planning a deeper, ethnographic study. The data were then mapped against a framework based on activity theory to examine the role of bounded communities in shifting professional practice towards more open educational practice. This second mapping enabled analysis of the motives inherent in educational communities releasing OERs (Falconer, Littlejohn & McGill, 2013).

Activity systems are socio-cultural settings where community members (*subjects*) work on some sort of *object* or 'problem space', transforming it into an *outcome* using *tools* which may be technological (such as software) or conceptual (such as pedagogic theory) (Engeström, 1987). The tool-mediated action may be constrained or enabled by implicit and explicit *rules* and the broader social context (*community*) within which the activity takes place. Labour is divided among the community members (*roles*). This framework allowed us to view the various UKOER projects in a coherent way, providing an analytic lens through which to understand the complex relationships within the programme. These relationships are illustrated in the context of one of the UKOER projects in Figure 4.1.

Figure 4.1 illustrates the UKOER Open Spires Project as an activity system. In this example, people within the project team (subjects) worked on open release of podcasts of public lectures and discussions by Oxford and visiting academics (objects). The outcomes of the activity were released as podcasts with new intellectual property rights (IPR) agreements. The team (subjects) used video capture and repository technologies (tools) to create and release OERs. Although the community (academics, visiting lecturers, support staff) had to adapt conventional rules (for example, rules around IPR) and re-adjust their roles to accommodate emerging practice, the difference between conventional rules and roles of the existent community and the rules and roles required for open professional practice was not significant. In this case the factors align very well with minimum disruption to existing community rules, roles and so on. Therefore, the community appears to be an ideal environment to encourage the release of OERs. However,

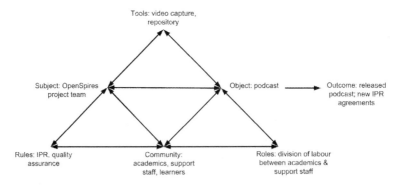

FIGURE 4.1 Activity System from the UKOER Open Spires Project

Source: http://openspires.oucs.ox.ac.uk/

we identified examples where there are significant contradictions in open release within bounded communities.

Using an activity theoretic framework has two advantages. First, it holds in view both the project teams (subject) and the social context within which they are working, illustrating that the subject's actions cannot be understood in isolation (Kuutti, 1996). Second, innovation can be seen to involve 'contradictions' or 'structural tensions' within the system, leading eventually to a divergence from present practice (Engeström, 2005, p. 313). Thus, we view the system as dynamic, changing in response to tensions or contradictions, and any activity triangle represents only a snapshot of the changing system.

The mapping of the coded data from the UKOER Phase 1 data against an activity framework is illustrated in Table 4.1.

In this analysis the *subject* is the project team that worked on OERs (*objects*), resulting both in the (intended) release of OERs and unintended impacts on institutions, cultures and communities (*outcomes* of the activity). A range of *tools* were used to act on the object to achieve the outcome. Technological tools ranged from online systems for storing OERs (for example repository, YouTube) to social media tools (for example Twitter) for publicising OERs. Conceptual tools included pedagogic approaches. This tool-mediated action was constrained or enabled by implicit and explicit *rules* of IPR, legal liability, quality assurance and institutional policy, as well as the broader cultural context of developers, users (for example teachers, enrolled students, prospective students, the public) and other stakeholders (for example university managers or professional associations) (*community*) within which the activity took place. Division of labour amongst the

TABLE 4.1 Mapping of UKOER Synthesis Framework Against an Activity Theoretic Framework

Top-level codes used in the UKOER synthesis framework (McGill et al., 2010)	Activity framework components
Project teams *	Subject
OER release	Object
Business models and benefits	Outcome
Technical and hosting issues	Tools
Pedagogy and end-use issues	
Cultural issues learner and other stakeholder engagement	Community
Developing managing and sharing OERs	
Legal issues	Rules
Quality issues	
Institutional issues-strategy policy practice	
Programme and project management issues	Roles
Guidance and support mechanisms	

Note: * Project teams were not a coding category, but have been included for completeness.

community members depended upon their *roles*, for example academic, technical developer, learner. The relationships and contradictions in each of these areas are further explored in the following sections.

Results and Discussion

Analysis of the UKOER programme highlighted a number of tensions in the release of OERs that are generated within bounded communities. These tensions are associated with the tools used by communities, community rules and roles and the pre-existing relationships within communities, and they have implications for changing professional practice.

Tensions around Communities

We found evidence that OER projects tended to have greatest impact in contexts where communities were already collaborating and good working relationships existed. For example, subject communities, where faculty previously shared discipline-specific teaching resources, provided good settings for OER development and release. In contrast, in situations where people did not have an existing working relationship, new collaborations were difficult to initiate. Communities associated with projects were sometimes reluctant to allow outsiders access to repositories to deposit resources. However, because trust was established within the community, it was more possible to develop genuinely open professional practices such as non-reciprocal sharing (Open Exeter: Browne, 2010).

Trust is a key factor enabling practice to change within communities. Our study provides evidence that trust expedites access to and sharing of knowledge within a community. Where trust did not exist within a community group, a common response was to resist change by exerting control over the new situation, and this presented a barrier to project development. For example, we came across situations where people in project teams were not convinced that the adoption of open professional practices would lead to enhancements or efficiencies in their professional practice, or improve their (personal or institutional) reputation—even though evidence of enhancement had been gathered from other teams within the UKOER programme.

Another critical factor in OER release was the motivation of the community to adopt open professional practices (Falconer, Littlejohn, & McGill, 2013). We found evidence that changes in professional practice were sometimes triggered by a specific event such as planning for a course review event or undertaking course (re)design. In the absence of such disruptive events, there was less motivation to change.

While the value of open exchange of knowledge was widely recognised, individuals were not always committed to sharing their own knowledge or teaching resources. Generally, faculty wanted to retain control over which communities or sub-communities they opened up their resources to. We found examples of communities preferring to release content only within a closed community; using a specific licence allowed depositors to choose the level of sharing they wanted (McGill, Currier, Duncan, & Douglas 2008). Some academics wanted to restrict some of the 'freedoms' available through the open licence options by choosing variants such as 'non-commercial use' or 'no derivatives'. Allowing these so-called 'degrees of openness' encouraged academics to make their resources openly available, as evidenced by some projects adopting 'phased release' (for example, Morris, 2010). However, controlled release of resources within closed communities is antithetical to the philosophy of open access to knowledge by all and can present barriers to the successful release of resources as OERs because of the continued reliance on shared cultural assumptions.

In general, those project teams that focused on improving the reputation of their institution tended to conserve traditional professional practices within predefined communities. By contrast, project teams that aimed to transform pedagogy tended to change professional practice more radically and redefine community roles (for example openSpace: di Savoia, 2010). For example, faculty changing pedagogical practice might consciously redefine students as resource reviewers or co-constructors of resources—so-called 'prosumers'—rather than content consumers (for example BERLiN: Beggan, Horton, Johnson, & Stapleton, 2010; Otter: Witthaus & Armellini, 2010). We identified contradictory views amongst faculty about whether all types of users of OERs (for example learners) are equal participants within the community. These differing views as to who is a community member and who is not may lead to divergence in the OER community.

Faculty remained largely unwilling to reuse or repurpose materials produced by others, particularly if the material had originated from outside communities with which they identified. The reasons ranged from low trust in the expertise of others not known to them to a lack of recognition of their own expertise (Evolution: Leeds, 2010).

In summary, the study identified significant tensions between the aim of the UKOER programme to release educational resources openly and the closed knowledge practices within established disciplines and academic cultures, resulting in release of OERs within closed communities. These tensions present major barriers to successful OER release.

Tensions around Tools

The changes in practices outlined in the previous section sometimes resulted in tensions around the ways people within communities used technology. For example, a perceived need for stable, archived content resources with good version tracking came into conflict with pedagogic approaches in which learners were co-creating resources (as prosumers). The tension between the need to maintain stable, archived resources and the opportunity for multiple users to contribute dynamically to a resource needs to be resolved if professional practice is to evolve towards open, participatory activities. We saw evidence of diverse relationships between project teams and user communities: producers of 'static' OER might encourage user feedback, review and ratings, while producers of 'situative environments'—settings within which resources evolved through on-going adaptation—wanted learners to contribute to a dynamic, changing, but less controlled resource (di Savoia, 2010).

Hosting solutions for OER were strongly influenced by the community within which each project was working. Open release of resources, with the aim of maximum uptake from the public, was supported by multiple dissemination and hosting solutions; building communities around resource collections was supported by digital platforms with user profiles and social facilities such as commenting, recommending, following and reviewing.

Therefore, we identified a tension between the release of resources by communities of people who primarily produce the resource for use within the community and the open release of resources that will be used by broad, potentially unknown, groups of people. At present, the technologies of choice reflect those tensions rather than helping to resolve them.

Tensions Around Rules

These evolving open professional practices blur the distinction between the 'creators', 'reusers' and 'adapters' of OERs, as illustrated in the previous sections. These changing roles render existing rules inappropriate. For example, rules around IPR break down in situations where teaching-content resources are evolving, rather than static. Creative Commons licences provide a basis for dealing with many difficult IPR issues but do not align with conventional professional practice in a number of ways. To alleviate this tension, some project teams set up written contracts with contributors in parallel with Creative Commons licensing. Consequently, there were a range of methods for accrediting individual contributors, which, rather than easing changes in professional practice, provided additional complications (for example Evolution: Leeds, 2010).

Further tensions were identified within communities around rules of quality. Just as disruptive events (for example the release of OERs) acted as a trigger for changes in professional practice, these events also prompted reconsideration of institutional policy (for example quality measures). Quality processes had to be reconceptualised, since the lifecycle of OERs is different from that of conventional teaching resources (open resources have no natural 'review' cycle). Some projects followed through this logic and initiated change to curriculum-development processes across the board (for example ChemistryFM: Winn, 2010 and also BERLiN, OCEP and Open staffs projects). Others used add-on solutions such as peer review or stakeholder and user review processes (for example Bioscience: McAndrew & Taylor, 2010). However, this solution could be problematic, since conventional quality processes tend to assess resources within a specific pedagogic context. It cannot be assumed that the materials themselves will 'carry' quality assurance into the open environment and range of contexts where they might be used by a number of users with different requirements (for example Humbox: Dickens et al., 2010).

There were tensions within communities when some members viewed change as risky, while others considered not adapting to carry a higher risk. For example, some individuals within the project teams faced resistance from colleagues within their institutions who did not wish to allow users from outside the institution to use resources hosted within collaborative forums supported by enterprise systems. This issue was problematic for projects where co-evolution of knowledge (for example through peer feedback) was built into the pedagogic design (openSpace: di Savoia, 2010). This issue raises problems for forms of learning, such as learning through knowledge co-construction (see Chapter 7 in this volume).

Therefore, it seems that applying new rules that fit with open professional practices is a source of continual tension. We found evidence of tensions between groups of people who wish to develop and release OERs to a broader community and others who affiliate themselves with the rules of particular institutions.

Tensions Around Roles

The communities within our study included people with a variety of roles: faculty, e-learning developers, library and learning resource staff, content developers, repository curators, legal (IPR) support staff and quality support staff. There were tensions between familiar and emerging practices in each of these roles, particularly where hybrid roles were emerging. These professionals involved in project activity almost always found that their roles changed, particularly as they became the 'experts' in the area of OERs, providing advice and support to colleagues. Some projects cascaded expertise to other faculty by supporting project staff to take on additional activities, such as third-party IPR clearance (for example BERLiN: Beggan et al., 2010); others encouraged faculty to take the lead in developing OERs, drawing on specialist expertise when required (for example Unicycle: Thomson, 2010). The devolved model used by the Unicycle project involved significant change in roles and professional practices. Whether practice change comes about through changing the boundaries of existing roles, or through creating new ones, significant engagement with OER does seem to entail organisational restructuring.

Within communities, changing the role of learners from being a 'consumer of content' to a 'prosumer' fundamentally changes learner–teacher relationships. We found evidence that faculty–student collaboration (for example ChemistryFM: Winn, 2010; BERLiN: Beggan et al., 2010) was associated with a less hierarchical relationship between the teacher and the learner. A change in cultural perceptions of learner agency and learner–teacher roles is required if OERs and associated practices are to reach their full potential (Falconer, Littlejohn, & McGill, 2013). After completing compulsory education, people may choose to direct their own learning, rather than turning automatically to formal institutions. It may become natural for learners to make use of open learning resources and opportunities throughout their lives, making their own decisions about what to learn, when and how. As they become proficient users of open resources, learners naturally want to augment and adapt existing content, enriching the experience for other users and eventually contributing to the learning of others as well as learning themselves.

Conclusions and Recommendations

We have analysed the experience of the HEA and JISC UKOER pilot programme, using an activity framework to draw out inherent tensions. Communities bound together by trust in common values, such as those that form around the UKOER projects, emerged as both drivers and inhibitors of change.

There is evidence that an open sharing approach, addressing issues of release, hosting and reuse, can be effective and sustainable, particularly where communities share clear common interests. In one interpretation, the most compelling case for open sharing exists at the level of a community (possibly even research-based) within a discipline. However, even within close-knit communities, sharing was impeded by the existence of different institutional quality processes, different levels of institutional commitment to OERs, and different levels of expertise and institutional support for role and practice change. Strong collaborations were needed to overcome such barriers and to give confidence in quality assurance processes.

In many cases the OER project served to bind together an existing or new community, and the excitement of belonging to a community with a commitment to sharing resources helped to drive change. Communities also provided a safe environment for those who were nervous about OERs, such as teachers who wished to release initially only to their own institutional or discipline colleagues. Indeed, it is notable how many projects released resources with a well-defined audience in mind, often of teachers within the discipline.

We have evidence that OER development and use challenges established community boundaries, especially where learners or international partners are involved. Traditionally these have been assigned the role of 'audience'—recipients of resources. There is evidence from some projects that this view is breaking down and that, for reasons both of sustainability and of enhancing the learner experience, learners and international partners are beginning to be seen as co-producers or re-purposers of OERs. There is a flattening of the former hierarchical relationship, which is coherent with the underlying philosophies of open access to knowledge and collaborative development. But this erosion of community boundaries requires new kinds of trust to be generated, in looser networks. This loss of existing community norms, along with nervousness about the technical and legal processes of release and concerns about OER quality, continues to undermine the potential for change.

However, while closely bound communities may encourage first steps into open practice, they are fundamentally antithetical to the basic philosophy of open access to knowledge by all. Resources developed within a community for a specific audience will tend to conform to the values and expectations of the community members; it is by those values that resource quality will be judged and decisions will be reached on whether to share, and the outcome may be coloured by assumptions that it is within the community's known and given contexts that resources will be reused. In this sense, over-reliance on trusted communities and community-based tools (that require a specific login) may inhibit long-term significant change.

Policy makers and practitioners implementing change initiatives to encourage the release of OERs should recognise that the creation and release of OERs within a community lowers barriers to professional practice change. Situating an appropriate and effective change initiative within an established community is likely to accelerate change in professional practice, particularly at the beginning of the change programme. However, resources may be produced with a specific user group in mind: limiting the use of resources; change may not develop beyond the existing practice of the community; communities may be impermeable to fresh knowledge; and ideas may stagnate. Therefore, change is likely to be limited.

The diffusion of knowledge across community boundaries is critical for transformational change. Strategies to encourage change include the following.

- *Changing community cultures.* It is critical to establish cultures and outlooks amongst community members to encourage them to source and apply new knowledge from outside their immediate community. Community members should be sufficiently confident and motivated to adopt change at regular intervals. People should be able—both culturally and cognitively—to move in and out of different community spaces, serendipitously finding others, and being alerted to concepts and ideas that may be of use to them.
- *Ensuring that communities regularly incorporate new people and ideas across different domains.* Community members should dynamically change their networks to either strengthen ties or strike out in new directions according to their needs. Community members need to be motivated to change connections regularly within their networks and understand how to move in and out of communities, developing in their new communities where appropriate. One way forward is for people from different communities to work on the same OERs at the same time. In this way, the resources become 'boundary objects' that support cross-community collaboration.
- *Changing societal perceptions of when learning takes place.* More fundamentally, there has to be a broader view within society of what constitutes learning. Universities, colleges and schools influence how people think about learning. Radically opening up these organisations, through strategic commitments to openness, reforming and developing new infrastructures, could

broaden people's understanding of what constitutes learning. Learning could be viewed as extending beyond formal, structured events to include unstructured, serendipitous, learning opportunities.

- *Changing organizational perceptions of where learning takes place.* It is important to recognise that a wide range of different organisations (private, public, professional bodies and third sector) have roles to play and can draw on experience of supporting learning. Opening new forms of conversation with these sectors through OERs or Open Educational Practice provides an opportunity for different communities to inform and enrich practice within the educational sectors.

Forms of learning which depend on OERs are inevitably fraught with challenges. They depend on a host of other social, economic and political systems producing relatively autonomous learners. Moving in this direction requires a radical change in cultural perceptions of learner agency and learner–teacher roles, associated with changes in networked technologies and resources. Whether recent areas of activity around OERs have been sufficient to trigger this sort of fundamental change is yet to be seen.

References

Atkins, D. E., Brown J. S., & Hammond, A. L. (2007). A review of the Open Educational Resources (OER) movement: Achievements, challenges, and new opportunities.https://oerknowledgecloud.org/sites/oerknowledgecloud.org/files/ReviewoftheOERMovement.pdf.

Beggan, A., Horton, J., Johnson, A., & Stapleton, S. (2010). *BERLiN project final report.* Retrieved 27 August 2011 from www.jisc.ac.uk/media/documents/programmes/oer/berlin_final_report_v1.0.pdf.

Browne, T. (2010). *Open Exeter project final report.* Retrieved 26 August 2011 from www.jisc.ac.uk/media/documents/programmes/oer/oer-final-report-exeter.doc.

Dickens, A., Borthwick, K., Richardson, S., Lavender, L., Mossley, D., Gawthrope, J., & Lucas, B. (2010). *Humbox project final report.* Retrieved 23 December 2011 from www.llas.ac.uk/resourcedownloads/3233/humbox_final_report.pdf.

di Savoia, A. (2010). *Open Space project final report.* Retrieved 27 August 2011 from www.heacademy.ac.uk/assets/York/documents/ourwork/oer/OER_final_report_openSpaceFinalMay2010v2FALMOUTH.doc.

Engeström, Y. (1987). *Learning by expanding,* Helsinki: Orienta-konsultit. Retrieved 23 December 2011 from http: //lchc.ucsd.edu/mca/Paper/Engestrom/expanding/toc.htm.

Engeström, Y. (2005). Knotworking to create collaborative intentionality capital in fluid organizational fields. In M. M. Beyerlein, S. T. Beyerlein, & F. A. Kennedy (Eds.), *Collaborative capital: Creating intangible value* (pp. 307–336). Amsterdam: Elsevier.

Falconer, I., Littlejohn, A., & McGill, L. (2013). *Fluid learning: A vision for lifelong learning in 2030.* Retrieved from http://blogs.ec.europa.eu/openeducation2030/files/2013/04/OE2030_LLL_Booklet.pdf.

Falconer, I., Littlejohn, A., McGill, L., & Beetham, H. (2013). Motives and tensions in the release of Open Educational Resources. Available from http://bit.ly/motivespaper.

Kuutti, K. (1996). Activity theory as a potential framework for human–computer interaction research. In B. Nardi (Ed.), *Context and consciousness: Activity theory and human–computer interaction* (pp. 17–44). Cambridge, MA: MIT Press.

Lane, A., & McAndrew, P. (2010). Are open educational resources systematic or systemic change agents for teaching practice? *British Journal of Educational Technology*, 41(6), 952–962.

Leeds, B. (2010). *Evolution project final report*. Retrieved 6 September 2011 from www.heacademy.ac.uk/assets/York/documents/ourwork/oer/UCLAN_final_rep.doc.

Littlejohn, A., & Margaryan, A. (2010). Sharing resources in educational communities. *International Journal of Emerging Technologies in Learning*, 5(2). DOI:10.3991/ijet.v5i2.857, Available from: http://online-journals.org/i-jet/article/view/857.

Littlejohn, A., Beetham, H., & McGill, L. (2012). Learning at the digital frontier: A review of digital literacies in theory and practice. *Journal of Computer Assisted Learning*, 24(4), 333–347

Margaryan, A., & Littlejohn, A. (2008). Repositories and communities at cross-purposes: Issues in sharing and reuse of digital learning resources. *Journal of Computer Assisted Learning*, 24(4), 333–347.

McAndrew, T., & Taylor, C. (2010). *Bioscience OER project report*. Retrieved 23 December 2011 from www.heacademy.ac.uk/assets/York/documents/ourwork/oer/Bioscience_final_rep.docx.

McGill, L., Beetham, H., Falconer, I., & Littlejohn, A. (2010). *JISC/HE Academy OER programme: Pilot phase synthesis and evaluation report*. Retrieved 23 December 2011 from https://oersynth.pbworks.com/w/page/29688444/Pilot%20Phase%20Synthesis%20and%20Evaluation%20Report.

McGill, L., Currier, S., Duncan, C., & Douglas, P. (2008). *Good intentions: Improving the evidence base in support of sharing learning materials*, report for the UK JISC. Retrieved 13 January 2011 from http://ie-repository.jisc.ac.uk/265/1/goodintentionspublic.pdf.

McGill, L., Falconer, I., Dempster, J. A., Littlejohn, A., & Beetham, H. (May, 2013). *Journeys to open educational practice: HEFCE OER review final report*. JISC. Retrieved 23 July 2013 from https://oersynth.pbworks.com/w/page/60338879/HEFCE-OER-Review-Final-Report.

Morris, D. (2010). *OCEP project final report*. Retrieved 23 December 2011 from www.jisc.ac.uk/media/documents/programmes/oer/ocepfinalcomplete_web.pdf.

OECD (2007). *Giving knowledge for free: The emergence of Open Educational Resources*. Retrieved 17 November 2011 from www.oecd.org/document/41/0,3746,en_2649_35845581_38659497_1_1_1_1,00.html.

Thomson, S. (2010). *Unicycle project final report*. Retrieved 6 September 2011 from www.jisc.ac.uk/media/documents/programmes/oer/unicycle_final_report.doc.

Winn, J. (2010). *ChemistryFM project final report*. Retrieved 27 August 2011 from wwheacademy.ac.uk/assets/documents/oer/OER_1_Lincoln_Final_Report.pdf.

Witthaus, G., & Armellini, A. (2010). *Otter project final report*. Retrieved 27 August 2011 from www.jisc.ac.uk/media/documents/programmes/oer/otterfinalreport27april2010_v2%201.pdf.

Yuan, L., MacNeil, S., & Kraan, W. (2008). *Open Educational resources—opportunities and challenges for higher education*, JISC CETIS report. Retrieved 23 December 2011 from http://wiki.cetis.ac.uk/images/6/6d/OER_Briefing_Paper_CETIS_without_recommendations_with_cover_page_.pdf.

5

OERs

A European Policy Perspective

Jesús Maria Alquézar Sabadie, Jonatan Castaño Muñoz, Yves Puni, Christine Redecker and Riina Vuorikari

Introduction

Education and training are changing radically all over the world. The increasing demand for education in emerging economies, however, contrasts with the financial cuts being implemented in Europe. At the same time, global competition between education providers for funding and talent is intensifying. Probably, the most disruptive pressure comes from information and communication technologies (ICT) which could be potential catalysts in the (near) future of education and training (Redecker et al., 2011). The question is whether the European players (institutions, governments and citizens) in education and training systems are ready to seize the opportunities offered by the digital revolution and overcome the challenges of the twenty-first century.

The Europe 2020 strategy[1] acknowledges that a fundamental transformation of education and training is needed to address the skills and competences required for Europe to remain competitive, overcome the current economic crisis and grasp new opportunities. The Europe 2020 strategy flagship initiatives underline the need for innovation in education and training. The European Commission has also established key educational targets for promoting creativity and innovation, reducing early school leaving, increasing participation in higher education and adult learning, fostering re-skilling and up-skilling and modernising education and training.

Educational stakeholders recognise the contribution ICT could make to achieving these targets. All European countries have implemented policies and activities which aim to promote the use of ICT in education and training. The Thematic Working Group on ICT and Education is reporting on these initiatives and sharing good practices. This group is made up of representatives of the Member States under the Open Method of Coordination on Education and Training 2010 (Van den Brande, Carlberg, & Good, 2010.).

Responding to these policy trends, the 'Rethinking Education' Communication (European Commission, 2012), launched by the European Commission in November 2012, emphasises the need to stimulate open and flexible learning in order to provide the skills needed in the twenty-first century economy and labour market. It points out that the quality of education relies on a mix of different educational approaches and materials. Therefore, the Communication calls for wider access to and use of open educational resources (OERs), accompanied by clear quality standards and mechanisms to assess and validate the skills and competences acquired.

OERs, as defined by UNESCO in 2002, are 'teaching, learning or research materials that are in the public domain or released with an intellectual property license that allows for free use, adaptation, and distribution'. According to this definition, OERs do not exclusively refer to digital resources, although the concept is usually restricted to ICT materials, as illustrated by the OECD definition (Hylén, Van Damme, Mulder, & D'Antoni, 2012).

Reflecting on these two commonly used definitions of OERs, at least four different characteristic dimensions can be distinguished, as illustrated in Figure 5.1. OERs are (digital) learning and teaching (and research) resources that are (1) free (as in 'gratis'); (2) open (i.e. freely accessible, publicly licensed, in the public domain); (3) can be shared and re-distributed; and (4) can be freely (or liberally) reused, adapted and mixed for individual learners' and teachers' purposes. The first two dimensions concern the content sphere of OER. The latter two dimensions, also referred to as the 4Rs of Open Content[2] (i.e. the right to reuse, revise, remix and redistribute content), point to the use of content through personalisation and collaboration. This is what we call the 'people' side of OERs. It is important to bear in mind, however, that not all educational materials commonly considered as OERs actually satisfy all four conditions.

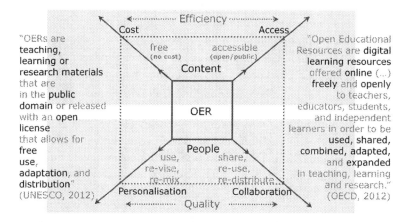

FIGURE 5.1 The IPTS OER Square

The importance of OERs for innovating in learning and teaching lies in the interconnectedness of these four dimensions and the fruitful interplay of free use and collaborative revision as a mechanism to improve quality and usability. As a consequence, the 2012 Paris OER Declaration by UNESCO encourages public institutions to: 'Promote and use OER to widen access to education at all levels, both formal and non-formal, in a perspective of lifelong learning, thus contributing to social inclusion, gender equity and special needs education' (UNESCO, 2012a). Disaggregating the UNESCO recommendation, we can state that OER provide a strategic opportunity for governments to:

• foster inclusion and democratisation of knowledge by extending access to education (Atkins, Brown, & Hammond, 2007; Lane, 2008);
• increase the efficacy (quality) and efficiency (cost-quality) of educational systems, by promoting innovations that OERs allow, and using their potential to reduce educational costs.

Furthermore the promotion of OERs can facilitate policy dialogue, knowledge sharing and collaboration between states and institutions at the pan-European level. This is one of the reasons why the European Commission decided to take action and launch a dedicated initiative for 'Opening up Education' in Europe.

This chapter aims to describe the landscape and the trends in OER policies and initiatives in Europe. It highlights the main challenges that OER policies have to overcome and, finally, presents and discusses the European 'Opening up Education' initiative.

Current Trends

There are distinctive differences in the use and promotion of OERs between school education and higher education. There is also a notable lack of awareness of how to seize the opportunities offered by OERs to promote lifelong learning. Higher education is currently the most advanced sector in the deployment of OERs, as shown by the boom in Massive Open Online Courses (MOOCs). However, Europe (aside from some exceptions, such as the UK) is not embracing OERs with as much enthusiasm as are other regions of the world, like the USA or Brazil.

In both these countries, public authorities are strongly committed and there is collaboration between stakeholders. In the USA, OERs and digital technologies are key elements of the Obama administration's National Education Technology Plan[3] and its goal to ensure that the United States has 'the best-educated, best-prepared workforce in the world by 2020'. A number of systemic initiatives, designed with a view to scale from the outset, have been implemented. They are based on a model of bottom-up/top-down innovation, in which all relevant stakeholders constitute an eco-system at the local/state level. All initiatives are accompanied by rigorous evaluation and controlled experiments so that an evidence base about what works can be built up (Shapiro, 2013). In Brazil, OER are seen as an opportunity to democratise access to education and their development goes hand in hand with the political objective to reduce the digital divide by extending the availability and use of internet. One of the success factors in Brazil's national initiatives is the close cooperation between universities, the Ministry of Education, local authorities and schools.

In Europe, the expected benefits of OERs have led most European governments to implement policies to encourage their creation and use (Hylén et al., 2012), especially in (upper) secondary education. Fewer policies of this kind have been directed at higher education, due to the institutional autonomy of universities (Hoosen, 2012), and even fewer at the supposedly strongest impact area of OER, lifelong learning. In the past, the policy focus has been on expanding the development of and access to OERs. However, there has been a growing awareness that this must be accompanied by a shift in pedagogical practices towards 'Open Educational Practices'. Only thus can their potential to promote quality and innovation in teaching and learning and to address individual learners' needs be realised.[4] The European Commission's (2013) Communication on 'Opening up Education' therefore follows a more comprehensive approach in which dedicated OER incentives are embedded in a broader strategy fostering the use of ICT for learning.

Higher Education

Higher education institutions, particularly in the USA, have been at the forefront of OER development and deployment since 2001, when the Massachusetts Institute of Technology (MIT) announced that nearly all its courses would be freely accessible to anyone on the internet. In 2002, as the number of institutions offering free or open courseware (OCW) increased, UNESCO organised the 1st Global OER Forum and the term 'OER' was adopted. Subsequently many universities worldwide started to offer open access to their courseware (Vlădoiu, 2011) (Figure 5.2).

UNESCO and the Commonwealth of Learning have developed guidelines for integrating OERs into higher education to encourage a systematic production, adaptation and use of OERs (COL & UNESCO, 2011). In Europe, initiatives such as SCORE[5] or OPAL,[6] amongst others, have provided support and advice to individuals, projects, institutions and programmes, helping them to create, publish, remix, reuse and redistribute OERs. These are examples of what we may consider the 'top-down' approach to developing OERs: initiatives funded by international organisations, educational funding bodies, public institutions or foundations.

The emergence and spread of MOOCs has brought the OER movement to a new high. MOOCs are, according to the definition provided by Wikipedia in

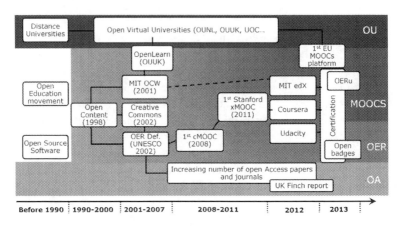

FIGURE 5.2 The Brief History of OER in Higher Education

January 2012, 'a type of online course aimed at large-scale participation via the web'. In 2013 the biggest MOOC platform was Coursera, initiated at Stanford University as a venture capital start-up in April 2012. It was followed by edX, a Harvard/MIT non-profit initiative launched in autumn 2012 with a starting capital of $30 million (see Chapter 10 in this volume). Coursera is growing exponentially: by August 2013, it already had 85 partner universities worldwide; 431 courses and 4.5 million users. EdX currently has 28 partner universities—several of them from Asia and 5 from Europe (TU Delft, EPF Lausanne, TU München, Karolinkska Institutet and the Université Catholique de Louvain)—offering 63 courses to more than one million students on its platform. In April 2013, the European Association of Distance Teaching Universities (EADTU) joined this global movement and launched the first pan-European MOOC platform,[7] which offers 40 courses in 12 different languages.[8]

While MOOCs are not strictly OERs (the resources provided rarely encourage adaptation or remix and are not always published under an open licence), they epitomise an unprecedented move towards greater accessibility of higher education at no (or low) additional cost based on high-quality theoretical content. Sir John Daniel and others therefore argue that OERs in general and MOOCs in particular can break the 'Iron Triangle' that has dominated past debates on higher education. The Iron Triangle refers to 'the assumption that that quality, exclusivity, and expense necessarily go together'.[9] Hence, it is impossible to widen access, lower cost and increase quality at the same time: any improvement along one of these axes will always be detrimental to at least one of the other axes (Figure 5.3). It is now believed that OERs will not only make high-quality higher education available at low cost to a large number of users, but it will also lead to innovation within universities.[10]

However, it is still unclear how this leap can be accomplished in practical terms. Universities and enterprises involved in MOOCs have not yet consolidated

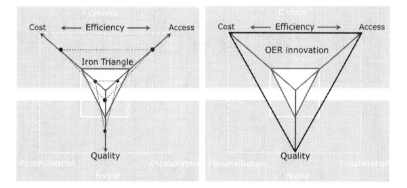

FIGURE 5.3 The Iron Triangle and OER Innovation

Note: Developed on the basis of the Iron Triangle by Sir John Daniel (www.col.org/SiteCollection Documents/Daniel_110308AustraliaHE.pdf) and Fred Mulder's argument for OER innovation in Higher Education (http://ministerialconference2012.linkevent.no/F%20Mulder%20parallel.pdf)

their business models. Coursera, for example, is currently experimenting with different funding lines, including the revenues paid by an Amazon.com affiliates programme if users buy books suggested by professors; an opt-in recruiting programme that matches students with employers, and verified course certificates offered for a fee. Thus, it remains to be seen how 'open' and 'free' MOOCs will be in in the future.

It is, however, clear that the MOOC movement is starting to undermine the traditional bricks-and-mortar university model (cf. Barber et al., 2013). Higher education institutions will have to seriously consider what kind of services they can offer their students and whether these will be better than or complementary to an online Ivy League MOOC. Most European universities and academics have not yet realised the extent to which their conventional approach to teaching and research is being challenged by open learning. According to a survey carried out by the European University Association (EUA) in 2013, the concept of the MOOC is unknown in one third of the 200 European universities consulted and only another third has discussed the topic internally.[11]

School Education

OERs also have much to offer primary, secondary and vocational education and training institutions in creating, sharing and adapting learning material. Open learning object repositories, digital libraries and collaborative authoring platforms where learning resources can be exchanged and reused have been around since the 1990s. Nowadays, all EU Member States have national gateways to digital learning resources for school education, and some also promote access to OERs (Figure 5.4). In many European countries, these include public broadcasting

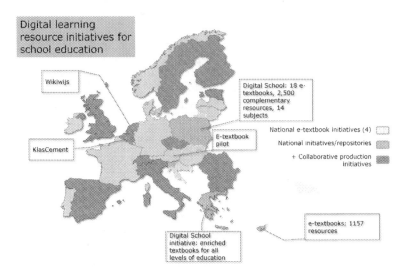

FIGURE 5.4 OER Initiatives and Strategies in School Education in Europe

corporations, cultural heritage funds and other national or public institutions. Most textbook publishers also make additional teaching and learning materials available for free online. Thus, there is a range of educational materials of different scope, focus and quality available to learners and teachers, sometimes scattered across the internet, sometimes, as in Denmark,[12] accessible via one central platform.

In some countries, a collaborative approach to producing and sharing OERs is being followed. The Wikiwijs project in the Netherlands, for example, is inspired by the idea of wikis and focuses on the collaborative development of content. It offers teachers from primary to university education an open platform where they can find, download, (further) develop and share educational resources. The whole project is based on open source software, open content and open standards. An important characteristic of Wikiwijs, perhaps the key to its success, is the collaboration with educational publishers, leading to a combination of OERs with more traditional materials. According to some national surveys, teachers prefer to combine traditional textbooks with resources from the internet.[13]

KlasCement in Flanders (Belgium),[14] on the other hand, is run by the non-profit organisation EduCentrum, mainly financed by the Ministry of Education of Flanders. KlasCement is a repository of teacher-generated learning materials (more than 26,000 resources), some of which are made available under open licences (variations of Creative Commons). In March 2011, it had 67,000 members, two-thirds of whom are teachers. The portal has a very active community of contributors with around 8 per cent of users sharing resources. Content and metadata submitted to KlasCement are moderated by a team of up to ten teachers. Furthermore, all resources are put into moderation every two years to ensure their relevance and quality.

Some European countries, for example Slovenia, Greece, Cyprus and Poland, are exploring free, digitally enriched e-textbooks as a means of saving money in times of crisis. In Poland in 2012, the Ministry of Education launched the 'Digital School' initiative, in which at least eighteen free textbook resources (including multimedia packages) will be published under a Creative Commons Attribution—Share Alike license. In Slovenia, the government is currently running an e-textbook pilot with four e-textbooks and is planning a further twenty-five new e-textbooks by the end of 2013. In total, €2 million are being invested in this project. In Greece, the 'Digital School' initiative by the Ministry of Education is part of the 'New School' reform and is the main vehicle for exploiting the potential of ICT and OERs. The scheme has been piloted in 800 primary and 1,250 lower secondary schools, with a view to providing a platform for digital content and tools and teacher training. One of the things offered by this initiative is an official repository of all available textbooks in the form of enriched e-books for all levels of education (primary, secondary, upper secondary and professional education). However, the initiative may not be fully implemented, as it is currently being undermined by major budgetary cuts in Greece.

At the pan-European level, a number of European-funded initiatives have tried to encourage the reuse of OERs, both at national and cross-border levels. LeMill,[15] for instance, already had over 7,500 members and over 8,500 reusable learning resources by 2009 (Leinonen et al., 2010). Another example is the Learning Resource Exchange by European Schoolnet, which provides a service that enables schools to find educational content from many different countries. The Scientix[16] platform contains teaching material on science education and also aims to enable teachers' communities to share knowledge and experiences. Open Discovery Space[17] provides a socially powered and multilingual open learning infrastructure to boost the adoption of e-learning resources in Europe. The SLOOP2Desc (2009–11) initiative[18] promoted the use of OERs among teachers in vocational education and training.

However, despite the large number of OERs available for schools and the high number of national and pan-European initiatives, OERs are not yet widely used in school education and less so across national borders. The overall picture of OER use in school education in Europe is mixed: there are different levels of deployment and different approaches towards making use of OERs, which usually depend on the national and local educational policy context. Two poles emerge when comparing different national approaches: on the one hand, there is a focus on the collaborative dimension of OERs, and on the other, there is the use of centrally commissioned interactive digital textbooks as a means of reducing public and private spending on textbooks.

2.3 Adult Education and Lifelong Learning

Surprisingly, OERs have not (yet) been exploited to support lifelong learning or adult education by making learning opportunities available openly and freely to a general audience (Minguillón, Rodríguez, & Conesa, 2010). Case studies with good examples and successful initiatives suggest that the development of innovative forms of teaching and learning is crucial for the success of OERs (Dinevski, 2008). Furthermore, heterogeneous interfaces, search engines and varying criteria hamper access to and retrieval of relevant resources that could assist enterprises in addressing the training needs of their employees (Niemann et al., 2010).

In a study conducted by the Glasgow Caledonian University on behalf of the Institute for Prospective Technological Studies, over 100 relevant lifelong learning and adult education initiatives were analysed to better understand the current use of OER (Falconer et al., 2013a). A detailed survey conducted with initiative organisers reveals that those offering OERs know very little about who is actually using these resources (Figure 5.5). Even for lifelong learning, pedagogic approaches envisaged by OER initiatives are rather traditional, institutional and teacher directed, which contrasts with current trends towards informal and self-directed learning. Furthermore, the concept of OERs is novel and still somewhat confusing to lifelong learning stakeholders. For example, the distinction between free (meaning 'no cost') and openly licensed is not well understood. It is therefore difficult for them to understand the potential of OERs and reap their benefits.

The ability of employers, and the wider public, to recognise the value of learning through OERs also requires, at least in the longer term, trusted forms of assessment, certification and accreditation. At present, the university degree

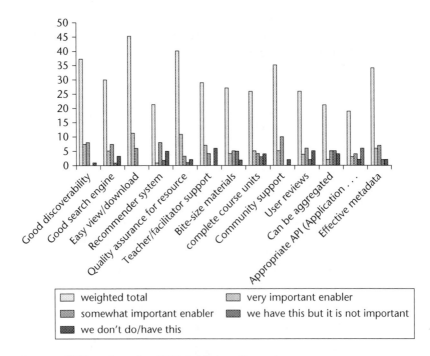

FIGURE 5.5 Lifelong Learning OER Initiatives: Focus Areas

is still the gold standard of post-compulsory education, although it is not an appropriate format for most lifelong learning activities. Thus, the European Council (2012) Recommendation on the validation of non-formal and informal learning and the UNESCO (2012a) Paris Declaration both call for the recognition and accreditation of competences acquired through OERs, for example by means of small units of credit, competency-based credits, peer reviews and wide availability of competency-based testing. Recognition is important for getting a better match between workers' skills and available job positions and it also has positive implications for equity, e.g. providing second chances for drop-outs, improving access to formal education and training, increasing self-confidence (Werquin, 2010).[19] Official recognition and quality schemes could increase the credibility of OERs at little cost, raising awareness and increasing uptake. Innovative tests and assessment formats can further increase the usefulness of OERs for lifelong learners.

Policy Challenges

Although OERs are high on the policy agenda and supported by many education and training stakeholders, their use in schools, universities and adult education institutions has not reached a critical threshold. Some of the bottlenecks and barriers to mainstreaming the use of OERs in education and training are elaborated below.

Content Aspect: Foster Adequate, Easy-to-Find and High-Quality Resources

Traditionally, national and regional policies have focused on the production of educational content and the creation of repositories to facilitate access. Thanks to these supply policies, there are a number of educational resources and OER platforms on the internet. The demand, however, is still lacking, due to the following factors.

- *Discoverability*. It is not easy for users to find quality resources that are appropriate to their teaching and learning needs (e.g. match of curriculum subjects across European countries remains a challenge).
- *Lack of quality assurance mechanisms*. The sheer number and nature of OERs make it difficult to employ quality assurance mechanisms across various repositories. Some European initiatives have addressed this issue by defining specific quality mechanisms for OERs (e.g. OPAL or OERtest[20]), highlighting the needs of a specific context of use and communities of users (i.e. an independent learner in a lifelong learning context may have different quality assurance needs from learners in an institutional context). In practice, quality assurance is the responsibility of each institution, teacher or learner who uses OERs (Kanwar & Uvalic-Trumbi, 2011).
- *Language*. Nearly half the OER initiatives surveyed in the international Poerup project supplied their resources in English. As a consequence, learners

who do not speak English have less choice, and there is a danger that the content developed will not reflect local contexts and lose cultural richness.

- *Lack of adoption of open standards.* Despite the efforts to develop open technical specifications for learning applications, the lack of adoption of agreed standards can hinder access to OERs. For example, the case of e-books shows that the business models of some major IT companies also represent a major obstacle to interoperability of content. For e-books, fully interoperable and compatible technical standards exist (e.g. EPUB-3), but enterprises like Apple or Amazon prefer to maintain closed ecosystems to defend their market shares (Bläsi & Rothlauf, 2013).

Legal Aspect: Clarify the Legal Framework

An important challenge to extending the use of OERs in European education is to implement a legal framework that clarifies the use, sharing and reuse of educational materials available on the internet. In the past, national copyright laws provided different types of exceptions for educational use of copyrighted material. In addition, there is the issue of cross-border use of publicly funded educational material which is free to use in one country but cannot be made publicly available to users in another country. Understandably, teachers and learners perceive copyright rules as too complex and not transparent, and thus choose not to use or reuse internet resources (Clements & Pawlowski, 2012).

On the other hand, moves, for example in the UK, to make all research, learning and teaching materials produced with public funds publicly and freely available (Finch, 2012) have been greeted with harsh criticism by publishers, who perceive these changes as a threat to their traditional business models. In this context, the key question is how OERs, commercial learning material and other types of learning materials will co-exist.

Societal Aspect: Foster Learners' and Teachers' Skills for Using OERs

The use of OERs is also hindered by access constraints and lack of skills. Five main issues arise:

1. *Uneven availability of ICT infrastructure.* In June 2012, internet penetration in Europe was 73 per cent overall, but this figure includes variations between countries, for example 44 per cent in Romania and 93 per cent in the Netherlands.[21]
2. *Different levels of digital skills.* According to Eurostat[22] in 2011, the proportion of the population with a high level of ICT skills varied between 43 per cent (Finland and Luxembourg) and 10 per cent (Romania). While 53 per cent of the European labour force as a whole felt confident in their computer

and/or ICT skills to look for or change jobs, this figure drops to below 30 per cent in several countries, such as Cyprus, Romania, Greece and Italy. Furthermore, the level of digital competence varies substantially according to age, education level and gender.

3. *Teachers' digital pedagogic skills.* Teachers need to be trained to exploit the potential of ICT and OERs for improving teaching and learning experiences. Currently, according to a joint EC–OECD study in 2010, 58 per cent of teachers surveyed said they had not received any training in how to use ICT in the classroom. Around 70 per cent of teachers in the EU, however, would like to have professional development in ICT skills (Scheerens, 2010).

4. *Developing innovative teaching practices and innovation-friendly teaching environments.* Teachers usually perceive OERs as resources that do not fit with teaching approaches (Carneiro, Nozes, Policarpo, & Correia, 2011; Harley, 2008). OERs are often adapted to traditional practices and therefore their potential to improve the quality of the learning process is not exploited. Furthermore, European education and training institutions often lack the vision or capacity to promote innovative teaching methods and an integrated use of technologies. Additionally, curricula and assessment schemes are often too restrictive to allow teachers to employ and experiment with innovative and creative pedagogies, especially in primary and secondary education (Petrides, Nguyen, Jimes, & Karaglani, 2008; Sahlberg, 2006; UNESCO 2012b). The fact that many teachers feel alone in their efforts is reflected by 74 per cent of respondents to an IPTS survey saying they needed more institutional support (Cachia, Ferrari, Ala-Mutka, & Punie 2010).

5. *Insufficient individual learning-to-learn skills.* OERs have an enormous potential for lifelong learning, but this requires learners to be able to identify and monitor their own learning needs and to know how to fulfil these (Falconer, Littlejohn, & McGill, 2013b).

Economic Aspect: Foster Sustainability and Increase Returns on Public Investment on OERs

In the next few decades, the level of worldwide demand for university studies will largely exceed the capacity of existing systems. It is predicted that the demand for higher education will rise from 97 million students in 2000 to over 262 million students by 2025. The magnitude of unsatisfied demand indicates that alternative learning and teaching concepts need to be developed. OERs can contribute by complementing existing post-secondary education provision, creating flexible pathways for learners (Athabasca University et al., 2011). As in other economic sectors, it is expected that digital technologies combined with new didactics will enhance resource productivity and economies of scale, expanding access to more people at lower costs (Butler Battaglino et al., 2012; SRI, 2012).

In Europe, against the background of the economic crisis which started in 2008, one of the main arguments for OERs is their potential to reduce the costs of education and training. One study indicates that correct use of open textbooks could save over 50 per cent of textbook costs without affecting educational outcomes (Wiley, Levi Hilton, Ellington, & Hall 2012). This could represent a partial solution,[23] though it should not be forgotten that the cost of educational materials (both paper based and digital) amounts to less than 10 per cent of the overall costs of education.

Despite the potential of OERs for reducing the costs of education, there are important debates on the sustainability of OER initiatives (cf. Downes, 2007; Meiszner, 2012). The current reliance on government and institutional funding, in particular, is a cause for concern, as it discourages the development of alternative revenue streams such as paid-for services, cross-sector partnerships, advertising or membership. Governments and institutions appear to lack confidence in OERs as a viable long-term investment, e.g. as a cheaper alternative to commercial textbooks. From a public policy perspective, it is important to understand how to integrate public and non-public funding models in order to reduce education costs and maximise public investment returns.

The European 'Opening up Education' Initiative

The European Commission has a long tradition of support for the integration of ICT into education and training. Since the main responsibility for designing, developing and implementing policies in education and training systems is a prerogative of its Member States, European policy has focused on:

- *Financing national initiatives and projects*, e.g. through the eLearning (2004–6) and Life Long Learning (2007–13) programmes, the Framework Programmes 5 (19982002), 6 (2002–6) and 7 (2006–13), and eContentPlus (2005–08);
- *Encouraging the exchange of experiences and benchmarking between Member States*, through the Open Method of Coordination (OMC) and, more concretely, in the Thematic Working Group on ICT and Education.

In September 2013, the European Commission launched its new initiative 'Opening up Education: Innovative teaching and learning for all through new technologies and Open Educational Resources' (European Commission 2013). This Communication 'sets out a European agenda for stimulating high-quality, innovative ways of learning and teaching through new technologies and digital content' (ibid.). It is based on the belief that embedding ICT and OERs in education will increase both efficiency and fairness of education and training in Europe.

The Communication responds to the fact that developments in the area of OERs, such as the rise of the MOOC movement, highlight the need to develop economies of scale and remove barriers to access, use and sharing of knowledge across borders for education, if Europe is to remain competitive globally. The Communication also acknowledges the need to overcome pertinent challenges to ICT access and skills in order to reap the benefits of OERs, and focuses more broadly on integrating ICT in education and training systems. Thus, incentives fostering OER development and availability are combined with measures for digital and pedagogical skills development for teachers, on the one hand, and, on the other, measures to improve ICT infrastructure and connectivity for schools, including interoperability and portability standards and incentives to stimulate the market for new interactive content and learning tools.

In these three areas, three different types of actions are combined: (i) financial support to organisations implementing projects in these fields; (ii) tools providing online solutions; and (iii) policy guidance for Member States to reform education and training systems. Most actions will be implemented through the new programmes Erasmus+ and Horizon 2020 (2014–20), which combine more general with rather concrete measures, and exploration with implementation. These include:

- ensuring that educational materials produced with public funding are made freely accessible to all citizens;
- launching a European OER portal called 'Open Education Europa', to increase the visibility of high-quality European OER in several languages;
- enhancing transparency of user rights and obligations regarding educational resources;
- promoting open licences among communities of both teachers and policy makers, and developing technical tools to integrate metadata in each resource available on the web, to increase transparency;
- defining interoperability and portability standards for educational resources and ensuring that these are applied across devices, platforms and brands to provide a level playing field for all market players;
- promoting organisational change across schools, universities and training institutions to support better integration of new technologies and high-quality OERs;
- launching large-scale research and policy experiments to test innovative pedagogical approaches, curriculum development and skills assessment;
- exploring how established and emerging tools for the validation and recognition of skills, such as 'open badges', can be tailored to the needs of learners.

The main objective is to create the political will among the Member States and stakeholders such as education and training institutions, publishers and the ICT industry to take coherent and coordinated action. The Commission needs to create common framework conditions to combat the traditional fragmentation and lack of continuity in national and regional policies, which is based on projects that are often financially unsustainable. Furthermore, it can serve as a catalyst for increasing the knowledge base on OERs in areas where uncertainties persist—like business models, the future role of teachers, the potential of learning analytics, the implications of copyright regulations for the implementation of collaborative and personalised practices, amongst others.

Launching a strong political message is considered particularly important in a period of economic crisis and financial austerity, when some public authorities may be tempted to stop supporting initiatives which aim to exploit the potential of technologies and digital content in education and training. At the same time, the explosion of MOOCs has dominated discussions on the future of higher education, even though few European universities are involved. If, on the other hand, fragmentation of policies and initiatives takes place, this would be a major obstacle to developing economies of scale at European level and to exploiting opportunities from public investments.

The new Communication aims to join forces and create synergies on the European level to make change happen in education and training and to reap the benefits of OERs in all countries and for all citizens. More holistically, opening up education is seen as a starting point for creating a more innovation-friendly education and training environment.

Discussion and Conclusions

Policies for the promotion of OERs have led to passionate debates. The mere existence of OER challenges both traditional teaching and learning practices and business models of education and training stakeholders, like publishers or universities. The very concept of OERs is often under scrutiny. To what extent are OERs actually free, if they are often funded by public institutions or foundations? How can their financial sustainability and constant update be ensured? Are teachers ready and really interested in creating, reusing and sharing their materials? Is there enough empirical evidence about the added value offered by OERs, as compared to traditional commercial content? Should public authorities intervene to promote an extensive use of OERs in education and training systems?

OERs are a disruptive phenomenon, comparable to open source, open access or internet file sharing, which also challenged the traditional business models of the software industry, scientific publishers and the audiovisual sector. After first considering these new phenomena as threats, these sectors were then able to integrate them as different models and practices that co-exist and reinforce each other. In the area of OERs, commercial and non-commercial actors need some time to establish common spaces in a marketplace that is radically evolving (ELIG, 2011). Similarly, education and training systems and institutions will need time to understand how best to seize to benefits of OERs to innovate in teaching and learning. Some teachers and learners will be fully committed to OERs and Open Educational Practices, while others will combine commercial content with OERs—or even just use traditional textbooks.

OERs, like the whole internet, represent a radical cultural change. Different visions of what the internet is and should be must be confronted. For some, the internet is a space of freedom, characterised by social relations that allow sharing, reusing and discussing content without necessarily any commercial interest. There are several examples of this vision, the most obvious of which is probably Wikipedia. Indeed, major companies have implemented fora on their websites where their clients can discuss their problems, with very little intervention from the provider. These enterprises have understood that the internet can be a disintermediated space that works on its own, and allows them to save money in post-sales services. For others, the internet is the continuation of traditional markets and requires adapted regulations with a centralised control. In the field of education and training, the position of policy makers, school leaders and teachers as regards these different divides will probably lead to the support and implementation of completely different pedagogical approaches and use of web-based resources and OERs.

The role of a public policy should be to create framework conditions that allow all sorts of practices and business models, without artificial barriers to innovation. A European-wide framework could stimulate the creation of digital technology tailored to education and training purposes and the supply of quality digital content, including OERs. This would allow individuals, schools, training institutions and universities to be better equipped to capitalise on (past or present) public investments in upgrading ICT infrastructure. European framework conditions could also boost synergies across countries in the development of innovative teaching and learning practices and thus help to improve the quality of European education.

Notes

1 http://ec.europa.eu/europe2020/index_en.htm.
2 www.opencontent.org/definition/.
3 www.ed.gov/technology/netp-2010.
4 According to the International Council for Open and Distance Education (ICDE), Open Educational Practices (OEP) are 'practices which support the production, use and reuse of high quality open educational resources through institutional policies, which promote innovative pedagogical models, and respect and empower learners as co-producers on their lifelong learning path'. OEP can enrich the quality of the learning experience, with practices based on collaboration, contextualisation and personalisation. See: www.icde.org/en/resources/open_educational_quality_inititiative/definition_of_open_educational_practices/
5 http://www8.open.ac.uk/score/.
6 www.oer-quality.org.
7 www.OpenupEd.eu.
8 http://europa.eu/rapid/press-release_IP-13-349_en.htm.
9 www.changemag.org/Archives/Back%20Issues/March-April%202009/full-iron-triangle.html.

10 http://ministerialconference2012.linkevent.no/F%20Mulder%20parallel.pdf.
11 See: www.eua.be/news/13-02-25/Massive_Open_Online_Courses_MOOCs_EUA_to_look_at_development_of_MOOCs_and_trends_in_innovative_learning.aspx.
12 www.emu.dk.
13 In France, for instance, teachers consider ICT instruments as complementary tools to traditional textbooks and very few think they will replace them (Savoir Livre and Syndicat National de l'Edition, 2010). This is confirmed by some anecdotal evidence about the use of Wikiwijs resources: it seems that those produced by commercial publishers are more successful. However, the opposite trends are appearing in other European countries. In Denmark, a survey of principals in general and vocational upper secondary education institutions, on the use of OERs, showed that 7 per cent of these institutions had replaced all their educational materials with OERs in 2011. Another 23 per cent expected to do so within the coming year and 47 per cent within three to five years. Only 10 per cent said that they expected that the gymnasium would never totally replace printed materials. See: www.emu.dk/gym/tvaers/it/2runde.html.
14 www.klascement.be/, about 69 per cent of materials are under Creative Commons licences.
15 http://lemill.net.
16 www.scientix.eu.
17 www.opendiscoveryspace.eu/.
18 www.sloop2desc.eu/.
19 E.g. ALISON offers a low-cost, always on, competency-based testing service to employers wishing to verify that an ALISON certificate holder possesses the relevant knowledge; the site freelancer.com offers low-cost, always on, competency-based tests to freelancers wishing to raise the credibility of their tenders; LinkedIn allows peer endorsement and recommendation.
20 See: www.oer-quality.org/ and www.oer-europe.net/.
21 www.internetworldstats.com/stats9.htm.
22 http://epp.eurostat.ec.europa.eu/portal/page/portal/eurostat/home/.
23 www.bgsu.edu/departments/english/cconline/open/introduction.html.

References

Athabasca University; OER Foundation; Otago Polytechnic; & University of Southern Queensland (2011). Open Educational Resource University. Towards a logic model and plan for action. Retrieved from: http://wikieducator.org/images/c/c2/Report_OERU-Final-version.pdf.

Atkins, D. E., Brown, J., & Hammond, A. (2007). A review of the open educational resources (OER) movement: Achievements, challenges, and new opportunities. Retrieved from: www.hewlett.org/uploads/files/ReviewoftheOERMovement.pdf.

Barber, M., Donnely, K., & Rizvi, S. (2013). *An avalanche is coming. Higher education and the revolution ahead*. London: Institute for Public Policy Research. Retrieved from: www.ippr.org/images/media/files/publication/2013/04/avalanche-is-coming_Mar2013_10432.pdf.

Bläsi, Ch., & Rothlauf, F. (2013). *On the interoperability of eBook formats*. Brussels: European and International Booksellers Federation.

Butler Battaglino, T., Haldeman, M., & Laurans, E. (2012). The costs of online learning. In *Creating sound policy for digital learning*. Working Paper Series, Thomas B. Fordham Institute. 2012. Retrieved from: http://larrycuban.files.wordpress.com/2012/11/the-costs-of-online-learning-1.pdf.

Cachia, R., Ferrari, A., Ala-Mutka, C. & Punie, Y. (2010). *Creative learning and innovative teaching. Final report on the study on creativity and innovation in education in the EU Member States*. Luxembourg: Publications Office of the European Union. Retrieved from: http://ftp.jrc.es/EURdoc/JRC62370.pdf.

Carneiro, R., Nozes, J., Policarpo, J. C., & Correia, T. (2011). *OPAL quantitative online survey*. Open Educational Quality Initiative (OPAL), deliverable 3.3. Retrieved from: www.oer-quality.org/wp-content/uploads/2011/05/D3.3-Study-on-OEP-acceptance.pdf.

Clements, K., & Pawlowski, J. M. (2012). User-oriented quality for OER: Understanding teachers' views on re-use, quality, and trust. *Journal of Computer Assisted Learning, 28*(1), 4–14.

COL & UNESCO (2011). Guidelines for open educational resources (OER) in higher education. Retrieved from: www.col.org/PublicationDocuments/Guidelines_OER_HE.pdf.

Dinevski, D. (2008). Open educational resources and lifelong learning. *30th International Conference on Information Technology Interfaces, 2008 (ITI 2008)*. Cavtat/Dubrovnik. Retrieved from: http://hnk.ffzg.hr/bibl/iti2008/PDF/(102)/102-02-034.pdf

Downes, S. (2007). Models for sustainable open educational resources. *Interdisciplinary Journal of Knowledge and Learning Objects, 3*, 29–44.

ELIG (2011). *Open education: A wake-up call for the learning industry? Is open education fundamental to a sustainable learning industry or a noble but commercially flawed cause?* European Learning Industry Group, White Paper. Retrieved from: www.elearningeuropa.info/sites/default/files/meeting20120713/ELIG%20WhitePaper_small.pdf.

European Commission (2012). Communication from the Commission to the European Parliament, the Council, the European Economic and Social Committee and the Committee of the regions. Rethinking Education: Investing in skills for better socio-economic outcomes. COM(2012) 669 final. Retrieved from: http://ec.europa.eu/education/news/rethinking/com669_en.pdf.

European Commission (2013). Communication from the Commission to the European Parliament, the Council, the European Economic and Social Committee and the Committee of the regions. Opening up Education: Innovative teaching and learning for all through new technologies and Open educational resources. COM(2013) 654 final. Retrieved from: http://ec.europa.eu/education/news/doc/openingcom_en.pdf.

European Council (2012). Council Recommendation of 20 December 2012 on the validation of non-formal and informal learning. Retrieved from: http://eur-lex.europa.eu/LexUriServ/LexUriServ.do?uri=OJ:C:2012:398:0001:0005:EN:PDF.

Falconer, I., McGill, L., Littlejohn, A., & Boursinou, E. (2013a) Overview and analysis of practices with open educational resources in adult education in Europe review, JRC Scientific and Policy Reports (Eds. Redecker, C., Castaño Muñoz, J., & Punie, Y.). European Commission. Retrieved from: http://tinyurl.com/pk6nuvt.

Falconer, I., Littlejohn, A., & McGill, L (2013b). Fluid learning: Vision for lifelong learning in 2030. *Open Education 2030: Lifelong Learning*. Retrieved from: http://blogs.ec.europa.eu/openeducation2030/files/2013/04/Falconer-et-al-OE2030-LLL.pdf.

Finch, D. J. (2012). *Accessibility, sustainability, excellence: how to expand access to research publications*. Report of the Working Group on Expanding Access to Published Research Findings. Retrieved from: www.researchinfonet.org/wp-content/uploads/2012/06/Finch-Group-report-FINAL-VERSION.pdf.

Harley, D. (2008). Why understanding the use and users of open education matters? In V. T. Iiyoshi, & V. Kumar (Eds.), *Opening up education: The collective advancement of education through open technology, open content and open knowledge*. The Carnegie Foundation for the Advancement of Teaching. Cambridge, MA: The MIT Press.

Hoosen, S. (2012). *Survey on government's open educational resources (OER) policies.* Vancouver: Commonwealth of Learning. Retrieved from: www.col.org/resources/publications/Pages/detail.aspx?PID=408.

Hylén, J., Van Damme, D., Mulder, F., & D'Antoni, S. (2012). Open educational resources: Analysis of responses to the OECD country questionnaire. *OECD Education Working Papers*, No. 76, Paris: OECD Publishing. Retrieved from http://dx.doi.org/10.1787/5k990rjhvtlv-en.

Kanwar, A., & Uvalic-Trumbi, S. (2011). A basic guide to open educational resources (OER). Vancouver: Commonwealth of Learning. Retrieved from: www.col.org/resources/publications/Pages/detail.aspx?PID=357.

Lane, A. (2008). Widening participation in education through open educational resources. In V. T. Iiyhoshi, & M. Vijay Kumar (Eds.), *Opening up education: The collective advancement of education through open technology, open content and open knowledge.* The Carnegie Foundation for the Advancement of Teaching. Cambridge: The MIT Press.

Leinonen, T., Purma, J., Poldoja, H., & Toikkanen, T. (2010). Information architecture and design solutions scaffolding authoring of open educational resources. *IEEE Transactions on Learning Technologies 3*(2), 116–128.

Meiszner, A. (2012). *Business and sustainability models in open education: Concepts and examples in 2012.* United Nations University, UNU-Merit, CCG, The Netherlands.

Minguillón, J., Rodríguez, M. E., & Conesa, J. (2010). Extending learning objects by means of social networking. *Lecture Notes in Computer Science, 6483*, 220–229.

Niemann, K., Schwertel, U., Kalz, M., Mikroyannidis, A., Fisichella, M., Friedrich, M., Dicerto, M., Ha, K., Holtkamp, P., Kawase, R., Parodi, E., Pawloski, J., Pirkkalainen, H., Pitsilis, V., Vidalis, A., Wolpers, M., & Zimmermann, V. (2010). Skill-based scouting of open management content. *Lecture Notes in Computer Science, 6383*, 632–637.

Petrides, L., Nguyen, L., Jimes, C., & Karaglani, A. (2008). Open educational resources: Inquiring into author use and reuse. *International Journal of Technology Enhanced Learning, 1*(1/2), 98–117.

Redecker, C., Leis, M., Leendertse, M., Punie, Y., Gijbers, G., Kirschner, P., Stoyanov, S., & Hoogveld, B. (2011). *The future of learning: Preparing for change.* Luxembourg: Publications Office of the European Union. Retrieved from: http://ftp.jrc.es/EURdoc/JRC66836.pdf.

Sahlberg, P. (2006). Education reforms for raising economic competitiveness. *Journal of Educational Change, 7*, 259–287.

Savoir Livre and Syndicat National de l'Edition (2010). Manuels numériques: Les premiers usages. Une enquête TNS-SOFRES/Savoir Livre auprès des professeurs utilisateurs. [Press release].

Scheerens, J. (ed.) (2010). *Teachers' professional development. Europe in international comparison. A secondary analysis based on TALIS dataset.* Luxembourg: Publications Office of the European Union. Retrieved from: http://ec.europa.eu/education/school-education/doc/talis/report_en.pdf.

Shapiro, H. (2013) *Case studies on OER: United States.* Paper produced by the Danish Technological Institute for the European Commission (unpublished).

SRI International–Center for Productivity in Learning (2012). *Understanding the Implications of Online Learning for Educational Productivity.* Washington, DC: US Department of Education, Office of Educational Technology. Retrieved from:www.sri.com/sites/default/files/publications/implications-online-learning.pdf.

UNESCO (2012a). 2012 Paris OER Declaration. Retrieved from: www.unesco. org/new/fileadmin/MULTIMEDIA/HQ/CI/CI/pdf/Events/Paris%20OER%20 Declaration_01.pdf.

UNESCO (2012b). *ICTs for curriculum change.* IITE Policy Brief, April. Retrieved from: http://iite.unesco.org/pics/publications/en/files/3214717.pdf.

Van den Brande, G., Carlberg, M., & Good, B. (eds.) (2010). Learning, innovation and ICT. Lessons learned by the ICT cluster Education & Training 2010 programme. Retrieved from: www.kslll.net/Documents/Key%20Lessons%20ICT%20cluster%20 final%20version.pdf.

Vladoiu, M. (2011). State-of-the-art in open courseware initiatives worldwide. *Informatics in Education, 10*(2), 271–294.

Werquin, P. (2010). *Recognising non-formal and informal learning, outcomes and practices.* Paris: OECD.

Wiley, D., Levi Hilton, J., Ellington, S., & Hall, T. (2012). A preliminary examination of the cost savings and learning impacts of using open textbooks in middle and high school science classes. *The International Review of Open and Distance Learning, 13*(3), 00–00. Retrieved from: www.irrodl.org/index.php/irrodl/article/view/1153/2256.

SECTION 2
Work

6

WORKPLACE LEARNING IN INFORMAL NETWORKS

Colin Milligan, Allison Littlejohn and Anoush Margaryan

Introduction

Traditional conceptions of learning focus on the formal learning that occurs in contexts such as school, college and university education. These, however, form only part of the learning experience for any individual. Indeed, for adults, most learning will occur outside formal contexts, either informally or incidentally (Marsick, Watkins, Callahan, & Volpe, 2009). Informal learning is typically unplanned, or highly embedded within other activities such as work. The workplace is increasingly recognised as a key locus for informal learning (Harteis & Billet, 2008), particularly in knowledge-intensive domains where classroom training approaches are unsuitable. In the workplace, an individual develops trusted networks of current and former colleagues that provide access to the knowledge and expertise necessary to perform their role. These networks may be internal to an organisation or can extend beyond organisational boundaries, and can be activated when new learning needs arise. However, to take advantage of the learning opportunities afforded by networks, individuals must be able to plan and structure their own learning, and to know how to interact effectively in order to learn.

This chapter explores workplace learning in informal networks. The chapter is structured into four main sections. First, we consider the context of informal learning in the workplace for knowledge workers (people who produce knowledge as an output through work) in knowledge-intensive environments (Davenport, 2005; Drucker, 1999). We explore how the changing nature of the workplace requires knowledge workers to be able to self-regulate their learning (Zimmerman, 2000). Second, we explore how people self-regulate their learning in practice. We outline people's learning behaviours—activities we have observed in individuals as they managed, monitored and optimised their interaction with the people and resources within their network. This analysis draws on our previous research in knowledge-intensive organisations in the petrochemical (Littlejohn, Milligan, & Margaryan, 2012) and financial services industries. Third, we consider how these behaviours are currently supported by the tools that make up an individual's personal work and learning environment. Functions that are missing from existing tools are highlighted and we explore how they might be provided. Finally, we conclude by considering the nature of knowledge workers' learning in an open, networked world.

Informal Learning in the Workplace

Since the early 2000s, the workplace has attracted increasing attention from learning researchers (Tynjälä, 2008). This increased interest has coincided with rapid changes in working life brought about by the advent of communications technologies and the expansion of the knowledge economy. Whereas work has conventionally been viewed as a context where learning was applied, much recent research has focused on workplaces as locations where learning actually takes place. Organisational structures designed to maximise productivity using the principles of Taylorism are being supplanted by new organisational structures and workplace practices that support continuous learning to maximise innovation (Clow, 2013). New knowledge is not written down and recorded in organisational knowledge bases, but is instead exchanged and created as work problems are solved by interdisciplinary teams. Workplace learning is therefore fundamentally social (Brown & Duguid, 2000; Eraut, 2007) and is supported and occurs through practices that are more open, recognising the expertise held by the individual and the personal networks they maintain. We are now in a 'Networked Society' (Castells, 1996) in which the connections between people, content and tools (especially in the workplace) are almost ubiquitous (in the Western world at least). Knowledge work is now routinely conducted in technology-rich environments. With the advent of Web 2.0 tools and the social web, learning in these informal networks is enacted through digital tools and in the open, across organisational boundaries rather than within closed silos. Personal networks do not follow organisational boundaries, and include not just co-workers, but also ex-colleagues and contacts made through professional bodies. While research exploring the nature of learning in workplaces has typically focused on organisational issues, research which adopts an individual, rather than organisational, perspective is also needed (Illeris, 2003).

Learning in the workplace is fundamentally different from formal learning. Sfard (1998) identified two distinct metaphors for learning. The first, *acquisition*, is characteristic of formal education and training, where there is clear transmission of knowledge from instructor to learner. The second metaphor, *participation*, is more typical of workplaces describing the transmission of knowledge through participation in stable communities of practice (Lave & Wenger,

1991). However, knowledge work is becoming increasingly cross-disciplinary, involving experts with different skills working collaboratively to solve novel problems. In such cases, a participation metaphor, while appropriate for passing stable knowledge from expert to novice is insufficient. Paavola, Lipponen, and Hakkarainen (2004) argued that a third metaphor, the *knowledge creation* metaphor, is needed to describe 'trialogical' learning (Paavola & Hakkarainen, 2005). This is the type of learning that occurs alongside the processes of '*deliberately creating and advancing knowledge*' that typify knowledge work in modern society (Hakkarainen, Palonen, Paavola, & Lehtinen, 2004, p. 11). In this view, learning is opportunistic, authentic and dynamic, occurring as a direct by-product of work (Chapter 7, this volume).

Self-Regulation in the Workplace

To work effectively in continually changing environments, knowledge workers have to self-regulate their learning through cycles of goal-setting, self-monitoring and self-reflection (Veen, van Staalduinen & Hennis, 2011; Zimmerman, 2000). Sitzmann and Ely (2011) conducted a meta-analysis of a number of different models of self-regulation that had been applied to learning in the workplace. Their analysis identified a core set of constructs common to all theories of self-regulation, concluding that differences between models largely reflect different theoretical traditions. One example originating from the domain of educational psychology is Zimmerman's Social Cognitive Model of Self-Regulated Learning (2000). Typical of many models of self-regulated learning, this example divides the Self-Regulated Learning (SRL) process into three phases (Puustinen & Pulkkinen, 2001), forming a cycle. During the *forethought* phase, the individual recognises gaps in their knowledge, formulates goals and plans their learning. In the *performance* phase, learners make decisions about effort and enact learning strategies, all the while monitoring their performance. In the *self-reflection* phase, the learner self-evaluates their learning based on internal or external criteria, driving further goal setting and planning. In knowledge-intensive workplaces, SRL is a highly social process, structured by and deeply integrated with work tasks (Billet, 2001; Margaryan, Littlejohn, & Milligan, 2013). However, it is difficult to understand how knowledge workers can apply self-regulated learning (SRL) strategies to achieve their learning goals.

Learning Behaviours in the Workplace

Knowledge workers are often unaware of the extent to which they are continually learning while working. We have explored the learning practices of knowledge workers, in both technical and non-technical roles, in the petrochemical industry (Margaryan, Milligan, Littlejohn, Hendrix, & Graeb-Koenneker, 2009; Littlejohn, Milligan, & Margaryan, 2011; Littlejohn et al., 2012). Through this research we identified four key learning behaviours that knowledge workers use when learning in informal networks.

The four behaviours are as follows:

1. *Consuming* knowledge and resources created by others. Individuals may discover new knowledge passively, through the knowledge sources (people and resources) they have incorporated into their personal learning environment—or in a more active way—through directed searching.
2. *Connecting* with people and resources (information sources) in a learner's personal learning network. This includes linking with peers who share interests or goals to develop ideas, share experience, provide peer-support, or work collaboratively to achieve shared goals. Connections can be loose and serendipitous or can be directed, as perhaps when an individual seeks out another individual with specific expertise. Connections may be reciprocal or unidirectional, and may be made between colleagues within an organisation, and also beyond it.
3. *Creating* new knowledge, by authoring and extending resources to elaborate and record current practice. The new knowledge and knowledge structures created represent a dynamic, faithful and individually focused view of the knowledge and understanding they possess about a given topic, and how different topics interrelate. Structuring knowledge and making these knowledge structures public adds a layer of value that others can benefit from. This sense-making process is continual and collaborative, generating collective knowledge that evolves and changes over time.
4. *Contributing* new knowledge back to the network. This can occur both formally (as reports, publications and other stand-alone artefacts) and informally (as reflections, ideas, ratings and other context-dependent content). Creating new knowledge and contributing knowledge resources back to the network are open processes, encouraging discovery and consumption by others in the network.

These four learning behaviours—*consume, connect, create, and contribute*:—are complex, and the classification here is somewhat simplified. However, together they represent the ways in which an individual interacts with other members of their network to achieve their learning goals. All four behaviours are most effective when conducted in the open, since 'openness' extends the reach of each individual's learning network and, therefore, maximises the potential benefits gained through interacting with others. Learning networks tend to be loosely bound. Connections between individuals can be formed or strengthened when people identify that they share a common learning goal. Other studies have identified similar behaviours to the four described here. For instance, Kop (2011) describes a set of behaviours that enhance learning in connectivist networks: *aggregation, relation, creation* and *sharing*. Similarly, Davenport (2005) outlines a typology of knowledge activities, including *creating, packaging, distributing* and *applying* knowledge. Table 6.1 maps these four learning behaviours to different

TABLE 6.1 Mapping of Learning Behaviours to Different Phases of Self-Regulated Learning

	Consume	Connect	Create	Contribute
Forethought	Explore learning requirements via a search engine or other trusted information sources.	Connect to personal learning network to seek advice, or identify others with similar learning goals.	Articulate and record goals and learning strategies.	Make goals or development plan or learning strategies public and accessible by all.
Performance	Discover new knowledge to help achieve learning goals.	Engage with others to achieve learning goals, through collecting and connecting knowledge and developing new knowledge structures.	Create new knowledge or augment existing knowledge.	Make new knowledge and knowledge structures public, through formal and informal mechanisms.
Self-reflection	Seek evidence to validate learning strategy.	Find others with similar experiences to establish/ confirm causality.	Write personal, reflection notes.	Public self-reflection through blogging or similar mechanisms.

phases of the self-regulated learning cycle, highlighting specific behaviours typical of each phase.

These learning behaviours represent the ways in which learners interact with the people and resources within their personal learning network. In effect, these describe how people self-regulate their learning. Together they illustrate how each individual plans, implements and reflects on their learning and development at work. We term this (metacognitive) process of planning and instantiating learning 'charting'. As people plan and manage their learning, they 'chart' their learning pathways. Therefore charting brings together these four behaviours (consume, connect, create and contribute; Figure 6.1).

Supporting Charting Through Technology

Increasingly, personal learning networks, mediated through tools such as Twitter and blogs, provide an important mechanism that allows workers to connect with

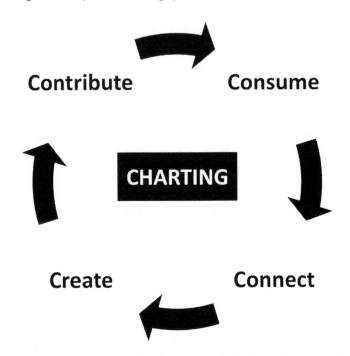

FIGURE 6.1 Charting Brings Together the Learning Behaviours Consume, Connect, Create and Contribute

other people from beyond their immediate group of colleagues. These open, informal, personal networks support learning in a variety of ways (Dron & Anderson, 2009): recommending new resources, filtering information streams, creating and augmenting knowledge structures. Digital tools influence people's learning behaviour, but the affordances of these tools can also limit the ways people are able to interact. We can map existing tools against each of the four learning behaviours identified above.

1. *Consuming*: **Search engines** provide powerful mechanisms for discovery of new knowledge and ideas. **RSS readers** and **social bookmarking** tools assist in interacting with trusted knowledge sources.
2. *Connecting*: **Microblogging** tools such as Twitter provide a method for establishing and maintaining personal learning networks. **Social book-marking** and tools such as Delicious, and Diigo allow sharing of resource collections, and creation of knowledge structures. **Communication** tools such as Gmail, Google Hangouts and Skype facilitate collaboration and peer support.
3. *Creating*: **Personal note taking tools** such as Evernote offer connected (accessible across devices) means to support personal annotation, knowledge creation and knowledge structuring.

4. *Contributing*: **Collaborative platforms** such as blogs, wikis and Google Docs provide mechanisms for personal and collaborative publishing of new knowledge and self-reflective content. **Cloud storage** such as Dropbox and **content hosting** such as Slideshare, YouTube and Soundcloud make it simple to share static files. **Social curation tools** such as Scoop.it and Pinterest allow resource collections to be developed, accompanied by reflection and synthesis.

These tools are inherently open, encouraging the learner to make the evidence of their learning (the resources they use, the artefacts they create) public and freely accessible to all by default. In this way, one individual's learning becomes available to their peers, and to future learners. A range of these tools would constitute a learner's Personal Learning Environment (Leslie, 2012; Milligan, Beauvoir, Johnson, Sharples, Wilson, & Liber, 2006), integrated alongside the tools an individual uses to perform their work role. The precise set of tools used depends on individual need and preference, but the full range of learning behaviours needs to be supported.

In compiling the list of tools that support the 4c learning behaviours, it becomes clear that some behaviours are poorly supported by existing tools—in particular, goal setting. While tools such as Outlook contain useful task management tools and the web is inundated with 'to do list' apps, tools for expressing and managing learning goals are less common. In the workplace, goal setting may be supported through individual development-planning tools. However, these tools are typically focused on organisational structures such as fixed timeframes (for example a one-year development review) and are viewed (largely) as a private, rather than a public resource to be openly shared.

Goal setting is a critical component of self-regulated learning, since it is the mechanism by which an individual recognises and articulates their learning needs and plans and monitors their subsequent learning. Learning is inherently social, so it seems incongruous that people's learning goals are not routinely shared. Articulating and sharing goals communicates learning intentions to other members of an individual's network. Goals provide a way of connecting with other learners. Charting is based on the idea that learners set and share their learning goals. Learning goals are individually set, but influenced heavily by others in the workplace and may be shared with co-workers or with colleagues outside the organisation. Furthermore, learning goals provide a purpose for interaction with other people and resources when learning. In other words, learning goals serve as a 'social object' around which people interact (Engeström, 2005; Knorr-Cetina, 2001). Therefore tools that support 'charting' should promote social goal setting and goal sharing.

A prototype charting tool has been developed (Milligan, Margaryan, & Littlejohn, 2012; http://charting.gcu.ac.uk/). This tool has been designed to support people in continually learning and expanding their work practice. The tool allows learners to articulate and share their learning goals, creating opportunities for connection and interaction with other people who may share the same or similar goals. The more learners there are in the network, the more effective goal discovery is likely to be. As the learner goes about their daily work, they can use a bookmarklet to associate resources with a specific goal. Providing simple ways to create and contribute new knowledge to the system emphasises that a user structures new knowledge by making his/her own connections between disparate resources. Over time, the user develops a set of resources and notes which constitute the knowledge and understanding they possess for that goal. Thus the charting tool allows individuals to collect and structure knowledge related to a specific learning goal. Through collecting (consuming), using (connecting), structuring (creating) and sharing (contributing) knowledge, people learn.

The charting tool is open and social: anyone in the network can view and adopt public goals contributed by other users. Once they are adopted, the learner gains access to all the public resources and notes created by the original user. This affords two usage scenarios. First, users can share goals which they are collaborating on; for example, two or more co-workers who are on the same project and need to develop a joint understanding of a new area. Second, learners can search and discover the goals and associated artefacts of other learners who are unknown to them. Finding others with similar goals allows them to gain an insight into how these learners achieved the goal they set, or to work with them to achieve goals together.

Conclusion

This chapter has highlighted that changes in the nature of knowledge work have placed increasing demands on knowledge workers to self-regulate their learning in the workplace. While self-regulating their learning, knowledge workers utilise four learning behaviours—consuming, connecting, creating and contributing knowledge. Together, these behaviours make up the processes of 'charting': a mechanism through which an individual regulates and participates in the learning and development and the knowledge management essential to their effective learning in the workplace. Although focused on the individual, the behaviours (like the learning they support) are fundamentally social, and are enacted online. Traditionally, learning networks in the workplace may have been closed and private, controlled by the organisation. With the learner in control, the locus of learning moves to where the expertise is, and expertise does not respect organisational boundaries. Executives in some organisations understand this and are moving towards greater use of open social networks by their employees. Furthermore, organisational leaders understand that if learning is viewed as something which occurs only 'within the organisation', then the possibilities for new types of knowledge interaction beyond organisational boundaries, as afforded by social networks, are missed (Tapscott & Williams, 2006).

Understanding the nature of knowledge workers' learning at work as a set of learning behaviours allows exploration of how technology can support the enactment of these behaviours. The role played by technology in mediating this learning in the workplace is critical. For knowledge workers, computers (and, increasingly, mobile devices) represent the primary tool through which they carry out their role. Social tools disrupt previously closed organisational networks, freeing knowledge from internal silos. The use of public social networks blurs the boundaries between peers within the organisation and colleagues in the wider network. Peripheral network connections can become important members of an individual's personal learning network as specific needs arise. For the learner, contributing new knowledge and reflections back to the network is a key activity, as it enables reputations to develop, trust-based relationships to form and networks to grow. This in turn leads to more effective knowledge flow and learning. The value of the knowledge in the network increases as paradata—such as ratings and usage data—are incorporated. Emergent knowledge structures provide additional signals about the quality and utility of resources. Over time, the knowledge held by the network is enriched by the contributions of its members. Individual members learn from each other's reflective practice, benefitting from seeing how others solved problems, the resources they used and the routes they took to learn.

Informal learning in networks occurs most effectively as the boundaries between work and learning dissolve, and where the individual is able to manage their learning in the context of their work. This facility to structure learning is not only critical for knowledge workers, but can also support lifelong learning. With an active aging population, more and more people want to plan, structure and take forward their own learning. Tools such as the charting tool described in this chapter provide a mechanism to discover others with similar interests who can provide support, advice and input in striving towards goals.

References

Billet, S. (2001). *Learning in the workplace: Strategies for effective practice.* Crow's Nest: Allen & Unwin.

Brown, J.S., & Duguid, P. (2000). *The social life of information.* Boston, MA: Harvard Business School Press.

Castells, M. (1996). *The information age: Economy, society and culture: The rise of the networked society.* Oxford, UK: Blackwell.

Clow, J. (2013). Work practices to support continuous organisational learning. In A. Littlejohn & A. Margaryan (Eds.), *Technology-enhanced professional learning: Processes, practices and tools.* London: Routledge.

Davenport, T.H. (2005). *Thinking for a living.* Boston, MA: Harvard Business School Press.

Dron, J., & Anderson, T. (2009). How the crowd can teach. In S. Hatzipanagos & S. Warburton (Eds.), *Handbook of research on social software and developing community ontologies* (pp. 1–17). London: IGI Global.

Drucker, P.F. (1999). *Management challenges for the 21st century*. Oxford: Butterworth-Heinemann.

Engeström, J. (2005). Why some social networks work, and others don't. Retrieved 19 March 2013, from www.zengestrom.com/blog/2005/04/why-some-social-network-services-work-and-others-dont-or-the-case-for-object-centered-sociality.html.

Eraut, M. (2007). Learning from other people in the workplace. *Oxford Review of Education*, *33*(4), 403–422.

Hakkarainen, K., Palonen, T., Paavola, S., & Lehtinen, E. (2004). *Communities of networked expertise: Professional and educational perspectives*. Advances in Learning and Instruction Series. Amsterdam: Elsevier.

Harteis, C., & Billet, S. (2008). The workplace as learning environment. *International Journal of Educational Research*, *47*(4), 209–212.

Illeris, K. (2003). Workplace learning and learning theory. *Journal of Workplace Learning*, *15*(4), 167–178.

Knorr-Cetina, K. (2001). Objectual practice. In K. Knorr-Cetina, E. von Savigny, & T. Schatzki (Eds,), *The practice turn in contemporary theory* (1st ed., pp. 175–188). New York: Routledge.

Kop, R. (2011). The challenges to connectivist learning on open online networks: Learning experiences during a massive open online course. *The International Review of Research in Open and Distance Learning*, *12*(3), 19–38.

Lave, J., & Wenger, E. (1991). *Situated learning: Legitimate peripheral participation*. New York: Cambridge University Press.

Leslie, S. (2012). Some observations on PLE diagrams. Retrieved 24 January 2013, from www.edtechpost.ca/wordpress/2012/12/19/ple-diagrams-observations.

Littlejohn, A., Milligan, C., & Margaryan, A. (2011). Collective learning in the workplace: Important knowledge sharing behaviours. *International Journal of Advanced Corporate Learning*, *4*(4), 26–31.

Littlejohn, A., Milligan, C., & Margaryan, A. (2012). Charting collective knowledge: Supporting self-regulated learning in the workplace. *Journal of Workplace Learning*, *24*(3), 226–238.

Margaryan, A., Milligan, C., Littlejohn, A., Hendrix, D., & Graeb-Koenneker, S. (2009). Self-regulated learning in the workplace: Enhancing knowledge flow between novices and experts. *4th International Conference on Organizational Learning, Knowledge and Capabilities (OLKC)*, Amsterdam, 26–28 April 2009.

Margaryan, A., Littlejohn, A., & Milligan, C. (2013). Self-regulated learning in the workplace: Learning goal attainment strategies and factors. *International Journal of Training and Development*, *17*(4), 254–259 DOI: 10.1111/ijtd.12013.

Marsick, V.J., Watkins, K.E., Callahan, M.W., & Volpe, M. (2009). Informal and incidental learning in the workplace. In M. C. Smith & N. DeFrates-Densch (Eds.), *Handbook of research on adult learning and development* (pp 570–599). New York: Routledge.

Milligan, C.D., Beauvoir, P., Johnson, M.W., Sharples, P., Wilson, S.B., & Liber, O. (2006). Developing a reference model to describe the personal learning environment. In W. Nejdl & K. Tochtermann (Eds.), *Proceedings of the 1st European Conference on Technology-Enhanced Learning (EC-TEL)*, (Lecture Notes in Computer Science 4227: pp. 506–511). Heidelberg: Springer.

Milligan, C., Margaryan, A., & Littlejohn, A. (2012). Supporting goal formation, sharing and learning of knowledge workers. In A. Ravenscroft, S. Lindstaedt, C. Delgado Kloos, & D. Hernández-Leo (Eds.), *Proceedings of the 7th European Conference on Technology-Enhanced Learning (EC-TEL)*, (Lecture Notes in Computer Science 7563: pp. 519–524). Heidelberg: Springer.

Paavola, S., & Hakkarainen, K. (2005). The knowledge creation metaphor: An emergent epistemological approach to learning. *Science and Education, 14*(6), 535–557.

Paavola, S., Lipponen, L., & Hakkarainen, K. (2004). Models of innovative knowledge communities and three metaphors of learning. *Review of Educational Research, 74*(4), 557–576.

Puustinen, M., and Pulkkinen, L. (2001). Models of self-regulated learning: A review. *Scandinavian Journal of Educational Research, 45*(3), 269–286.

Sfard, A. (1998). On two metaphors for learning and the dangers of choosing just one. *Educational Researcher, 27*(2), 4–13.

Sitzmann, T., & Ely, K. (2011). A meta-analysis of self-regulated learning in work-related training and educational attainment: What we know and where we need to go. *Psychological Bulletin, 137*(3), 421–442.

Tapscott, D., & Williams, A.D. (2006). *Wikinomics: How mass collaboration changes everything.* New York: Portfolio.

Tynjälä, P. (2008). Perspectives into learning at the workplace. *Educational Research Review, 3*(2), 130–154.

Veen, W., van Staalduinen, J-P., & Hennis, T. (2011). Informal self-regulated learning in corporate organizations. In G. Dettori & D. Persico (Eds.), *Fostering Self-regulated learning through ICT,* (pp. 364–379). Hershey, PA: IGI Global.

Zimmerman, B.J. (2000). Attaining self-regulation: A social cognitive perspective. In M. Boekaerts, M. Zeidner, & P.R. Pintrich (Eds.), *Handbook of self-regulation* (pp. 13–39). San Diego, CA: Academic Press.

7

CHALLENGES OF COLLABORATIVE KNOWLEDGE CREATION

Work with Shared Objects

Sami Paavola

The so-called *Meno paradox* (or the *learning paradox*) is a classic way of formulating the quandary of newness; that is, how can we make inquiries into something which does not yet exist (Bereiter, 1985)? How can we learn things which are more complex than our existing knowledge and extend beyond knowledge we have previously encountered? The *knowledge creation metaphor* refers to those theories and approaches to learning where learning is understood as the process of developing new knowledge together (Paavola, Lipponen, & Hakkarainen, 2004). This metaphor extends across a range of diverse theories and conceptions of learning. However, the basic concept is not as challenging as it might seem at first glance, if we view learning as being based on practices and processes of inquiry and work. Unlike formal learning, these practices and processes do not require any *special* creativity, but are focused around real-world problems and solutions. These object-oriented and artefact-centred activities provide examples of reusing online resources.

There is clearly a need, or at least a call, for understanding those processes of learning where people develop new knowledge artefacts or solve existing problems creatively together. According to Nonaka, a knowledge society 'calls for a shift in our thinking concerning innovation in large business organizations. It raises questions about how organizations process knowledge and, more importantly, how they create new knowledge' (Nonaka, 1994, p. 14). Scardamalia and Bereiter (2010) suggest that *knowledge building* focuses on 'the 21st century need to work creatively with knowledge'. The basis for *expansive learning* (Engeström & Sannino, 2010) is a broader societal need: 'The ultimate test of any learning theory is how it helps us to generate learning that penetrates and grasps pressing issues the [sic] humankind is facing today and tomorrow' (ibid., p. 21). It can be argued that, for good or bad, modern society builds on the capabilities of its citizens to produce new knowledge, solve problems, and develop new kinds of practices.

Collaborative knowledge creation is often (although not always) linked to the role of new digital technologies that support collaboration. It can be argued that, until fairly recently, digital technology has been used largely for specialised and specific purposes and has been relatively marginal in education. However, technology use is changing rapidly, at least in Western countries. Increasingly, digital techologies provide an *infrastructure* for our everyday lives, or 'the environments within which we act and interact' (Wiltse & Stolterman, 2010). Technology is a medium for all kinds of activities in our lives: to communicate with people around the world, to give and receive information, to buy things, to understand and to communicate what we or others are doing, and so on. These new and emerging affordances of technology tools as a (potential) means for collaboration foster a need to rethink collaborative learning. There are many examples where technology is used in new ways for effective collaboration (see, for example, Hemetsberger & Reinhardt, 2009). On the other hand, new technology is emerging all the time, triggering the search for new forms of collaboration (see, for example, McLoughlin & Lee, 2008). Consequently, technology is not only an enabler of collaboration, but requires (in parallel) the development of new *knowledge practices* that capitalise on the affordances of the technologies (Hakkarainen, 2009), and new *pedagogical practices* for utilising available learning materials (Ilomäki, Lakkala, & Paavola 2006; Chapter 1, this volume).

A third reason for collaborative knowledge creation (closely related to the previous reasons) is the increasing complexity of modern society, which necessitates collaboration. There has been a tradition in Western thinking to attribute creativity and intelligence to solitary thinkers, but this custom is changing (John-Steiner, 2000). Celebrated 'geniuses' have built their work on the work of others, capitalising on various kinds of collaborative relationships (John-Steiner's (2000) book presents a multitude of eloquent examples of creative couples and partnerships in science and art). This is not to downplay the role of individuals' agency and creativity; in other words, the role of the learner in his or her own learning. However, it can be argued that one key aspect of developing new models of collaborative knowledge creation is to find ways of aligning individuals' activities with social and cultural processes (Hemetsberger & Reinhardt, 2009; Stetsenko, 2005).

Promoting Collaborative Knowledge Creation: Design Principles for Trialogical Learning

The author, along with a group of collegues, is developing a novel pedagogical approach to learning, called *trialogical learning*. Trialogical learning is already embedded in many forms of authentic learning practices and processes, including informal, work-based learning, as outlined earlier. However, a central idea is to ensure that collaborative knowledge creation is also a focus for formal learning within educational contexts (see for example Paavola & Hakkarainen, 2009). Trialogical learning builds on the idea that modern digital technology is providing new means and resources for collaboration, including open collaborations. So the challenge is to organise work around collaboratively developed artefacts and objects. Therefore, instead of 'monologues' (how individuals process information in their heads), and in addition to 'dialogues' (how people communicate with each other or learn by interacting with the environment), the *trialogical approach* aims at supporting collaborative, 'object-oriented' work which produces various types of knowledge artefacts (using jointly developed knowledge practices) that can subsequently be used by others. According to the trialogical approach to learning, the availability of learning resources is not in itself sufficient to trigger learning, if the use of these materials is not connected to advanced pedagogical practices (Ilomäki et al., 2006). The challenge is to organise collaboration such that it supports object-oriented collaboration, and does not simply connect networks of people (cf. Engeström, 2005). An important motivating factor is that the knowledge artefacts and practices created while learning are meant for subsequent use (often beyond the immediate, specific educational context).

Therefore the trialogical approach promotes collaborative work that capitalises on external (knowledge) artefacts and jointly developed practices. Human cognition is distributed in a fundamental sense. Traditional conceptions of schooling suggest that learning involves thinking (within an individual's mind) and externalising what has been learned through conversations or writing (within a social context). However, a critical aspect of learning is the processes of developing and modifying external artefacts by using various kinds of 'external memory fields' (Donald, 2001), working 'on paper' (Olson, 2009), or 'on screen'. The use of computers means that these external memory fields can function as 'external *working* fields', that is, something with which we can easily use, modify, and develop artefacts such as texts, presentations, figures, models, and so on, by ourselves or with others.

One basic example of trialogical collaboration is the process of collaboratively developing and modifying journal articles, or other collaborative texts or documents. The process typically begins with dialogue around the focus, content, and structure of the text. Someone (usually someone who has a grasp of the focus area) takes the lead responsibility for developing the text, producing an initial draft, which may—or may not—be advanced. At this point the main trialogical work begins. The document is circulated amongst all the authors, who comment upon and modify the text. The lead author has the main authority to evaluate and decide upon the final formulation of these changes, on the basis of others' suggestions and comments. There are, of course, many ways documents, and other sorts of artefacts, are produced collaboratively. Examples include a text document circulated by e-mail, or a Wikipedia article. However, a key feature of the trialogical approach is the role of the different versions of the artefact. The main agency is that of the authors; however, the versions of the artefact (as different stages of artefact development) play a prominent (even active) role in learning.

The trialogical approach builds on previous approaches to learning where artefacts and practices have a central role in human cognition. Object-orientedness and artefact-mediated activities have been emphasised in activity theory (see, for example, Engeström & Blackler, 2005; Miettinen & Virkkunen, 2005), although nowadays many other approaches to human cognition also emphasise the role of artefacts and objects (see, for example, Engeström, 2005; Ewenstein & Whyte, 2009; Knorr-Cetina, 2001). These approaches to cognition view human activity as 'object-oriented' or 'object-centred'. Human activity is targeted at specific outcomes, around particular interests, and on using and producing external objects and artefacts. An 'artifact is to cultural evolution what the gene is to biological evolution' (Wartofsky, 1979, p. 205; see also Cole, 1996). We are not merely using different kinds of artefacts (such as tables, books, pens and paper, computers) but can also produce artefacts ourselves for subsequent use. This provides a compelling argument that students should be able to engage in collaborative, object-oriented and artefact-producing practices, as well as participating in 'dialogue' and 'meaning making' (Lund & Hauge, 2011; Muukkonen, Lakkala, & Paavola, 2011; Paavola & Hakkarainen, 2009).

Through our research, we have developed six *design principles* (DPs) (or knowledge practices that should be supported) for trialogical learning. These design principles arose from analyses of the commonalities across learning theories associated with the knowledge creation metaphor of learning (see Paavola et al., 2011; and on the knowledge creation metaphor above). The design principles are described in this section, along with an outline of anticipated challenges in implementing each of the principles. It should be noted that these design principles are *not* defined separately for online and offline activities, which could be an extra dimension to be looked at in the future.

DP1: Organising Activities Around Shared 'Objects'

DP1 is a central characteristic of the trialogical approach. The aim is to design courses where learners collaboratively develop useful knowledge artefacts, practices, or outcomes. Examples include client briefs or prototype products, wiki pages, models, plans, or other types of documents. The purpose is to create something which will be used after the course by the learners themselves or by others. The potential usefulness of the outputs provides motivation for the work. Collaborative work around knowledge artefacts is highlighted where there are versioning of the documents, 'object-oriented' discussions, joint planning and reflections on processes and practices.

Expected challenges:

- How can learners find shared objects (to be developed collaboratively) which are meaningful and relevant, but at the same time produced within (often) relatively short courses?
- How can learners promote collaborative ways of working with shared objects, if they have limited prior experience of working in this way?

DP2: Supporting the Integration of Personal and Collective Agency and Work (Through Developing Shared Objects)

The aim is to organise work such that the learners take responsibility not only for their own learning, but also for the collaborative processes and products of learning. This means that participants should be able to utilise their own expertise and areas of interest while constructing collaborative outputs, and while learning the processes used during collaboration. The idea is to leave room for personal space (working with one's own topics and resources) and link this space as easily as possible with work in the collaborative space.

Expected challenges:

- How can learners find shared objects of interests which support their own interests where participants' areas of knowledge are varied?
- How can learners coordinate different ways of working and schedules to combine effectively their individual and collaborative work?

DP3: Fostering Long-Term Processes of Knowledge Advancement with Shared Objects (Artefacts and Practices)

The aim is to develop knowledge artefacts and knowledge practices which can be reused across diverse courses and situations, and to find continuity between different pedagogical situations. A simple basis for this is the claim that novel ideas and development requires long-term, iterative work. This requirement is both for the development of the pedagogical settings themselves, and for the knowledge artefacts created. Long-term processes are fostered by developing knowledge artefacts and knowledge practices which are 'authentic' (in other words they are made by taking into account the subsequent use outside a specific educational setting).

Expected challenges:

- How can learners combine separate short courses with long-term development?
- How can teachers create continuity across courses?
- How can learners reuse the contributions of others?

DP4: Emphasising Development and Creativity in Working on Shared Objects Through Transformations and Reflection

The aim is to support working with open problems. This work involves practices where detailed ideas, questions, and practical knowledge are combined with reflection, conceptualisations, and documenting. To create new knowledge or new ideas, topics and shared objects must be developed from various perspectives utilising different media (for example, texts, figures, conceptualisations, pictures, videos, models, questions).

Expected challenges:

- How can learners combine different ways of dealing with a topic within an integrated, shared object?
- How can learners support work with new ideas and suggestions and—at the same time—deal with the versioning of specific knowledge artefacts?

DP5: Promoting Cross-Fertilisation of Various Knowledge Practices and Artefacts Across Communities and Institutions

The aim is to learn to work with 'authentic' knowledge artefacts and practices by collaborating with partners (for example, with real-world clients or with experts in the field) whose ways of working one is learning. This kind of collaboration supports trialogical work. The term 'cross-fertilisation' refers to the aim of developing one's own practices by learning from practices in different communities.
    Expected challenges:

- How can learners establish collaboration with different organisations, experts, and educational institutions?
- How to combine different ways of working and get enough resources and time for collaboration across institutions.

DP6: Providing Flexible Tools for Developing Artefacts and Practices

The aim is to use technologies that provide opportunities and 'affordances' for trialogical work (that is, issues emphasised in other design principles above). Trialogical practices can be implemented without any special technology. However, these design principles can be facilitated using digital technologies that support flexible and long-term work with shared objects (see more in the next section on the Knowledge Practices Environment technology). Digital technology is primarily used for information sharing and communication, but can also provide a mechanism for object-oriented, focused work with knowledge artefacts and related practices.
    Expected challenges:

- How to obtain technological support for long-term work with shared objects.
- How to flexibly combine object-oriented work carried out with different tools.

Developing Collaborative Knowledge Creation in the KP-Lab Project

The trialogical approach to learning has been developed for technology-enhanced courses in higher education, building on broad concepts around human learning and cognition. The approach has been informed by a large-scale research and development project, the Knowledge Practices Laboratory (KP-Lab), which was a five-year (2006–11), EU-funded project with twenty-two partners from fourteen countries (see Moen, Morch, & Paavola, 2012). The trialogical design principles were used to guide technology development within the KP-Lab project. The principles were specifically used to analyse and develop higher education courses and pedagogical settings in which student groups engaged in the collaborative development of diverse products and outputs.

The design principles of the trialogical approach provided the pedagogical underpinning for a virtual environment developed through the KP-Lab project: the Knowledge Practices Environment (KPE) (Bauters et al., 2012; Lakkala et al., 2009). The KPE comprised 'shared spaces', that is, virtual areas where groups of learners could contribute diverse knowledge artefacts (such as text documents, slide presentations, wiki pages). These shared spaces were akin to 'desktop areas' in which various ways of organising different versions of knowledge artefacts were (spatially and visually) supported. The KPE aimed at promoting collaborative work with a diverse range of documents and files, rather than only encouraging discussion or argumentation. Therefore the KPE included a set of tools that supported learners' work with knowledge artefacts. These tools included a note editor, commenting, chat, linking, wiki, and filtering functions. The shared spaces could be open or closed to other learners, depending on how the group wanted to organise their work.

The design principles of the trialogical approach provided a heuristic basis for developing diverse pedagogical settings (see Moen et al., 2012; Paavola et al., 2011). These design principles were extended during the project to produce a framework and guidelines to evaluate the pedagogical setting of the courses. These courses were largely contextualised within higher education and involved students' collaborative development of knowledge artefacts and outcomes. Examples of student activity include the production of design assignments for real-world clients in a media engineering course, or the development of concept maps by student pairs selecting their own methodological approach (see, for example, Kosonen, Muukkonen, Lakkala, & Paavola, 2012; Lakkala et al., 2012). The trialogical design principles were also used as a basis for the development of medical simulation training, in which student teams used a simulation manikin that replicated the behaviours of a newborn baby (see Karlgren, 2012).

A significant criticism of the trialogical design principles is that they are broad and general and, therefore, ambiguous. The design principles alone do not provide clear guidelines for pedagogical or technological development. This problem was overcome in the KP-Lab project through provision of additional guidelines that could be interpreted according to the context of application (see Paavola et al., 2011). The application of the trialogical design principles proved to be overly demanding where the aim was to achieve every principle within one single course. A solution was for teachers and developers to focus on a narrow range of principles, depending on the context. For example, some developers focused on the principles that govern collaborative work, while others concentrated on individual work, since these two modes of working were difficult to combine (see DP2). Others focused on implementing long-term work that would continue after the end of the course (see DP3).

Therefore the trialogical approach should not be viewed as a specific pedagogical model, but rather as a set of design principles that can be used to transform trialogical elements into a range of different pedagogical settings. The trialogical approach aims to inspire the development of diverse pedagogical approaches that focus on learning through collaboration around knowledge artefacts, using specific knowledge practices. The approach provides a mechanism for reflection on pedagogical practices and on how these practices might be extended around 'object-oriented collaboration'.

Object-oriented collaboration, which emphasises collaboratively developed knowledge artefacts, may take various forms (see also Lund & Hauge, 2011; Muukkonen et al., 2011). Analysis of cases within the KP-Lab project identified three main ways in which 'shared objects' were co-constructed (Paavola et al., 2012).

1. The co-creation of knowledge artefacts using specific knowledge practices. Learners' activities are organised around the iterative co-development and versioning of knowledge artefacts. This clearly exemplifies the trialogical approach. For example, students making versions of their presentation for a client.
2. Collaboration around a certain topic or phenomenon. Work with knowledge artefacts, such as project plans, presentations, timetables, and so on, provides means of materialising work outputs. In this case the aim is more abstract—for example, to improve learners' understanding around a specific topic. These examples illustrate a broad perspective on 'shared objects' which supports learning around an abstract phenomenon studied during a course (the topic can be, for example, methodologies of collaborative design).
3. The aim here is the same as in case 1, to co-create knowledge artefacts. However, collaboration is through learners' negotiations, rather than collaborative versions of the artefacts. An example of this type of activity is the collaborative development of specific knowledge artefacts in face-to-face meetings or by using chat tools.

To summarise, object-oriented ways of working are increasingly important in knowledge work (Engeström & Sannino, 2010; Ewenstein & Whyte, 2009). It is therefore critical that students can develop object-orientated knowledge practices in their studies, rather than have to transform how they learn when they transition to working life.

Conclusion

Digital technologies provide new opportunities for collaborative learning and work practices. The co-development of technologies, work, and learning practices is transforming deep-rooted concepts about human cognition and learning. This transformation requires the development of new approaches to learning that support the sorts of skills, competencies, and practices required in the modern world, such as collaborative knowledge creation. This chapter has outlined one approach to further developing elements of collaborative knowledge creation through trialogical learning.

Object-oriented and artefact-centred activities provide examples of reusing online and open resources. These activities can take many forms, and this chapter has briefly presented some interpretations of them. The trialogical approach does not (yet) provide a specific pedagogical approach, but offers ideas and directions around learning to be developed further in specific contexts. Further research is needed on different types of object-oriented activities and how these can be applied in different contexts. The trialogical approach builds on current societal trends that emphasise the role of objects and artefacts for knowledge work. The unique aspect of trialogical learning is that it aims to extend the role of objects and artefacts in educational contexts, specifically in higher education.

References

Bauters, M., Lakkala, M., Paavola, S., Kosonen, K., & Markkanen, H. (2012). KPE (Knowledge Practices Environment) supporting knowledge creation practices in education. In A. Moen, A. Morch, & S. Paavola (Eds.), *Collaborative knowledge creation: Practices, tools, concepts* (pp. 53–74). Rotterdam: Sense Publishers.

Bereiter, C. (1985). Towards a solution of the learning paradox. *Review of Educational Research 55*(2), 201–226. DOI: 10.3102/00346543055002201.

Cole, M. (1996). *Cultural psychology. A once and future discipline*. Cambridge, MA: The Belknap Press of Harvard University Press.

Donald, M. (2001). *A mind so rare: The evolution of human consciousness*. New York: Norton.

Engeström, J. (2005, 13 April). Why some social network services work and others don't — Or: The case for object-centered sociality [Blog post with comments]. Retrieved from www.zengestrom.com/blog/2005/04/why-some-social-network-services-work-and-others-dont-or-the-case-for-object-centered-sociality.html.

Engeström, Y., & Blackler, F. (2005). On the life of the object. *Organization 12*(3), 307–330. DOI: 10.1177/1350508405051268.

Engeström, Y., & Sannino, A. (2010). Studies of expansive learning: Foundations, findings and future challenges. *Educational Research Review 5*(1), 1–24. DOI:10.1016/j.edurev.2009.12.002

Ewenstein, B., & Whyte, J. (2009). Knowledge practices in design: The role of visual representations as 'epistemic objects'. *Organization Studies 30*(1), 7–30. DOI: 10.1177/0170840608083014.

Hakkarainen, K. (2009). A knowledge-practice perspective on technology-mediated learning. *International Journal of Computer Supported Collaborative Learning 4*(2), 213–231. DOI: 10.1007/s11412-009-9064-x,

Hemetsberger, A., & Reinhardt, C. (2009). Collective development in open-source communities: An activity theoretical perspective on successful online collaboration. *Organization Studies 30*(9), 987–1008. DOI: 10.1177/0170840609339241.

Ilomäki, L., Lakkala, M., & Paavola, S. (2006). Case studies of learning objects used in school settings. *Learning, Media, and Technology 31*(3), 249–267. DOI: 10.1080/17439880600893291.

John-Steiner, V. (2000). *Creative collaboration.* Oxford: Oxford University Press.

Karlgren, K. (2012). Trialogical design principles as inspiration for designing knowledge practices for medical simulation training. In A. Moen, A. Morch, & S. Paavola (Eds.), *Collaborative knowledge creation: Practices, tools, concepts* (pp. 163–183). Rotterdam: Sense Publishers.

Knorr-Cetina, K. (2001). Objectual practice. In T. R. Schatzki, C. K. Knorr, & E. von Savigny (Eds.), *The practice turn in contemporary theory* (pp. 175–188). London and New York: Routledge.

Kosonen, K., Muukkonen, H., Lakkala, M., & Paavola, S. (2012). Product development course as a pedagogical setting for multidisciplinary professional learning. In A. Moen, A. Morch, & S. Paavola (Eds.), *Collaborative knowledge creation: Practices, tools, concepts* (pp. 185–202). Rotterdam: Sense Publishers.

Lakkala, M., Paavola, S., Kosonen, K., Muukkonen, H., Bauters, M., & Markkanen, H. (2009). Main functionalities of the Knowledge Practices Environment (KPE) affording knowledge creation practices in education. In C. O'Malley, D. Suthers, P. Reimann, & A. Dimitracopoulou (Eds.), *Computer Supported Collaborative Learning Practices: CSCL2009 Conference Proceedings* (pp. 297–306). Rhodes, Greece: International Society of the Learning Sciences (ISLS).

Lakkala, L., Ilomäki, L., Paavola, S., Kosonen, K., & Muukkonen S. (2012). Using trialogical design principles to assess pedagogical practices in higher education. In A. Moen A, A. Morch, & S. Paavola (Eds.), *Collaborative knowledge creation: Practices, tools, concepts* (pp. 141–161). Rotterdam: Sense Publishers.

Lund, A., & Hauge, T. E. (2011). Changing objects in knowledge-creation practices. In S. Ludvigsen, A. Lund, I. Rasmussen, & R. Säljö (Eds.), *Learning across sites: New tools, infrastructures and practices* (pp. 206–221). New York: Routledge.

McLoughlin, C., & Lee, M. J. W. (2008). The three P's of pedagogy for the networked society: Personalization, participation, and productivity. *International Journal of Teaching and Learning in Higher Education 20*(1), 10–27. Retrieved from www.isetl.org/ijtlhe/pdf/IJTLHE395.pdf,

Miettinen, R., & Virkkunen, J. (2005). Epistemic objects, artefacts and organizational change. *Organization 12*(3), 437–456. DOI: 10.1177/1350508405051279.

Moen, A., Morch, A., & Paavola S. (Eds.) (2012). *Collaborative knowledge creation: Practices, tools, concepts.* Rotterdam: Sense Publishers.

Muukkonen, H., Lakkala, M., & Paavola, S. (2011). Promoting knowledge creation and object-oriented inquiry in university courses. In S. Ludvigsen, A. Lund, I. Rasmussen, & R. Säljö (Eds.), *Learning across sites. New tools, infrastructures and practices* (pp. 172–189). EARLI series: New Perspectives on Learning and Instruction. New York: Routledge.

Nonaka, I. (1994). A dynamic theory of organizational knowledge creation. *Organization Science 5*(1), 14–37. DOI: 10.1287/orsc.5.1.14.

Olson, D. R. (2009). A theory of reading/writing: From literacy to literature. *Writing Systems Research 1*(1), 51–64. DOI: 10.1093/wsr/wsp005.

Paavola, S., & Hakkarainen, K. (2009). From meaning making to joint construction of knowledge practices and artefacts: A trialogical approach to CSCL. In C. O'Malley, D. Suthers, P. Reimann, & A. Dimitracopoulou (Eds.), *Computer Supported Collaborative Learning Practices: CSCL2009 Conference Proceedings* (pp. 83–92). Rhodes, Greece: International Society of the Learning Sciences (ISLS).

Paavola, S., Engeström, R., & Hakkarainen, K. (2012). The trialogical approach as a new form of mediation. In A. Moen, A. Morch, & S. Paavola (Eds.), *Collaborative knowledge creation: Practices, tools, concepts* (pp. 1–14). Rotterdam: Sense Publishers.

Paavola, S., Lipponen, L., & Hakkarainen, K. (2004). Models of innovative knowledge communities and three metaphors of learning. *Review of Educational Research 74*(4), 557–576. DOI: 10.3102/00346543074004557,

Paavola, S., Lakkala, M., Muukkonen, H., Kosonen, K., & Karlgren, K. (2011). The roles and uses of design principles for developing the trialogical approach on learning. *Research in Learning Technology 19*(3), 233–246. DOI: 10.1080/21567069.2011.624171.

Scardamalia, M., & Bereiter, C. (2010). A brief history of knowledge building. *Canadian Journal of Learning and Technology 36*(1), Fall 2010. Retrieved from http://cjlt.csj.ualberta.ca/index.php/cjlt/article/view/574.

Stetsenko, A. (2005). Activity as object-related: Resolving the dichotomy of individual and collective planes of activity. *Mind, Culture, and Activity 12*(1), 70–88. DOI: 10.1207/s15327884mca1201_6.

Wartofsky, M. (1979). *Models: Representation and scientific understanding*. Dordrecht: Reidel.

Wiltse, H., & Stolterman, E. (2010). Architectures of interaction: An architectural perspective on digital experience. *Proceedings of the NordiCHI 2010, 16–20 October, Reykjavik, Iceland.*

8

OPEN, LIFEWIDE LEARNING

A Vision

Allison Littlejohn, Isobel Falconer and Lou McGill

Open, lifewide learning is critical in a world where knowledge, professions and practices are continually changing. It bridges all areas of life including education, work or general interest. Examples are becoming commonplace and are not always recognised as learning: Reviewing new concepts in an open course, building fresh ideas at work through reading and commenting on a blog, or coding an algorithm within an open source community. A commonality across these examples is that the learner, rather than a teacher or instructor, is the active agent.

While there is evidence that society is moving towards open, lifewide learning, this chapter provides a vision of its potential over the coming decade, rather than examining current practice. It is suited to a world that has seen a radical change in cultural perceptions of learner agency and learner–teacher roles, associated with changes in technology. Learners are autonomous and able to make choices about their own learning. After completing compulsory education, the focus of each learner ideally moves from learning predefined knowledge to filling gaps between areas of knowledge, integrating different areas of expertise, and learning new knowledge. People do not turn automatically to formal institutions for large blocks of learning. Instead they consider it natural to make use of open learning resources and open courses, making their own decisions about what to learn, when and how. Learners naturally employ open learning practices, creating new knowledge for future learners to benefit from. They expect to contribute to the learning of others as well as learning themselves, viewing themselves as the experts in their own situation. In some cases they may elect to take a short formal course, but this is always for a specific reason rather than as a cultural norm. Rather than managing multiple identities in the different groups/communities to which they belong, they see their unique identity as a unifying factor that integrates their activities in various groups, including work and leisure groups, that they move easily between. In doing so they accrue new knowledge, integrating it with their current understanding, such that their expertise changes dynamically to match their current needs.

This vision of open, lifewide learning requires significant cultural change in most societies such that:

- *The learner is in control of choices over his/her learning.* Learners are able—both culturally and cognitively—to structure and tailor their own learning, moving fluidly between learning contexts to fit their individual needs. Intelligent, networked systems enable learners to operate across networked spaces, serendipitously finding others, or being alerted to others with similar motivations and needs. Open learning practices are commonplace. This condition becomes critical when learners, rather than institutions, structure their own learning, particularly in social contexts, and through connections with different communities and networks.

- *Learning contexts are continually in flux.* Learners dynamically change their networks to either strengthen ties or strike out in new directions according to their needs. Even when learners sometimes choose to learn on their own, they may draw knowledge from networks. Learners understand how to move in and out of groups and networks fluidly, developing close ties in tightly knit groups, while recognising that a critical aspect of learning is extending links to new people and knowledge. Hence, their connections change over time.

- *Organisations that provide formal education radically open up.* These organisations influence how people think about learning, so their involvement in and understanding of the need for change is critical. They support the move to open, lifewide learning through strategic commitments to openness, reforming and developing new infrastructures.

- *A broad variety of organisations increase involvement in learning.* Private, public, professional bodies and third sector organisations all have a role to play in learning. These organisations work together routinely, rather than acting independently, as roles become increasingly connected.

- *As learning broadens, so too must assessment and accreditation.* Assessment is performed by a range of different types of people, including peers and experts in companies, not just by teachers. Learners themselves provide their own feedback through self-reflection as they progress (sometimes autonomously) their learning pathways. Open technologies offer new means of accreditation through expert consensus and/or online activity tracing.

Meeting this vision presents cultural challenges that require a radical change in how learning is viewed by societies, learners, communities, groups, universities and organisations globally.

The vision of open, lifewide learning presented here is shaped by a number of trends. First, the *rapid expansion in the number of active lifewide learners* around the world. This growth in lifewide learners is governed by active aging increasing the number of older learners; the need for continual learning at work, extending workplace learning; the inclusion of previously disadvantaged groups, such as disabled people, in lifewide learning. Second, the *proliferation of opportunities for lifewide learning*, visible through the increase in the number and range of open educational resources, open courses, escalation of 'edutainment', proliferation of networked communities for lifewide learning alongside a scaling up of networked technologies (see Chapters 9 and 10, this volume). *Expanding openness*, which is blurring boundaries. Geographic, disciplinary, sectoral borders are becoming difficult to identify, and shift constantly. The opening up of knowledge intensifies this shift, changing social behaviour, work, learning patterns and mindsets (see Chapter 1, this volume). As people collaborate in networks, knowledge is captured and exchanged more easily than before. Knowledge is released as articles, blogs, podcasts, images, datasets, geotags or bio-information, shifting the balance from consumption to the co-creation of knowledge. *Open knowledge, data and analytics* are providing new ways of connecting and informing learners (see Chapter 11, this volume). As boundaries break down, *knowledge becomes more specialised*. Cross-boundary translation of knowledge has created new knowledge domains, which, in turn, has led to an ever-increasing division of labour with new specialist disciplines and roles. In the past learners could become knowledgeable in a discipline only when they had access to the specialist libraries and discipline experts. In a world with open, specialist knowledge and easy access to experts, anyone (potentially) can learn to become a specialist in one or more domains. Specialists in one branch of a discipline can expand their knowledge to other areas, to a level they feel is useful.

This idea of learner autonomy leads us to question how people can *demonstrate competence*. Historically, examination of competence by 'experts' provided a low-resource means of measuring educational outcomes. Recognition of the need for assessment to be authentic, the ability of systems to track performance, and of learners to assess peers, is changing the nature of assessment. All these trends impact on our understanding of what constitutes 'learning'. Learning is no longer within educational domains. It has broadened from formal, structured events to unstructured, serendipitous learning opportunities (see Chapter 3, this volume).

For open lifewide learning to be successful, learners should be able—both culturally and cognitively—to structure and plan their own learning. Ideally, school learning prepares learners for open, lifewide learning, and their participation in open learning communities allows practices to be transferred to others. However, within 'schooled societies' learners tend to rely on being taught rather than engaging in active learning (Billet, 2013; Chapter 3, this volume). In some societies other (non-formal) pathways to learning and expertise development are already recognised, such as home learning, community learning or memetic learning (Billet, 2013).

Literacy and Identity Management for Lifewide Learning

Digital literacy is a critical element of open, lifewide learning. While structuring and regulating their learning, learners have to have the (cognitive and affective) ability to move between individual (solitary) or social environments and across structured or non-structured settings. Learners must develop the capability to work productively with others in different knowledge domains as they collaborate within intersecting networks of co-creation (Candy, 1991; Hiemstra & Brockett, 1994). While this is true in any setting, whether face-to-face or digital, it becomes more pronounced in digital networks, where learners can be simultaneously situated in multiple settings and can move rapidly in and out of different contexts.

Literacies can be viewed as knowledge practices situated in specific social and cultural contexts, from which they derive their meaning and on which they are significantly dependent for their performance (Street, 1996). The situatedness of literacies is complex in situations where learners move between different learning situations, many of which may be 'open'. In these circumstances multiple modes of meaning making are an essential aspect (Brown & Adler, 2008; Kress, 2003, Siemens, 2006). Different disciplines demand proficiency in different combinations of media, creating and sharing meaning in different ways. Therefore, as they move in and out of different disciplinary contexts, learners have to become proficient in self-expression and in critical argumentation in ways that connect with different disciplines, using a range of media as these evolve (Buckingham, 2007; Kress, 2003).

Learners should be able to manage their own identity across different social, cultural and disciplinary boundaries, sometimes in multiple forms. Specific forms of identity management include social network identity (Boyd, 2013), disembodiment through the use of avatars (Bayne, 2008) or use of IP addresses (sometimes tracked by 'cookies' on social network sites). Identities are managed through explicit or prescriptive data often entered by the users, such as the information on a social media profile; activity or behavioural data generated through the user's online behaviours, choices and preferences; and relationship data, based on connections and interactions. Some learners prefer to use their real identifies online, while others prefer to be anonymous, identifying themselves through pseudonyms and avatars. Online identities can be fluid, as users alter aspects of their identity, including name, age, location, gender, ethnicity, abilities and disabilities, preferences and so on (Boyd, 2007).

The ability to engage in different forms of meaning and to manage online identity is critical for open, lifewide learning, where learners move across different learning contexts.

An Illustration of Open Lifewide Learning: The Creative Writing Group

Open, lifewide learning can be understood using Engeström's (1987) model of expansive learning. The four basic, expansive steps each learner undertakes are:

1. analysis of the current situation and why it no longer meets their needs;
2. transforming the learning approach;
3. implementing a new learning approach;
4. reflecting on the new practice, consolidating and spreading it.

Expansive learning provides a relevant conceptual basis, because it takes into account the social context of learning, while emphasising the transformative agency of each learner as he/she moves from one learning context to another, as illustrated in the case example below.

The year is 2030. Networked technologies and internet access are ubiquitous. Open resources, courses and knowledge are abundant. Cultural and practice change has enabled learners to take control of their learning, structuring and expanding their learning pathways and moving fluidly from one learning context to another.

Amelie, Berndt, Carla and Dominic meet weekly in a French creative writing group. They share an interest in learning to write poetry, but their motivations for joining the group are different. Amelie and Berndt have been encouraged to join by their employer, who sees the heterogeneous and diverse group as a more effective means than in-house training days to enhance their report-writing skills. Carla has recently moved to France in search of work; she believes that her social interaction with the group, and the writing she produces, will help her to learn French and enhance her job prospects. Dominic aspires to make a name for himself as an author now that he has retired. For him, the writing is an end in itself.

The learning group was initiated through an online system that connects learners with similar interests. Their meetings, and activities, have been based on an open course comprised of open learning resources. The learners restructured elements of the online course to suit their learning needs. They are now *analysing their current situation, identifying to what extent it no longer meets their needs*. Carla initiates a discussion of their learning activity to date, acting as an informal group mentor. Some aspects have worked well, and the group agrees that it will continue with these. The group makes suggestions as to how the resources themselves could be improved and Amelie and Berndt volunteer to *transform the learning approach* used by the group. They see the relevance of open resource authoring to the development of their writing skills, and volunteer to develop the resources jointly and contribute them back to the wider community.

Meanwhile Berndt observes that colleagues have been promoted on the basis of peer endorsement and so, through recommendations from an intelligent system, he *implements a new learning approach*, joining an open resource development group that provides endorsements for his contributions. He finds that while the group can provide the evidence he anticipated—in ways that work well for most members—he, as a person with autistic spectrum disorder, needs more structure.

He moves to a facilitated group offering micro-credits, which supports his need for structure.

Dominic feels ready to publish his poetry. However, while writing to the web is an everyday activity for all, quality publishing that will make his work stand out is sophisticated and his technical skills are insufficient. He believes he will gain the skills faster if he enrols on a course led by an experienced publisher. His personal recommender system suggests a twelve-week open course with weekly videos and publisher tracking that provides what he needs. Activity tracing is used as a learning aid and for authentic assessment. He *implements the new learning approach* and is able to help Amelie and Berndt with technical aspects of their resource development.

Carla, *reflecting on her new practice*, wants to share her experience and newly developed language skills in a job that will help people who are moving country to work. She realises the next step is a certificate of professional practice and for this the Social Workers Institute stipulates a practice-based course. Assessment is based on observation of her practice, both face to face and traces on the web. She suggests to the writing group that a good way of enhancing their skills further might be to run a monthly writing club for socially disadvantaged people—providing a context for her professional practice and further recognition for all of them. Over time, her network changes as she links with other relevant learners.

The group operates within an inherently unstructured but social learning environment, fostered by cultural acceptance of open learning practices. However, the expansive actions that they choose take them to learning experiences in different contexts. They may have reasons for choosing to move temporarily into a more structured context: Berndt does so because of special needs; Carla requires professional certification; and Dominic believes it offers an efficient route. Their choices are illustrated in Figure 8.1

In terms of Engeström's four expansive steps:

1. *Analysis of the current situation*: The group recognised that they had reached the limits of the resources they were using, that the learning approach was ineffective in some ways, and that, as well as group needs, they had individual learning needs.
2. *Transforming the learning model*: The group (or, on occasion, individual learners) decided which aspects of the current model to keep, and how to expand the process to bring in new actions.
3. *Implementing the new model*: For various reasons, each member of the group explores a new learning context, and each brings new actions into the group learning activity.
4. *Reflecting on new practice*: The group reviewed and made modifications to its actions.

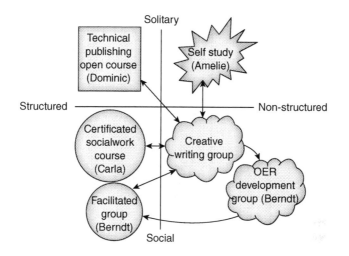

FIGURE 8.1 Movement of Active Learners Across Diverse Learning Contexts

Challenges and Tensions of Open, Lifewide Learning

Although trends in lifewide learning are evident, the outcome of their interaction with each other within society is unpredictable. Change will be decided by the way in which societal and technological tensions, which are already obvious, are resolved. The resolution may be more, or less, favourable to the cultural acceptance of learner agency crucial to open, lifewide learning. This section unfolds some of these tensions.

First, learners may not have the literacies to plan and structure their learning. The narrative illustrates how learners select resources for specific learning needs, and learn through serendipitous connections. Planning for learning and understanding how to integrate and move between different sorts of learning opportunities is a feature of open, lifewide learning. Currently many learners are not equipped to structure their own learning effectively (Littlejohn, Beetham, & McGill, 2013; Margaryan, Littlejohn, & Vojt, 2011). Even in situations where learners are given the freedom to plan a learning pathway, we find that they do not always want to take it (Milligan, Margaryan, & Littlejohn, 2013). There are a number of possible reasons: Lack of confidence can be one, but even confident learners may choose to surrender their autonomy to a formal course. Another reason can be the cultural expectation that learning should be directed by an instructor, rather than the learner (Billet, 2013). Thus, preparation as learners requires a shift in perspective within early formal education and beyond.

Learners have to be capable of expanding their own learning, understanding why it is vital to move between learning contexts. They have to have the confidence and ability to structure their own learning or, where appropriate, elect to participate in formal education. Radical changes within school systems are needed such that, by the end of compulsory education, learners are able to structure their own learning (Facer, 2009). Instructors should focus on helping learners to prepare to learn throughout their lives, rather than preparing them with information or enculturation into a discipline (ibid.). Adults who have already completed formal education can be mentored within open, lifewide learning communities to help them develop as autonomous learners. Both these scenarios are advanced through the *introduction of diverse, authentic learning opportunities in schools where teachers or mentors encourage learners to take control of their own learning. Critically, schools and universities have to change the metrics by which they are measured to include measurement of learner autonomy.*

Second, standardisation of education programmes in some countries restricts learner agency. The learners in the narrative choose what, when and how to learn. This flexibility runs counter to the trend towards the implementation of standard accreditation frameworks to allow accreditation across programmes in different countries, as exemplified through the European Qualifications Framework (Young, 2008). A move too far in the direction of imposed standards could impact on education in ways that are unforeseen or unintended.

Third, standardisation of learning restricts the broadening of what we understand as learning. Currently, educational institutions hold a pole position in cultural definitions of learning, to the extent that in situations such as the workplace, where learners frequently do plan their own aims and the actions needed to achieve these, the activity is often not recognised as 'learning'. Thus the recognition of what constitutes learning needs to be broadened to encompass activity outside formal educational institutions if learners are to recognise that this is what they are doing and gain the corresponding confidence in their ability to do it. Organisations that support formal learning must be encouraged to take a wide view of their place in the learning ecosystem (McGill, Falconer, Littlejohn, & Beetham, 2013). This may require changes in policy and legal frameworks. *Agencies worldwide could facilitate dialogue across private, third sector and public agencies (including formal education) to influence the development of cross-sectoral and cross-national frameworks aligned with societal changes. All types of organisations should be encouraged to consider their contributions to societal learning, triggering a re-evaluation of interrelationships.*

Fourth, current accreditation processes may restrict authentic and flexible assessment. The narrative illustrates the need for assessment to be more authentic for lifewide learning. There is little point in assessing memory of factual information, since this is readily and openly available. What matters is one's ability to practise effectively, and this is what should be assessed. This leaves unspecified the answer to the open question of who does the assessment—an institution, a professional body, a peer group, the community, or the learner—and how is this accredited (Knight, 2013). Assessment and accreditation has to be recast as integral to learning events. *Holistic assessment processes can be implemented through inclusion of a broader range of organisations in learning, capitalising on the opinions of peers and experts as to how well learners are expanding their competence through a combination of peripheral participation and coaching* (Eraut, 2004).

Fifth, open access may destabilise closed organisations. For the creative writing group, the ability to work across boundaries routinely and understand how to create resources that will be used by unknown groups of people in unseen ways is critical. Open access to resources could be problematic if the educational institutions that currently largely provide such resources either retain or adopt closed protectionist policies which may be undermined by openness (McGill et al., 2013). Broad elements of society (business, professions, individuals) need to prioritise learning and assume the responsibility for providing open resources (ibid.). *Formal education organisations should continue to open up knowledge, resources and courses to a wider group of learners by linking their strategies to a collaborative strategic vision of lifewide learning. Viable funding and business models will have to be developed and tested.*

Sixth, learning analytics may continue to focus on administrative rather than learning processes. The learners in the creative writing group create new knowledge as artefacts and as user traces. These objects and traces are an external expression of their learning that can be analysed to gauge their progress. In 2013, learning analytics is in its infancy and tends to focus on the administrative processes (for example the learner dashboards described in Chapter 11, this volume), rather than learning. *For learning analytics to become significant as a learning aid, system design has to take a quantum leap and incorporate intelligent analysis based on artificial intelligence.*

Taking forward the vision requires a radical change in cultural perceptions of learner agency and learner–teacher roles, associated with changes in technology. Government agencies and organisations worldwide have a key role to play in facilitating and supporting a vision which depends on increased collaboration across sectors and national boundaries, and on meaningful conversations between learners and formal education providers. Cultural differences across countries significantly impact on the ability to move towards this vision of open, lifewide learning. Any vision for learning is inevitably fraught with challenges around diverse social, economic and political systems, which may or may not support individuals' autonomy, an essential principle for successful lifewide, open learning.

References

Bayne, S. (2008). Higher education as a visual practice: Seeing through the virtual learning environment. *Teaching in Higher Education, 13*(4), 395–410.

Billet, S. (2013). Mimetic learning. Chapter 4 in A. Littlejohn & A. Margaryan (Eds.), *Technology-enhanced professional learning: Processes, practices and tools.* London: Routledge.

Boyd, D. (2007). Why youth (heart) social network sites: The role of networked publics in teenage social life. Berkman Research Publication No. 2007-16, Harvard university Available from: http://sjudmc.net/lyons/civicmedia1/wp-content/uploads/2013/09/boyd-Why-teens-heart-social-media.pdf.

Boyd, D. (2013). *It's complicated: The social lives of networked teens.* New Haven, CT: Yale University Press.

Brown, J. S., & Adler, R. (2008). Minds on fire: Open education, the long tail, and Learning 2.0, *EDUCAUSE Review, 43*(1). Retrieved 28 December 2013, from http://net.educause.edu/ir/library/pdf/ERM0811.pdf.

Buckingham, D. (2007). Digital media literacies: Rethinking media education in the age of the internet. *Research in Comparative and International Education, 2*(1), 43–55.

Candy, P. C. (1991). *Self-direction for lifelong learning: A comprehensive guide to theory and practice.* San Francisco, CA: Jossey-Bass.

Engeström, Y. (1987). *Learning by expanding. An activity-theoretical approach to developmental research.* Helsinki: Orienta-Konsultit.

Eraut, M. (2004). Informal learning in the workplace. *Studies in Continuing Education, 26*(2), 247–273.

Facer, K (2009). Beyond current horizons. Retrieved from www.beyondcurrenthorizons.org.uk/scenarios/.

Hiemstra, R., & Brockett, R. G. (1994). *Overcoming resistance to self-direction in adult learning.* San Francisco, CA: Jossey-Bass Inc.

Knight, E. (2013). RFC: An open distributed system for badge validation. Retrieved from http://tinyurl.com/d82s5eh.

Kress, G. (2003). *Literacy in the new media age.* London: Routledge.

Littlejohn, A., Beetham, H., & McGill, L. (2013). *Digital literacies as situated knowledge practices: Academics' influence on learners' behaviours.* In R. Goodfellow & M. Lea (Eds.), *Learning in the digital university.* London: Routledge.

Margaryan, A., Littlejohn, A., & Vojt, G. (2011). Are digital natives a myth or reality? University students' use of digital technologies. *Computers and Education, 56*(2), 429–440.

McGill, L., Falconer, I., Littlejohn, A., & Beetham, H. (2013). *Synthesis and evaluation report of the JISC UKOER3 programme.* Retrieved from http://bit.ly/UKOER3SynthesisReport.

Milligan, C., Margaryan, A., & Littlejohn, A. (2013). Patterns of engagement in massive open online courses. *Journal of Online Learning and Teaching (JOLT), 9*(2), 149–159, http://jolt.merlot.org/vol9no2/milligan_0613.pdf.

Siemens, G. (2006). *Knowing knowledge.* Lulu.com.

Street, B. (1996). Academic literacies. In D. Baker, J. Clay, & C. Fox (Eds.), *Challenging ways of knowing: In English, mathematics and science.* London: Routledge.

Young, (2008). Towards a European qualifications framework: Some cautionary observations. *Journal of European Industrial Training, 32*(2/3), 128–13.

SECTION 3
Education

9

LEARNING ACROSS SITES THROUGH LEARNING BY DESIGN IN USE

Marisa Ponti, Magnus Bergquist and Ebba Ossiannilsson

This chapter provides a perspective on designing open educational resources (OERs) as an activity interweaving use, design and learning. When educators decide to use OERs, one of the decisions they need to make is whether to reuse them as originally designed, or to repurpose them to fit different educational contexts. By reuse we refer to using resources again in another context but with the same content, while repurposing refers to modifying the content or learning design (Bond, Ingram, & Ryan, 2008). Depending on what educators want to do, OER can be seen either as matters of fact or matters of concern (Latour, 2005). As matters of fact, they can be seen as providing users with access to some discrete and reified content, such as, for example, *video* and audio *lectures* from faculty at the Massachusetts Institute of Technology (MIT) available in MIT OpenCourseware. However, OERs can also be seen as matters of concern, raising unexpected issues and challenges, modifying the space of interactions for learners and educators using such resources, and opening up new ways of thinking and learning. While the format and content of print textbooks are fixed beforehand, with authors trying to specify future uses of their products, many OERs can be changed and repurposed to fit existing and evolving educational activities. Viewing OERs as matters of concern implies a creative and investigative process to discover issues and work out solutions to address them, in order to meet local needs and accommodate diversity of educational practices. Inspired by the A.Telier's (2011) *Architecture and Technology for Inspirational Living* research project, this creative and investigative process is seen here as a process of designing in which emphasis is placed on inquiry, rather than professional competences or a particular domain of expertise. Thus the focus will be on '*designing* rather than on the designers or design' (emphasis in the original, A.Telier, 2011, p. 1). Taking this view of designing, educators and learners face a twofold challenge.

First, they need to foster this creative and investigative process. Second, they need to find ways to turn issues raised by the use of OERs within situated educational practices into learning opportunities. This chapter provides a perspective on designing OERs which draws from design in use and learning by design. Design in use is a concept that directs attention towards users acting as designers, and objects that must evolve continuously to accommodate future unexpected needs. To introduce this concept, the experience of open source software (OSS) is presented. Learning by design is a process supporting inquiry and problem solving, and directs attention towards turning issues arising from unforeseen teaching and learning problems into opportunities for supporting an inquiry process in which dialogue and collaboration play a critical role. Consideration of design in use and learning by design provides opportunities to critically and creatively rethink designing of OERs for reuse and repurposing. It also raises dilemmas though, such as the characteristics of OSS which make it easier—compared with OERs—to repurpose them in different contexts of use; the lack of collaborative design and sharing culture in the OERs community; and motivational issues and the role of participants in the development of repurposable OERs. These are complex issues with no easy solutions. However, this chapter begins to fill the gap between designing OERs 'at project time'—that is, when OERs are designed for the first time—and designing OERs when they are used, moving designing towards use time, and learners and educators as designers in use.

The Emergence of Open Learning Landscapes and the Need of New Frameworks for Education

The OER movement has its origin in open and distance learning and in the wider context of the culture of open knowledge, open source and open access which emerged in the late twentieth century. While initially the notion of openness in the term OER was meant to indicate increased access to educational content, especially in developing countries, in recent years this notion has broadened up to include shared and collaborative development and ownership of educational resources and content. Over the past few years, several international projects have emerged to encourage development, sharing and improvement of OERs. These projects include OPAL (Andrade et al., 2011); OLCOS (Geser, 2007); OLnet (www.olnet.org) an international research hub supported by the William and Flora Hewlett Foundation; POERUP (http://oer13.wordpress.com/tag/poerup/), a project for policies for OER uptake; OER4Adults, which provided a knowledge base for opening up adult and lifelong learning across Europe (http://oer4adults.org); and OERU (http://creativecommons.org/tag/oeru), an initiative aimed to provide pathways to accredited learning to all students worldwide using OER learning materials These projects promote a use of OERs that goes beyond access to content, and attempt to situate OER in forms of learning in networked arenas, where openness and flexibility are primary values and participants are expected to connect and collaborate (Conole, 2012; Downes, 2010; Ossiannilsson, 2012). A step forward in this direction is the definition of OER by Kanwar, Kodhandaraman, and Umar (2010), who envisioned OERs as an empowerment process facilitated by technology, in which several stakeholders can interact, collaborate, and create and use materials. Compared with the definitions initially coined by UNESCO (2002) and recalled in the Paris Declaration (UNESCO, 2012), the definition by Kanwar et al. does not focus on OERs as artefacts to be accessed, used and adapted, but rather on OERs as a sociomaterial process engaging a variety of stakeholders involved in educational practices. This processual approach to OERs is in line with the assumptions underpinning the notions of open educational practices. These practices are understood as supporting learner-centred and collaborative forms of learning, in which learners engage constructively with OERs to address and solve problems and not for reproducing content (Geser, 2007). Therefore, with the growing number of OERs made increasingly accessible online through a wide range of emerging technologies, the focus of interest has become how to incorporate OERs in educational practices to support these learner-centred and collaborative forms of learning (Geser, 2007).

The next two sections present concepts from the two approaches, design in use in the experience of the OSS projects and learning by design. Then, a discussion follows that brings them together with some initial ideas from evolutionary application development, to organise learning activities around the design of OERs in use and to understand the role of participants in this process.

Design in Use in Open Source Software

OSS development has its origin as a social movement claiming the right to protect the openness of software and ensure users' right to use, redistribute and modify the source code. The source code is available to anyone who wants to obtain it and must be licensed in ways that allow modification and the creation of derived work. OSS is developed in an open and collaborative way by a decentralised community of developers (Bergquist & Ljungberg, 2001). OSS development offers participants a space that is a potential design situation in which they can act as co-designers (Ye & Fischer, 2007). In this space, design takes place both at the start of a project ('at project time') and when designed applications are used ('design in use') (Fischer & Scharff, 2000). Therefore, application development does not end at the time of deployment but requires continuous user participation and contribution (Gasser, Scacchi, Penne, & Ripoche, 2003). According to their specific needs, community participants can redesign the source code and create new applications.

In OSS projects, two artefacts are fundamental to engaging users in design in use and encouraging continuous contributions: the source code and the licence. The Free Software Foundation, which was an early and important organisation for disseminating the idea of open source software, stated explicitly that 'access to the source code is a precondition' for running, changing and redistributing the software to benefit the whole community (www.gnu.org/philosophy/free-sw. html). Hence, free and open access to the source code became a tool to protect the possibilities for users to create, reuse, repurpose but also commercialise the software. An important underlying principle is the idea of reciprocality. The GNU General Public License (GPL), which is one of the most permissive of existing licences, is reciprocal because it takes an active stance towards sharing of software code in allowing only software distributed under a reciprocal licence to be combined with other reciprocal licences (Alspaugh, Scacchi, & Asuncion, 2010), which secures freedom to share, change and redistribute modified versions of software (Lakhani & Panetta, 2007). Incremental and cumulative contributions according to the philosophy of free and open software make possible a twofold evolutionary process: the development of applications to meet changing needs, and the development of knowledge and learning occurring as software is developed.

OSS development is also a process of learning and knowledge development. OSS projects are examples of arenas where design in use creates affordances for learning. In these communities, various participants, including users, 'power users', developers and testers, continuously and collectively develop and transform their knowledge of what the target application is, how it works, what it should be and how it should work (Gasser et al., 2003). This process of learning is collaborative, because participants need to interact to build a common understanding that is necessary for newcomers to contribute and participate actively in the community (Fugelli, Lahn, & Mørch, 2013). Shared external artefacts, including wikis, mailing lists and other means of communication, serve as important mediators of interaction and learning, because they allow the community to accumulate, organise, make sense of and use the wide variety of knowledge contributed by the many people involved (Gasser et al., 2003).

Learning by Design

Learning by design is the other approach applied in this chapter to understanding design of OERs as an activity of intertwined design, learning and use. A brief review of the literature points to a lack of commonly accepted meaning of the term 'learning by design', as apparently there is no univocal definition, nor a single perspective on this term. For example, learning by design is used to define a project-based inquiry approach initiated by Kolodner et al. (2003) to design science curricula for middle school to help students learn science content and scientific reasoning, communication and collaboration skills. Kalantzis, Cope, and the Learning by Design Group (2005) used the term instead to refer to an experiment aimed at transforming the pedagogical practices and the professional learning of teachers who participated in that experiment. Other researchers interested in linking design and learning have not used the term 'learning by design' at all. For instance, the notion of collaborative learning as design activity combines collaboration and artefacts, such as social media, to blur any sharp division between consumers of information and content producers and design collaborative learning systems (Kluge, Leinonen, Mørch, & Zhu, 2012). Similarly, in mutual development, professionals and users actively collaborate to develop an object in both design and use, and learn from each other through their interactions (Andersen & Mørch, 2009). Design plays a crucial role in organising artefacts and actions into a space able to connect playing and learning (Jahreie, Arnseth, Krange, Smørdal, & Kluge, 2011). The concept of 'learning design' is used by Conole (2012), who argues for making design processes more explicit and sharable to help teachers to develop more effective learning environments and learners to become more aware of their learning paths. To this end, Conole proposes a learning design framework, covering design, delivery and assessment, and called the 7C model (consider, collaborate, consolidate, communicate, capture, create and conceptualise). Finally, Koper (2003) discusses issues related to the reuse of learning resources in teaching within the context of major changes in education that emphasise the ability of teachers to design activities for learners, instead of transmitting content to learners through teachers' activities.

Amidst all the differences emerging from this brief review, a commonality can be traced to the need to design activities that support learning through dialogue, collaboration and product creation, and to the crucial role played by artefacts in these activities. The view of learning by design advocated here is that of a collaboratively organised setting supporting the potential of artefacts and actions for learning. In this collaboratively organised world, learners and educators can generate ideas, learn new concepts, build and test models, analyse solutions and revise ideas. Thus, learning by design is seen as supporting inquiry and problem solving, encouraging learners and educators to go beyond the content of available resources to examine complex situations and identify solvable problems within them.

The Way Forward: Evolutionary Development to Organize Design in Use and Learning by Design

As described earlier, in OSS projects design and use are closely intertwined. There is no separation between design time, led by experts who design a complete application, and use time, led by end-users who evolve an artefact to meet unforeseen changes. Furthermore, design in use is inherently a process of learning by design, because interactions among participants and between participants and shared external artefacts provide each project member the opportunity to contribute to design, learn something new, adapt and evolve applications continuously. Therefore, OSS projects can provide educators and learners with a good example of a collaborative environment where they can contribute to an ongoing creative and investigative process centred on altering the OERs in use.

However, it can be a challenge to organise learning activities aimed at designing OERs in use and to understand the role of participants in this process. At the same time, many OERs do not provide users yet with the ability to integrate their personal contexts into the content. This challenge raises the question of how to help educators and learners to link design in use and learning by design when unanticipated issues arise from the use of OERs. Educators may not have the experience and skills needed to adapt OERs in a creative and investigative process. In this respect, it has been noted that educators may lack the time and skills needed to find, evaluate and repurpose resources, and that they need guidance on how to rethink their design processes so as to make better use of technologies (Conole & McAndrew, 2010; Geser, 2007). To address this challenge, an approach to evolutionary application development (EAD) (Mørch, 2011) is suggested to provide initial ideas for empowering educators and learners to contribute to and participate more actively in the design process. EAD is a type of end-user development, which is defined as a 'set of methods, activities, techniques, and tools that allow people who are non professional software developers, at some point, to create or modify a software artefact' (Lieberman, Paternò, & Wulf, 2006, p. 2). The rationale for end-user development rests in the need to organise development activities involving a diversity of users. Users can have different cultural, educational and employment backgrounds, and can include novices and experienced computer users, and young and mature individuals with different abilities and disabilities (Mørch, 2011, p. 153). A useful example of EAD described by Mørch (2011) is cloning. New components of an application can be developed by cloning an existing component that resembles what designers want to create or modify. An example of cloning applied to OERs is the attempt made by the Peer-to-Peer University (P2PU) to provide users with a feature to clone existing courses. Cloning would allow users to take a copy of an existing course offered by P2PU and start independent development on it by altering it or creating a new course. Cloning can create a fertile ground for trial and error, offering educators and learners opportunities for reusing and repurposing resources themselves, for example through remixing content from various sources, adapting it to their specific learning environments and combining it with their own products, such as different exercises and topic descriptions.

Another useful example is the development of a generic application for graphics drawing into kitchen design (Mørch, 2011). Using tailoring tools built into the drawing application, an end-user can act as developer during use time and use the techniques for accessing, viewing and modifying the user interface, the design rationale and the program code of an application. The learning challenges involved in the use of the tailoring tools should be proportional to the skills people have (Repenning & Ioannidou, 2006). By integrating an easy-to-use builder tool into it, an educational resource, e.g. a course or a textbook, can arguably become a playground for alterations, keeping the process open to a wide range of contributions (Mørch et al., 2004). This process of repurposing can feed on the potential of openness allowed by the licence and the potentially high number of contributors who can interact with the resources. Furthermore, a builder tool integrated into a resource may also trigger a collaborative learning process in which participants can ask each other questions and share and discuss ideas.

The Role of Openness for Design in Use and Learning by Design with OERs: Opportunities and Dilemmas

As the two examples above suggest, openness is the premise for alterations of resources that make it possible to connect design in use and learning by design. Two critical features in the process should be highlighted. Firstly, instead of seeing OERs as finished resources, they can be seen as potential design activity, which can modify the space of interaction for learners and educators and open up new ways of thinking, solving problems and learning. This potential is relevant at a time in which it is difficult to predict what one may need to know in the future, or what may be useful in future educational activities.

Secondly, the movement towards OERs as potential design activity means to 'unpack' the resources and go back to the world in which they were developed in the first place, understand what is being inscribed in them, evaluate their content and significance in a new context and propose new solutions. Communication, collaboration and imagination are at the heart of this design process, involving an assembly of materials and people coming from different backgrounds and motives despite having a common interest. This assembly is an ecology of interdependent people, materials and techniques, where people acting as designers need to select and use materials and techniques in innovative ways to repurpose OERs. The use of emergent technologies in the design process can help learners and educators redraw the boundaries between design 'at project time' and 'design in use', that is, between producers and consumers of resources. Geser (2007) observed that there are different views on who should create and share OERs, specifically on what role educators—supposedly, one of the main user groups—should play in developing content. Oblinger and Lombardi (2008) criticised those commentators who argue that the development of OERs should remain 'centrally developed, "fixed" in form and closed to modification in order to preserve their integrity as learning experience' (p. 396). Instead Oblinger and Lombardi asserted that a top-down approach to content creation places an undue burden on creators of content and thus limits usability for those who wish to add OERs to their specific learning environment by reusing and repurposing the material. Linking design in use and learning by design reverses the traditional sequence of design, then build, then use, and turns it into 'use, evaluate, design'.

Combining the two approaches offers learners and educators opportunities for sharing ideas, solving problems, collaboration and reflection, in order to repurpose OERs in the contexts of their existing and evolving practices. The design process remains open to needs and demands that by necessity are evolving, as well as to the possibility to work out new and sometimes unexpected solutions (A.Telier, 2011).

Exciting as it may seem, the movement towards designing OERs is not without dilemmas. Three are mentioned here: the characteristics of OERs; the lack of a collaborative design and sharing culture; and the possible unwillingness of educators to put time and effort into repurposing OERs. First, in relation to the characteristics of OERs, what matters is whether OERs are sufficiently modular, extensible and capable of allowing learners and educators to repurpose them at use time. In OSS projects, access to source code, the reciprocal GPL licence and the modularity of software are tools that support repurposing of software for new and unanticipated use contexts. Although OERs are flexible and can be reused in novel combinations, not all of them can be repurposed easily. For example, even if it is relatively easy to manipulate a digital video and that video is released under a permissive Creative Commons licence, it can be difficult to modify the learning content of a recorded campus lecture, with its fixed and linear structure.

Second, the design of OERs seems still to be by and large one of individual practice and relatively little team work and peer review, while OSS software development is the product of many contributors who constantly work on a project, and change and extend it. An important and significant dimension of OSS development is the actual *process* of creating software based on a release-early, release-often and peer-to-peer-based work method. In OSS, development relies on a process of constant revision and refinement by the community to perfect the results, but more important from a learning perspective is the possibility to recontextualise the project in relation to emergent user needs. In OERs the use and modifications of resources are highly contextual. It has been argued that this is an important reason why the OSS development model does not work well with OERs. Mackie (2008) pointed out that a teacher who adapts a piece of OER to his/her local needs often contributes back this derivative work, but without merging it into the OER main project in the same way that a software patch is merged into a OSS original project. However, from the perspective of the central principles of OSS, two of the most important freedoms are the possibility for users to study the mechanisms by which a program operates to be able to modify it to a specific purpose, and the possibility to adapt and improve the program and release adaptations and improvements to the public.

Finally, most participants in OSS projects are volunteers, participants in a culture of sharing and gift-giving, in which social status is determined not by what you own or control but by what you give away (Bergquist & Ljungberg, 2001). It remains to be seen whether educators are willing to engage actively in repurposing OERs on top of their ordinary work unless support and appropriate incentives exist.

Conclusion

This chapter has brought concepts from design in use and learning by design together with ideas from EAD to understand how OERs can be repurposed through active engagement of participants, use of tailoring tools and interaction across multiple settings and contexts. Designing OERs to allow many potential contributors to act as designers in personally meaningful educational activities can help the transformation of educational practices led by the expectations and perspectives of the people involved. However, fostering EAD is not without challenges, as it depends on a fine balance between participant motivation, effective and easy-to-use tools for repurposing of OERs and organisational support. The opportunities and dilemmas explored here need to be addressed in future work on designing OERs, and this chapter hopes to be a step toward the development of a conceptual framework for an evolutionary development of OERs.

Acknowledgements

We are very grateful to Anders Mørch and the reviewers for providing valuable comments on a previous draft of this chapter. One of the authors acknowledges the financial support of the Swedish Research Council, Grant no. 350-2012-346.

References

Alspaugh, T.A., Scacchi, W., & Asuncion, H.U. (2010). Software licenses in context: The challenge of heterogeneously-licensed systems. *Journal of the Association for Information Systems, 11*(11/12), 730–755.

Andersen, R., & Mørch, A.I. (2009). Mutual development: A case study in customer-initiated software product development. *Second International Symposium on End User Development (EUD 2009)*. Lecture Notes in Computer Science. Heidelberg, Germany: Springer.

Andrade, A., Ehlers, U.-D., Caine, A., Carneiro, R., Conole, G., Kairamo, A-K., . . . Holmberg, C. (2011). *Beyond OER: Shifting focus to open educational practices—OPAL report 2011*. Retrieved from http://duepublico.uni-duisburg-essen.de/servlets/DerivateServlet/Derivate-25907/OPALReport2011-Beyond-OER.pdf.

A.Telier (Binder, T., De Michelis, G., Ehn, P. Jacucci, G., Linde, P., & Wagner, I.) (2011). *Design things*. Cambridge, MA: The MIT Press.

Bergquist, M., & Ljungberg, J. (2001). The power of gifts: Organizing social relationships in open source communities. *Information Systems Journal, 11*(4), 305–320. doi: 10.1046/j.1365-2575.2001.00111.x.

Bond, S.T., Ingram, C., & Ryan, S. (2008). Reuse, repurposing and learning design—lessons from the DART project. *Computers & Education, 50*(2), 601– 612.

Conole, G. (2012). *Designing for learning in an open world*. New York: Springer.

Conole, G., & McAndrew, P. (2010). OLnet: A new approach to supporting the design and use of open educational resources. In M. Ebner & M. Schiefner (Eds.), *Looking toward the future of technology-enhanced education: Ubiquitous learning and the digital native* (pp. 123–144). Hershey, PA: IGI Global.

Downes, S. (2010, 12 April). Collaboration and cooperation [Web log comment]. Retrieved from www.downes.ca/post/53303.

Fischer, G., & Scharff, E. (2000). Meta-design: Design for designers. In D. Boyarski & W.A. Kellogg (Eds.), *Proceedings of the 3rd International Conference on Designing Interactive Systems* (pp. 396–405). New York: ACM Publishing.

Fugelli, P., Lahn, L.C., & Mørch, A.I. (2013). Shared prolepsis and intersubjectivity in open source development: Expansive grounding in distributed work. Paper accepted at the *16th ACM Conference on Computer Supported Cooperative Work and Social Computing (CSCW 2013), San Antonio, TX, 23–27 February 2013.* ACM Press.

Gasser, L., Scacchi, W., Penne, B., Ripoche, G. (2003). Understanding continuous design in F/LOSS projects. In *Proceedings of the 16th International Conference on Software & Systems Engineering and their Applications (ICSSEA-03), Paris, France.*

Geser, G. (Ed.) (2007). *Open educational practices and resources: OLCOS roadmap to 2012.* Open e-Learning Content Observatory Services (OLCOS). Transversal action under the European eLearning programme. Retrieved from www.olcos.org/cms/upload/docs/olcos_roadmap.pdf.

Jahreie, C.F., Arnseth, H.C., Krange, K., Smørdal, O., & Kluge, A. (2011). Designing for play-based learning of scientific concepts: Digital tools for bridging school and science museum contexts. *Children, Youth and Environments, 21*(2). Retrieved from www.colorado.edu/journals/cye/21_2/index.htm.

Kalantzis, M., Cope, B., & the Learning by Design Group (2005). *Learning by design.* Melbourne and Altona, Australia: Victorian Schools Innovation Commission and Common Ground Publishing.

Kanwar, A., Kodhandaraman, B., & Umar, A. (2010). Towards sustainable open education resources: A perspective from the global south. *American Journal of Distance Education, 24*(2), 6580.

Kluge, A., Leinonen, T., Mørch, A., & Zhu, L. (2012). Collaborative learning as design activity. Workshop presented *at NordiCHI 2012, Copenhagen, Denmark.* Abstract retrieved from www.intermedia.uio.no/www-data-public/NordiCHI/.

Kolodner, J.L., Crismond, D., Fasse, B., Gray, J., Holbrook, J., & Puntembakar, S. (2003). Putting a student-centered learning by design™ curriculum into practice: Lessons learned. *Journal of the Learning Sciences, 12*(4), 495–547.

Koper, E.J.R. (2003). Combining re-usable learning resources and services to pedagogical purposeful units of learning. In A. Littlejohn (Ed.), *Reusing online resources: A sustainable approach to elearning* (pp. 46–59). London: Kogan Page.

Lakhani, K.R., & Panetta, J.A. (2007). The principles of distributed innovation. *Innovations, 2*(3), 97–112.

Latour, B. (2005). *Reassembling the social: An introduction to actor-network-theory.* Oxford, UK: Oxford University Press.

Lieberman, H., Paternò, F., & Wulf, V. (Eds.) (2006). *End-user development: Empowering people to flexibly employ advanced information and communication technology.* Dordrecht, Netherlands: Springer.

Mackie, C.J. (2008). Open source in open education: Promises and challenges. In T. Iiyoshi & M.S. Kumar Vijay (Eds.), *Opening up education: The collective advancement of education through open technology, open content, and open knowledge* (pp. 119–131). Cambridge, MA: The MIT Press.

Mørch, A.I. (2011). Evolutionary application development: Tools to make tools and boundary crossing. In H. Isomäki & S. Pekkola (Eds.), *Reframing humans in information systems development* (pp. 151–171). London, UK: Springer-Verlag.

Mørch, A.I., Stevens, G., Won, M., Klann, M., Dittrich, Y., & Wulf, V. (2004). Component-based technologies for end-user development. *Communications of the ACM, 47*(9), 59–62.

Oblinger, D.G., & Lombardi, M.M. (2008). Common knowledge: Openness in higher education. In T. Iiyoshi & M.S. Kumar Vijay (Eds.), *Opening up education: The collective advancement of education through open technology, open content, and open knowledge* (pp. 389–409). Cambridge, MA: The MIT Press.

Ossiannilsson, E. (2012). *Benchmarking e-learning in higher education: Lessons learned from international projects.* Doctoral Dissertation. Faculty of Technology, Department of Industrial Engineering and Management, University of Oulu, Finland.

Repenning, A., & Ioannidou, A. (2006). What makes end-user development tick? 13 design guidelines. In H. Lieberman, F. Paternò, & V. Wulf (Eds.), *End-user development: Empowering people to flexibly employ advanced information and communication technology* (pp. 51–86). Dordrecht, Netherlands: Springer.

UNESCO (2002). *Forum on the impact of Open Courseware for higher education in developing countries: Final report.* UNESCO, Paris, 1–3 July 2002.

UNESCO (2012). *2012 Paris OER declaration.* 2012 World Open Educational Resources (OER) Congress, UNESCO, Paris, June 20–22, 2012.

Ye, Y., & Fischer, G. (2007). Designing for participation in socio-technical software systems. In D. Hutchison et al. (Eds.), *Lecture Notes in Computer Science: Vol. 4554, Universal Access in Human Computer Interaction. Coping with Diversity* (pp. 312–321). Berlin, Germany: Springer. doi: 10.1007/978-3-540-73279-2_35.

10

MASSIVE OPEN ONLINE COURSES

A Traditional or Transformative
Approach to Learning?

Katie Vale and Allison Littlejohn

Massive Open Online Courses (MOOCs) are viewed by some as a game changer, radically shifting expectations around the ways in which people can access education (Daniel, 2012). But there are questions around whether and how MOOCs radically shift learning. A MOOC is an online course, free of charge and open to anyone, regardless of their prior knowledge or qualifications. As such they have the potential to transform—or even destabilise—societies, since learning and education play a central role in societal development (Brennan, King, & Lebeau, 2004; Hardt & Negri, 2003).

Many analyses of MOOCs agree that open courses are potentially threatening to current models of higher education (OBHE, 2013, p. 5). MOOCs disrupt the traditional form of course delivery to residential, campus-based students and open up opportunities for for-profit education providers to offer scaled-up courses (ibid., p. 48). The response from universities has been attempts at agile innovation, testing business models and pursuing brand enhancement through open courses. There has been a marked escalation in the number of MOOCs offered by universities over the two-year period 2011–13. MOOC learner experiences have been reported as (largely) positive, emphasising the expansion of learner access, learner empowerment and relationship building with individuals who may want to extend their studies through enrolment on formal educational programmes (ibid.).

Despite the excitement, conflicting perspectives around MOOCs divide education communities. Not all learning professionals agree on the value of MOOCs, voicing concerns around instructional design, quality and accreditation (ibid.). Learning researchers have evidence of poor engagement in online learning by those learners who have relatively low levels of digital literacies (Kop & Fournier, 2011) and may have limited ability to self-regulate their learning

(Milligan, Littlejohn, & Margaryan, 2013). Other researchers are critical that many MOOCs are based on the production and consumption of 'formal educational content', missing opportunities to empower learners to self-direct their own learning (see Chapter 3, this volume). The ability of learners to direct their own learning could trigger a significant shift in the position of the academy in society, therefore it is not surprising that universities may want to influence the direction of MOOC development.

This chapter examines potential benefits and limitations of MOOCs, using a case example of a major MOOC initiative: edX. The chapter begins by examining conflicting perspectives around MOOCs from the literature. Then the HarvardX course design workflow model is outlined. HarvardX is at the centre of a variety of activities at Harvard University associated with open educational resources and open courses. The first five HarvardX MOOCs are described and learner behaviours in these MOOCs are analysed. Finally, the benefits and limitations of open courses are reported.

Conflicting Perspectives Around MOOCs

The conflicting opinions and perspectives around MOOCs are rooted in the diverse origins of the concept of open education and open learning. Ideas around open courses emerged from three different arenas: universities, open learning researchers and the Open Access social movement.

The Open Access movement is a global network of people who support the transformation of work and learning practices towards free sharing and peer collaboration in society through open sourcing, open resources and the (re)use of open knowledge. A central aim is to change societal expectations of how, when and where people learn. One strategy has been to eliminate barriers to entry into university-level education through opening access to the 'fundamental building blocks' of learning (Brown & Adler, 2008). These building blocks are viewed as open educational resources (OERs)—digital materials that can be used, re-used and repurposed for teaching, learning or research, made available online through open licences, such as Creative Commons (McGill, Falconer, Littlejohn, & Beetham 2013). OERs and open courses are a lever sometimes used by universities to attract learners to move from informal to formal learning programmes, encouraging them to pay for subsequent, follow-on courses (Gillet, Law, & Chatterjee, 2010). Thus, motivations to develop and openly release OERs are complex and can be placed on a spectrum ranging from 'academic commons' to the marketisation of courses (Falconer, Littlejohn, McGill, & Beetham, 2013).

A second arena promoting the open courses are learning researchers and advocates of a pedagogical approach termed 'connectivism'. Connectivist principles emphasise that learning occurs through network connections, as learners connect with experts, peers and knowledge resources (Siemens, 2005). MOOCs can be viewed as an instantiation of the pedagogic approach of 'connectivism' (Downes,

2008; Siemens, 2005), opening up opportunities for learning as part of a learning community or group of learners (Downes, 2008). Despite these key principles, discussions around informal *open learning*, emphasising the learner, are sometimes conflated with formal *open education*, highlighting the design of activities, environments, networks, tools and resources. Some MOOC designs can mimic university courses, rather than focusing on building learner autonomy (Milligan et al., 2013; Nurmohamed, Gillani, & Lenox, 2013).

A third origin of the MOOC concept is the educational activity of the academy. Universities, often operating as consortia, have provided most open courses and open educational resources. An early example is the Open CourseWare Consortium (established in 2003), a consortium of universities committed to the open release of educational resources, often from contemporary, campus-based courses (OCW, 2013) This initiative has had significant impact in terms of opening access to a broad spectrum of resources, ranging from syllabi, lecture notes and supplemental materials to video materials (Forward, 2012). For example, the founding partner, the Massachusetts Institute of Technology, has released resources from 2,180 courses that have been viewed by over 100 million people (MIT, 2013). Funding organisations such as UNESCO, the Bill and Melinda Gates Foundation and the William and Flora Hewlett Foundation collectively have donated millions of dollars to the development and release of OERs. There are numerous examples of consortia and collections of educational resource materials around the world, including OER Africa,[1] OER Asia,[2] Open Education Europa,[3] Latin America Learning,[4] DEHub Australia,[5] Nordic OER,[6] MERLOT[7] and Jorum UK.[8] Some MOOC design teams attempt to capitalise upon these resource collections by packaging OERs around specific learning objectives and activities, then sequencing these activities in orchestrated, synchronous courses with regular, automated assessments. Course design may be based on equivalent campus-based courses. The design teams often recognise that exposure to the course's resource materials is not a sufficient condition for learning. However, an assumption is that learners can self-regulate their own learning, utilising learning resources with limited instructor interaction.

Interest in the potential of open courses to open up access to universities led to a fourth origin of MOOCs: MOOC platform providers. A number of platforms were established during the period 2011–13, mainly in the US and UK. Some are 'for profit' organisations such as Udacity (https://www.udacity.com) and Coursera (https://www.coursera.org). Others are organisations operated within non-profit universities, notably edX (https://www.edx.org/) and Futurelearn (https://www.futurelearn.com/).

Thus, some of the perspectives around MOOCs can be expressed as follows.

- *Universities*—particularly elite institutions—recognise the competitive advantages of MOOCs in branding, marketisation and extending reach. Their response is often to open up established courses to learners globally, seeking to imitate the 'campus experience'.

- *Practitioners* acknowledge the potential of MOOCs, viewing them as a sustaining rather than a disruptive innovation. They habitually align MOOC development and implementation within the confines of existing higher education models. Recognising that the student experience is changed and that their own workflow models are not sustainable in MOOCs, practitioners are concerned with problems of student engagement, feedback, quality and assessment, focusing efforts on improving the quality and engagement potential of educational content.

- Open Access activists are concerned that the view of MOOCs as a marketisation tool for traditional university education blocks alternative, viable futures for learning and learners. As MOOCs mature as a platform for learning, there is a growing acceptance that conventional metrics (completion rates, contributions to forums) are not useful to measure the effectiveness of open learning. Metrics and models have to be reconceptualised, drawing on learning analytics (Chapter 11, this volume).

- *Learners* have enthusiastically embraced MOOCs, signing up in their thousands to participate. Many act as passive observers or 'lurkers' (Milligan et al., 2013), raising concerns amongst practitioners and universities around completion rates. However, motivations across diverse groups of learners are broadly defined and extend beyond gaining credit (OBHE, 2013). A more pressing concern are the baseline capabilities—literacies, skills and dispositions—of learners as they learn in a new environment (Kop & Fournier, 2011; Mackness, Mak, & Williams, 2010; Milligan et al., 2013).

- Educational and learning *researchers* are sceptical of this learner enthusiasm, recognising that social expectations of 'university schooling' constrain transformative opportunities around learning (Chapter 3, this volume). In their view, recognition of what constitutes learning needs to be broadened (McGill et al., 2013).

- *Governments* hold pole position in cultural definitions of learning, but few seem willing to radically redefine learning and redraw business and workflow models. All the same, it is governments' view that MOOCs merit serious attention because of their potential for significant disruption and, at the same time, widening access to higher education (OBHE, p. 53).

The HarvardX MOOC Design Workflow Model

The first universities to experiment with MOOC business and workflow models at an institutional level were the Massachusetts Institute of Technology (MIT) and Harvard. In 2012 MIT and Harvard launched edX, which by fall 2013 had grown into a consortium of twenty-nine universities around the world. edX was set up to build upon the key operating principle of the MIT OpenCourseWare initiative that learners can effectively self-regulate their own learning, utilising learning resources without instructor interaction or assessment. This assumption is extended through the creation of HarvardX and MITX open access courses that are run on a platform called edX Studio. The design and development workflow processes used for campus-based, conventional courses at Harvard had to be redefined for open courses.

HarvardX and MITX open courses are broadly based on campus-based courses, though conventional course content is redeveloped for the MOOC environment. The development and publishing process is entirely in-house, drawing upon university-based instructional design teams. The development teams are university funded, for example HarvardX is funded through start-up funding from the Harvard University President's Office. Faculty at MIT and Harvard also have access to existing institutionally based support structures to help them with instructional design, copyright, multimedia, videography, communications, technology and student assessments. The magnitude of this support structure reflects the large resource base required to repurpose traditional courses as open courses. Future business support and sustainability models for HarvardX are still being considered and formulated.

edX is a non-profit organisation which draws funding from the participating institutions. It offers a significant resource base: in 2013 there were sixty employees—primarily software engineers and project managers—who provide the MOOC platform. The course development process for edX-based MOOCs follows a highly standardised process to select, design and publish courses. The HarvardX workflow is as follows.

- *Outreach*: Campus-based town hall forums are organised to disseminate the aims of HarvardX, what it takes to produce, publish and run a course, and what resources are available to help them. If a faculty member wants to run a MOOC, he or she submits a course proposal.
- *Approval and prioritization*: A course committee reviews and prioritises course proposals. The aim is to offer a diverse range of courses from different schools.
- *Roadmap*: Faculty meet with the HarvardX team to define the learning goals and instructional design, and to identify potential copyright, intellectual property or technical concerns. Faculty can hire part-time course-development staff funded through HarvardX. Faculty also draw on existing campus support for videography, software development and other needs, as outlined above.
- *Planning and production*: Faculty and course development staff are trained in how to use the edX platform. In circumstances where the MOOC is a modified version of an on-campus course, the learning goals and instructional design may be reviewed and adapted for an open audience. For new or significantly adapted courses, the instructional design is planned using a 'backwards design' methodology (Wiggins & McTighe, 2005). Whenever copyrighted material is used, an intellectual property specialist from the

Harvard Law Library assists in determining intellectual property rights and copyright, advises on the use of Creative Commons open licences and identifies alternative OER.

- *Review and launch*: When the first week's course content has been uploaded to the edX platform, a review meeting is held with the faculty member, course team, HarvardX and edX technical staff to surface any technical, legal or pedagogical issues. A course description is drafted and the launch date is agreed upon.

Like many practitioners, Harvard faculty want evidence that MOOCs contribute to positive learning outcomes and that time invested in preparing content materials for open courses will benefit on-campus teaching as well (see Cox, 2013). Faculty want multiple channels for releasing educational resources, including MOOCs, iTunesU, e-books and as OERs. The starting point for many of the HarvardX MOOCs has been to redesign conventional courses to a MOOC format.

Analysis of the HarvardX MOOC

The first five HarvardX courses, run in 2012 and 2013, are described in this section. The course designs are analysed using the framework for analysis of learning behaviours outlined in Chapter 6: the charting model.

MOOCs Focusing on Consuming and Connecting Content Resources: Public Health and Philosophy

One of Harvard's early courses on the edX platform was Quantitative Methods in Clinical and Public Health Research (PH207X), which first ran in 2012. This course aims to enable learners to discover the basic principles of biostatistics and epidemiology, including outcomes measurement, study design options and survey techniques. Course faculty had little experience of distance learning and decided to use an instructivist learning design (Joyce & Weil, 1992). The course was created by repurposing sections of campus-based courses using video lecture sequences interspersed with pictorial or interactive examples, online articles, chapters from a free e-textbook and exercise examples (Figure 10.1). Learning tasks were assigned automatically via the edX platform. Some tasks involved data analysis, therefore a licensed version of a statistical application Stata, provided by the Statacorp company free of charge for the duration of the course, was made available to learners. Progress was monitored by the learner via a personal progress page.

Learner behaviours were analysed using the charting model (see Chapter 6, this volume). During the course learners spend most time consuming and connecting the various course materials. There is also scope for learner interactions, through *creating* statistical analysis data (using the Stata software) and *contributing*

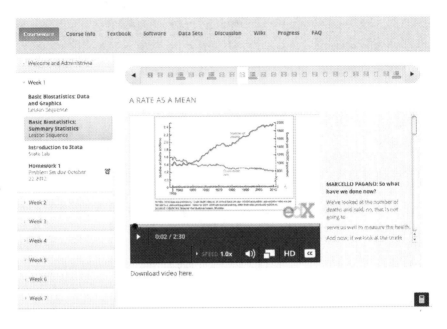

FIGURE 10.1 A Video Clip in the PH207x MOOC

This image is reproduced with kind permission from edX.

ideas about the analyses and the course via the course discussion forums. There was evidence of learners interacting outside the main course environment, as people used self-selected tools such as meetup.com to self-organise into face-to-face study groups. One such event in Bangalore drew over 100 attendees. Interaction and peer support was also evident in the course forums and via the course wiki, where learners contributed assistance and encouragement to each other. In one case, a PH20X learner became such a frequent and useful respondent to fellow students' queries that the faculty gave her an honorary Community Teaching Fellow title in recognition of her efforts.

Another of Harvard's early MOOCs was Justice: a course in political and ethical philosophy. The open course was based on the on-campus course, which regularly draws 600–700 students in each cohort. The Justice course is based on the Socratic method, to help students develop an understanding of complex legal issues. On-campus students use a range of resources, including a textbook, lectures, iTunesU resources and televised lectures broadcast on American public television. These resources were repurposed for the MOOC. In an attempt to replicate the Socratic method online, course producers worked with the edX team to add conditional branching to the MOOC platform, so that MOOC learners are posed with an ethical dilemma and are forced to make a decision. Students then 'work through' learning materials (lectures and discussion boards) examining the consequences of their decision.

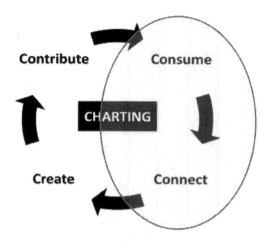

FIGURE 10.2 MOOCs Focusing on Consuming and Connecting

Analysis of learner behaviours in the MOOC indicate that learners primarily spend time consuming and connecting content resources (Figure 10.2). There are limitations in the ways learners can *create*, *contribute* and share their own knowledge, which is a drawback in learning Justice in this modality.

MOOCs Focusing on Creating and Contributing: Computer Science and Humanities

The first HarvardX course was Computer Science 50 (CS50), which ran in the fall of 2012; Vale, 2012). The on-campus course is one of Harvard's largest, involving around 100 teaching fellows and course assistants. The on-campus course uses an apprenticeship learning approach (Malan, 2010). Learners can self-select one of three tracks, depending on their knowledge of coding. Within each track learners pursue goals set by the course designers, rather than formulating their own goals. Pre-set goals were considered important by the course designers, because the course is at an introductory level. It was assumed that learners would have difficulty in setting their own goals. However, the option of three tracks means that learner progress, rather than relative knowledge, is assessed. Final course grades are in relation to the student's knowledge at the start of the course.

The MOOC version of the course is based on this apprenticeship model. Each learner had six months in which to complete the course activities and assignments (two interactive quizzes and a final project assignment), interacting with peers and teaching assistants. Analysis of learner behaviours shows that learners consume and connect course content over a twelve-week period: each week they view two video lectures, work through a course section or track (experienced learners could choose a faster-paced track, while a slower-paced one was available for novices), commence a programming assignment and view one or more videos on a specific topic (Figure 10.3). Learners are also encouraged to *connect* and interact with peers. Students ask and answer others' questions throughout the course using a discussion tool that mimics social media tools such as Reddit (www.reddit.com) and Piazza (www.piazza.com). Further opportunities for learners to *connect* with peers are via the CS50 social media streams in Facebook and Twitter. The apprenticeship approach encourages learners to *create and contribute* knowledge as they interact with peers and with teaching assistants.

The apprenticeship model encourages collaboration in part of the environment called 'Spaces'. There, learners can select and work on existing snippets of code, collaborating with peers and teaching assistants as they expand and debug code. Learners *contribute* to peer learning as they *create* new knowledge that peers benefit from. Teaching assistants work real-time shifts to scaffold learning in the discussion forums and Spaces. The teaching assistants grade problem sets in the form of coding assignments.

HeroesX was the first Humanities course to be offered via the edX platform. The MOOC is based on an on-campus course: The Ancient Greek Hero. The course is designed to facilitate learning within a twenty-four-hour period divided into one-hour segments. Learners consume and connect content in an electronic textbook, then complete sequenced assignments by participating in online quizzes. Course assessment requires demonstration of critical thinking, argument construction and

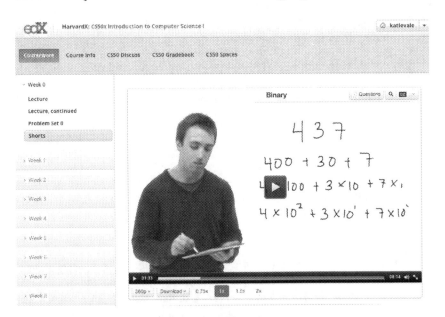

FIGURE 10.3 A Short Video Clip in the CS50x MOOC

This image is reproduced with kind permission from edX.

modes of thought not easily assessed via multiple-choice tests. A large number of Harvard alumni have completed the campus-based version of the course since its inception in 1970. Therefore alumni of The Ancient Greek Hero (campus-based) course were recruited via the Alumni Association to form a Board of Readers to provide feedback to learners in the open course. The Board of Readers was formed in response to online discussions being of an unacceptable quality, leading to low-level interactions and an inconsistent learner experience in the first HeroesX MOOC. Alumni were asked to monitor online discussions, ask questions and provide feedback aimed to complement teaching efforts from the course team (OBHE, p. 38).

Learners are assigned to cohort groups within which they participate in discussions under the guidance of their assigned Reader. HeroesX allows learners to *create and contribute* knowledge as they interact with peers and alumni (Figure 10.4). Assessments involve the use of the collaborative annotation tool to create and contribute philologic knowledge.

'Closed' MOOC: CopyrightX

Another HarvardX open course is CopyrightX, which is arguably a MOCC (Mid-sized Online Closed Course) (Catropa & Andrews, 2012) or SPOC (Small Private Online Course). The course is not fully open, as enrolment is limited to 500 learners who apply via a lottery. Limited enrolment means that learners tend to be more committed and motivated to completing the course, as compared with other MOOCs, where completion rates are typically low. The first cohort of learners completed the course in fall 2012. Of the 500 students, 247 chose to attempt the final exam, and of those 195 scored a passing grade. Similar to CS50x, learning goals are predefined by the faculty member, who wanted the course to retain as much of the 'feel' of an on-campus, law school seminar as possible.

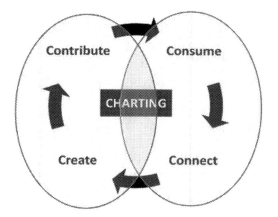

FIGURE 10.4 MOOCs Focusing on Creating and Contributing

In CopyrightX learners consume and connect course materials, including videos, readings and supplemental material via the faculty member's personal website (Fisher, 2013). Learners are divided into four cohorts, each following a slightly different curriculum in terms of content or scaffolding. Course sections are based on different syllabi and utilise various pedagogical methods to allow learners to *create* and *contribute* new knowledge. Teaching assistants interact with learners as they perform formative and summative review of the approaches and outcomes. Each teaching assistant oversees a cohort of twenty-five learners, in an effort to replicate face-to-face discussions in the on-campus course, which can be difficult, given the asynchronous nature of the class. Learners not fortunate enough to win a spot via the lottery are still able to access the online resources, but are not able to participate in the discussion forums. Course materials are available as open courseware even when the course is not 'live'.

Analysis of the learner behaviours shows that learners consume and connect with pre-prescribed content. They also have access to knowledge that their peers *create* and *contribute*.

Overall, these first five HarvardX courses faced common issues in their inaugural semesters, particularly attrition, teaching staff capacity and opportunities for student feedback and collaboration. The Copyright course—offered as a limited enrolment private course—saw fewer than half of the learners pass the final exam. The other MOOCs had a 10 per cent or smaller completion rate. Some faculty, unused to teaching online, grew concerned about early drop-out rates and wrote encouraging letters on the discussion boards in order to convince students to stay engaged with the course. Others were less concerned about the numbers, as they reckoned that the number of students who finished was ten to twenty times higher than they would normally teach in a year. These figures are similar to those experienced by other MOOC providers, and the issue of attrition continues to raise important questions about student motivation, self-regulated learning and the amount of effort and money it takes to design and teach a MOOC (Chronicle of Higher Education, 2013a).

This section provides a brief analysis of Harvard's initial experience of implementing and running open courses. It is difficult to draw hard conclusions without more empirical data. However, some general findings are useful in guiding future MOOC development.

Discussion of Constraints and Opportunities around HarvardX

Analysis of the first five HarvardX open courses points to some successes.

- *HarvardX courses are of interest to learners worldwide.* Learners seem to want to participate in the courses, as verified by the large numbers of people who register for open courses. Even allowing for high attrition rates, hundreds have completed edX courses. There is evidence of continual and persistent engagement by some learners, though there is (as yet) limited data on whether learners who are less active are benefitting or learning. One problem is that conventional course metrics, such as completion rates, are not an effective measurement of the success of MOOCs (OBHE, 2013). These measures do not provide data around the reasons why learners are registering for edX courses, nor do they give an indication of whether students learn in MOOCs, particularly learners who are not actively engaging within the edX environment. Designing HarvardX MOOCs around equivalent campus-based courses may encourage people to participate, as learners may be curious about students' experiences of Harvard. Alternatively, they may want to be associated with the Harvard 'brand'. Faculty from other universities or from commercial education providers may also be interested in Harvard educational materials. Analytics to identify who is accessing the resources are already available. However, understanding how materials are being used by educators and by learners and whether their use results in learning is more challenging (see Chapter 11, this volume).

- *Basing MOOC design on campus-based courses fits with societal attitudes towards formal learning.* That is, the designs are broadly based around conventional teaching and learning roles, where faculty 'deliver' course content which learners 'consume' (Chapter 3, this volume). Designing MOOCs around campus-based courses fits with the expectations and teaching practices of Harvard faculty. There is evidence that faculty involved in HarvardX are changing their professional practice. However, moving teaching practice beyond the application of new technologies to conventional teaching methods is difficult, even for faculty who are known for innovative teaching. Data gathered by the HarvardX development teams verifies that encouraging faculty, instructional designers and support staff to work outside of the norms of current professional practice is challenging. This finding aligns with developmental research work examining issues associated with changing professional teaching practice in universities across the UK (see Chapter 4, this volume). One way to convince faculty that practice change is worthwhile is to demonstrate benefits for mainstream, campus-based courses. To this end, Harvard is encouraging MOOC resources and professional practices to be implemented within conventional courses. However, formally registered, campus-based students are unsettled by changes in teaching practice. Preliminary studies report that Harvard students are uncomfortable with MOOC materials being repurposed in 'flipped classroom' settings on campus (Hashimi & Shim, 2013).

This analysis points to a number of limitations.

- *Scaling up campus-based courses diminishes opportunities for personalised learning in MOOCs.* Conventional courses are designed to support large numbers of students to reach a specific level of competency, largely ignoring any learning that takes place outside the curriculum. Competence-based curricula are becoming the norm around the world, a development which has been accelerated by the standardisation of qualifications (for an example of cross-national standardisation of courses see ECTS, 2013). Computer Science 50 (CS50) attempts to provide learners with different options and learning pathways by offering three learning tracks, depending on their expertise.

- *Basing HarvardX MOOCs on campus classes resulted in scaling issues.* It was generally believed that MOOCs would extend learners' use of OERs, educational resources that were openly and (generally) freely available for use (Daniel, 2012). However, in reality MOOCs have largely not extended the use of OER because many MOOCs comprise content specifically designed and produced for the course, rather than using available OERs. Significant resource has gone into developing MOOC course materials, due to faculty preference in developing bespoke materials, rather than reusing available OERs. One of the key differences between developing an in-house enterprise platform (edX) rather than outsourcing to private enterprises is that Harvard faculty can directly influence the development of the MOOC platform. It could be more difficult to influence the development of Coursera and Udacity than to work directly with the edX development team. However, in-house development means that the overall development cost per MOOC is considerably higher. In fall 2013 Harvard began experimenting with a number of options including creating open learning materials outside the full course format, creating smaller educational resources, content modules, or educational applets, and reusing MOOC resources within campus-based courses, as outlined earlier in this section.

- *There are difficulties with providing feedback to thousands of learners.* There is some justification for the criticism that MOOCs emphasise open access to educational resources, rather than providing opportunities for learner interaction and assessment (Daniel, 2012). HarvardX has tried to overcome this scaling problem, but providing feedback has proved challenging. One example is the Justice MOOC, which could not provide individualised, Socratic instruction to thousands of students. Instead students were asked to watch videos of a faculty member interacting with an on-campus student. Learners could then discuss issues with peers in the discussion forums. Justice teaching assistants provided weekly webcast responses to the top questions in the forums, but (as they numbered only two) were unable to answer every student query individually. HarvardX has tried to resource courses with Teaching Assistants (TAs), but the ratio of learners to TAs is very high. Use of alumni or peers may be a way forward. Peer interaction could also be an effective option, but learners have to understand how to interact and have to be in contact with knowledgeable peers.

- *There is limited evidence that some learners have the dispositions necessary to learn autonomously in MOOC settings.* For example, the Public Health Research (PH207X) students who met outside the edX environment and the PH20X learner who responded to fellow students' questions. However, these are exceptional cases amongst the tens of thousands of learners who register for the open courses. Harvard faculty are used to selecting students from a large number of applicants and potentially (unknowingly) may select those that are able to plan and direct their own learning. Many of these Harvard students have the confidence, mindset and ability to self-regulate their own learning. By opening up courses, universities have to find ways to encourage large numbers of learners to self-regulate their learning in unstructured, networked environments or provide highly structured courses. The second option is easier in the short term, yet it is only by moving beyond current forms of teaching that societal transformative opportunities can be achieved. Decoupling teaching from learning, as described in Chapter 3 in this volume, offers a way forward that includes formal teaching and education opportunities alongside informal learning pathways.

Next Steps for HarvardX

HarvardX offers a way of making Harvard education available to large numbers of people. However, the conceptualisation of HarvardX MOOCs as 'courses', the focus on 'content', the teaching model of direct instruction and the limited ability of some learners to self-regulate their own learning restricts future opportunities to transform learning.

Capitalising on the transformative opportunities around new forms of learning activity afforded by networked environments is complex. Major barriers are not only the inflexible organisational structures of universities and expectations of faculty (Chronicle of Higher Education, 2013b), but the beliefs and abilities of learners.

Harvard thinks of its educational offerings as occurring in three related modalities (Residential, Extended, and Open) and believes that learning materials can be shared amongst them. *Residential* refers to conventional methods of teaching tuition-paying students who are campus based. *Extended* includes existing continuing, distance and professional development courses, all of which are fee based. *Open* is a new category for Harvard, and includes not only HarvardX MOOCs but also materials made available through iTunesU,[9] GitHub,[10] MERLOT[11] or other sources. The goal of the Harvard development team when assessing the feasibility of course development is to determine first which modality is best suited to the intended learning approach. There are now three different versions of the courses CS50 and Heroes, and a current line of research is whether and how the teaching methods and outcomes vary across the different modalities.

As the initial hype around MOOCs wanes, the climate is ripe for experimentations with other types of open learning resources. Whether universities, faculty and learners can capitalise on these opportunities is yet to be seen.

Notes

1 OER Africa www.oerafrica.org/
2 OER Asia www.oerasia.org/
3 Open Education Europa www.openeducationeuropa.eu/
4 Latin America Learning www.latinamericalearning.org/
5 DEHub www.dehub.edu.au/
6 Nordic OER http://nordicoer.org/
7 MERLOT www.merlot.org/
8 JORUM www.jorum.ac.uk/
9 iTunesU www.apple.com/education/itunes-u/
10 GitHub https://github.com/
11 MERLOT www.merlot.org

References

Brennan, J., King, R., & Lebeau, Y. (2004). The role of universities in the transformation of societies. *An international research project. Synthesis Report*. London. Available at: www. open. ac. uk/cheri/documents/transf-final-report. pdf.

Brown, J. S., & Adler, R. P. (2008). Open education, the long tail, and Learning 2.0. *EDUCAUSE Review, 43*(1), 16–20.

Catropa, D., & Andrews, M. (2012). MOOCs to MOCCs. Retrieved from www.inside-highered.com/blogs/stratedgy/moocs-moccs.

Chronicle of Higher Education. (2013a). Coursera takes a nuanced view of MOOC dropout rates. Retrieved from http://chronicle.com/blogs/wiredcampus/coursera-takes-a-nuanced-view-of-mooc-dropout-rates/43341.

Chronicle of Higher Education. (2013b). An open letter to Professor Michael Sandel from the Philosophy Department at San Jose State U. Retrieved from http://chronicle.com/article/The-Document-an-Open-Letter/138937/.

Cox, M. (2013). Interview with David Cox, creator of HarvardX's Fundamentals of Neuroscience MOOC. *Degree of Freedom*. Retrieved 5 November 2013 from http://degreeoffreedom.org/interview-david-cox-creator-harvardxs-fundamentals-neuroscience-mooc/,

Daniel, J. (2012). Making sense of MOOCs: Musings in a maze of myth, paradox and possibility. *Journal of Interactive Media in Education, 3*. Retrieved from http://jime.open.ac.uk/jime/issue/view/Perspective-MOOCs/showToc.

Downes, S. (2008). Places to go: Connectivism and connective knowledge. *Innovate, 5*(1). Retrieved from www.innovateonline.info/index.php?view=article&id=668.

ECTS (2013). European Credit Transfer and Accumulation. Retrieved 26 October 2013 from http://ec.europa.eu/education/lifelong-learning-policy/doc48_en.htm.

Falconer, I., Littlejohn, A., McGill, L., & Beetham, H. (2013). Motives and tensions in the release of Open educational resources: The JISC UKOER programme. Available from http://bit.ly/motivespaper.

Fisher, W. (2013). CopyrightX2013. Retrieved 13 August 2013 from http://cyber.law.harvard.edu/people/tfisher/CopyrightX_Homepage_2013.htm.

Forward, M. L. (2012). OpenCourseWare. In D. Oblinger, *Game changers* (pp. 291–300). Lawrence, KS: Educause/Allen Press. Retrieved 5 November 2013 from www.educause.edu/library/resources/case-study-8-opencourseware.

Gillet, D., Law, E. C., & Chatterjee, A. (2010, April). Personal learning environments in a global higher engineering education Web 2.0 realm. In *Education Engineering (EDUCON), 2010 IEEE* (pp. 897–906). IEEE.

Hardt, M., & Negri, A. (2003). *Empire.* Cambridge, MA: Harvard University Press.

Hashimi, A. H., & Shim, C. W. (2013). The Harvard classroom, digitized. *The Harvard Crimson.* Retrieved 31 October 2013 from www.thecrimson.com/article/2013/10/31/harvard-classroom-virtual-learning/#.

Joyce, B., & Weil, M. (1992). *Models of teaching.* Boston, MA: Allyn and Bacon.

Kop, R., & Fournier, H. (2011). New dimensions to self-directed learning in an open networked learning environment. *International Journal of Self-Directed Learning, 7*(2), 1–18.

Mackness, J., Mak, S., & Williams, R. (2010). The ideals and reality of participating in a MOOC. *Proceedings of the 7th International Conference on Networked Learning 2010* (pp. 266–275). Lancaster: University of Lancaster.

Malan, D. (2010). Reinventing CS50. *Proceedings of the 41st ACM Technical Symposium on Computer Science Education, 152–156.*

McGill, L., Falconer, I., Littlejohn, A., & Beetham, H. (2013). JISC/HE Academy OER Programme: Phase 3 synthesis and evaluation report. Retrieved from https://oersynth.pbworks.com/w/page/60338879/HEFCE-OER-Review-Final-Report

Milligan, C., Littlejohn A., & Margaryan, A. (2013). Patterns of engagement in massive open online courses. *Journal of Online Learning and Teaching, 9*(2), 149–159. Available from http://jolt.merlot.org/vol9no2/milligan_0613.htm.

MIT (2013). MIT OpenCourseWare celebrates 10th anniversary. Retrieved 13 August 2013 from http://ocw.mit.edu/about/media-coverage/press-releases/tenth-anniversary/.

Nurmohamed, Z., Gillani, N., & Lenox, M. (2013). A new use for MOOCs: Real-world problem solving. Harvard Business Review Blog. Retrieved 5 November 2013 from http://blogs.hbr.org/cs/2013/07/a_new_use_for_moocs_real-world.html.

OBHE (2013). The maturing of the MOOC. Observatory on Borderless Higher Education, BIS Research paper No. 130. Retrieved 25 October 2013 from www.obhe.ac.uk/documents/download?id=933.

OCW (2013). OCW Consortium. Retrieved 13 August 2013 from www.ocwconsortium.org/en/aboutus/abouttheocwc.

Siemens, G. (2005). Connectivism: A learning theory for the digital age. *International Journal of Instructional Technology and Distance Learning, 2*(1), 3–10.

Vale, K. (2012). CS50 at Harvard: 'The most rewarding class I have taken . . . ever!'. In D. Oblinger (Ed.), *Game changers* (pp. 361–368). Lawrence, KS: Educause/Allen Press. Retrieved from http://net.educause.edu/ir/library/pdf/pub7203cs19.pdf.

Wiggins, G., & McTighe, J. (2005). *Understanding by design.* USA: ASCD.

11

ANALYTICS FOR EDUCATION

Sheila MacNeill, Lorna M. Campbell and Martin Hawksey

Introduction and Overview

Over the past five years a number of factors, not least the changing economic climate and its impact on the educational sector, have led to increased awareness of the need for greater research, analysis and understanding of all aspects of data relating to education. Researchers in the emerging fields of educational data mining (EDM) and learning analytics have been active in exploring the potential of data created through the processes of teaching and learning. In parallel with these developments, interest has also increased in the potential of 'big data' and the application of business intelligence approaches to the educational sector. For example, can the recommendation systems commonly used by companies such as Amazon and Netflix be employed in educational contexts? The emergence of MOOCs (massive open online courses) can be seen as a key area where big data approaches can be applied to learning data sets, due to the massive scale of participation. In wider society the 'quantified self movement'(*Quantified Self*, 2012), which involves using wearable sensors to self-monitor and gather data on different aspects of an individual's life, physical state and performance, is giving rise to increased access to and reuse of personal data from multiple sources, including social network sites, geolocation services and data collected from mobile devices.

This chapter will provide an overview of analytics within the domain of education, highlighting potential areas of development and the challenges faced by the education sector. Given the plethora of data available and the growing number of technologies and terminologies being used, it can be difficult for practitioners to gain a comprehensive overview of the education sector data landscape. The chapter draws heavily on the Analytics Series (*Cetis Analytics Series*, 2012), produced by Cetis, the UK Centre for Education Technology, Interoperability and Standards, which provides a broad perspective of the role and potential of analytics within higher education, together with an overview of current practice across the sector.

Analytics in the Context of Education

As MacNeill (2012) highlights, the use of analytics is far from new to education; the collection, use and sharing of data is well established in the sector. Despite generating increasing volumes of data, until recently, few institutions have been able to exploit the wealth of information they routinely collect through the core business of teaching and learning. This position is starting to change, partly as a result of growing interest in big data and business intelligence and partly due to the development of increasingly accessible analytics tools and applications. However, Cooper (2012) has cautioned that this increased interest in analytics comes at a cost:

> The problem with defining any buzz-word, including 'analytics' is that over-use and band-wagon jumping reduces the specificity of the word. This problem is not new and any attempt to create a detailed definition seems to be doomed, no matter how careful one might be, because there will always be someone with a different perspective or a personal or commercial motivation to emphasise a particular aspect or nuance. The rather rambling Wikipedia entry for analytics illustrates this difficulty.
>
> (p. 3)

Cooper (2012) goes on to propose a working definition of 'analytics', which we will adopt within the context of this chapter:

> Analytics is the process of developing actionable insights through problem definition and the application of statistical models and analysis against existing and/or simulated future data.
>
> (p. 3)

When discussing analytics within the domain of education it is also useful to consider how these techniques are being applied within the context of the institution. Buckingham Shum (2012) has introduced the concept of three levels of learning analytics.

- Macro-level analytics enable data sharing across institutions for a range of purposes including benchmarking.
- Meso-level analytics work at the level of individual institutions, and include analytics based on business intelligence approaches.
- Micro-level analytics support the tracking and interpretation of process-level data for individual learners.

Long and Siemens (2011) make a similar distinction between academic analytics and learner analytics. Academic analytics equates to Buckingham Shum's macro- and meso-level analytics, and learner analytics to micro-level analytics. In Long and Siemens' view, learning analytics focuses explicitly on the learning process.

Analytics can also be applied to educational content, and can be used to track and record how and in what context resources are used. Such information, which may be referred to as 'paradata', has the potential to provide a useful supplement to educational metadata and may help to address the problem of effectively describing educational context, a problem that formal educational metadata standards have struggled to address.

Learning Analytics

In terms of analytics relating specifically to teaching and learning, two main areas of research are emerging: educational data mining and learning analytics. The two are complementary, but have a different emphasis.

Bienkowski, Feng and Means' (2012) report, *Enhancing Teaching and Learning Through Educational Data Mining and Learning Analytics*, for the US Department of Education defines data mining and learning analytics as follows:

> Educational data mining (EDM) develops methods and applies techniques from statistics, machine learning, and data mining to analyze data collected during teaching and learning. EDM tests learning theories and informs educational practice.

> Learning analytics applies techniques from information science, sociology, psychology, statistics, machine learning and data mining to analyze data collected during education administration and services, teaching and learning. Learning analytics creates applications that directly influence educational practice.

> (p. 9)

Learning analytics may also incorporate data from formal and informal learning environments, and Ferguson and Buckingham Shum (2012) have introduced the concept of social learning analytics to provide mechanisms for identifying patterns and behaviours at both individual and group level.

As these research fields are developing, commercial vendors are introducing new analytics tools into their educational systems and applications, e.g. Blackboard Learn (*Blackboard Learn*, n.d.). These tools promise to improve the performance and engagement of both staff and students, and to provide measurable insights into the educational process. However, these applications are still in their infancy, and further research is required in order to quantify the impact of the dashboard views of data that these systems provide. In addition, it is debatable whether these tools are currently capable of engaging students and enhancing their learning experience, as they are often based on data that can be collected easily rather than on any substantiated pedagogical theory.

Learning analytics is an emerging field and, to date, there have been relatively few large-scale implementations of the potential approaches that comprise much of the body of the research literature. There are a few notable exceptions, including the Course Signals project (*Course Signals*, 2013), initially developed at Purdue University, which has amassed almost a decade's worth of evidence, and from which a commercial product has been created. Such examples are the exception rather than the rule and considerable work is still required to translate current research into the wide-scale adoption and application of learning analytics approaches to teaching and learning.

Macro-Level Analytics

Education authorities and funding bodies are increasingly aware of the need to be able to identify nuanced sector-level patterns, e.g. overall attrition levels, geographical and socio-economic trends to help determine priorities for spending and development.

At the institutional level, senior managers are increasingly aware of the need to integrate analytic approaches with current business intelligence methodologies. This would enable them to gain actionable insights that would allow them to make effective decisions in terms of operating within new economic models, while addressing strategic priorities such as student retention and achievement.

Meso-Level Analytics

A number of issues need to be considered when attempting to align business intelligence solutions. For example, it is not uncommon for problems to arise when attempting to share data between centrally managed administrative systems, such as student record systems, and teaching and learning applications, such as virtual learning environments, due to lack of data interoperability. Consequently, institutional approaches to data management, sharing, reuse and data protection need to be considered at the strategic level. Serious consideration needs to be given to apparently simple questions such as: Which systems hold the most useful and valuable data? Which formats are the data available in? Who has access to the data and how can it be used to develop actionable insights? In addition to considering technical issues such as data formats, it is equally important to develop the cultural and human capacity of the institution to enable it to make effective use of this data. Policies are required to govern the ethical use of data and opportunities need to be provided for staff and students to develop their knowledge and understanding of data and analytics.

Micro-Level Analytics

Powell and MacNeill (2012) have identified a number of drivers for the application for learning analytics. These include:

- individual learners using analytics to reflect on their achievements and patterns of behaviour in relation to their peers;
- identification of students who may require extra support and attention;
- helping teachers and support staff to plan supporting interventions with individuals and groups;
- enabling functional groups, such as course teams, to improve current courses or develop new curriculum offerings;
- providing information to help institutional administrators to take decisions on matters such as marketing and recruitment or efficiency and effectiveness measures.

As previously highlighted, the use of analytics within the education sector is still in its infancy. Different institutional stakeholders may have very different motivations for employing analytics and, in some instances, the needs of one group of stakeholders, e.g. individual learners, may be in conflict with the needs of other stakeholders, e.g. managers and administrators. Educational institutions have a duty of care towards students and staff and must be aware that certain data can only be used sensitively, appropriately and with consent (MacNeill & Ellis, 2013). Koulocheri and Xenos (2013) have demonstrated that using social network analysis visualisation techniques within learning environments could have a positive impact on learning. However, they have also highlighted ethical issues, including student consent, that must be considered when sharing individual assessment data.

Despite these reservations, there are a growing number of examples of how analytics can be used to have a positive impact on teaching, learning and the wider student experience. The University of Huddersfield in the UK is developing innovative approaches to team assessment and learning design by sharing data from its e-assessment system with students to help them improve their grades and overall achievement (MacNeill & Ellis, 2013). E-submission and e-marking tools have made this possible by collecting and providing access to more detailed assessment data than has previously been available. In addition, staff are developing pre- and post-assessment workshops where assessment rubrics are shared with students alongside real (anonymised) data, to highlight the impact of common mistakes on overall grades. Although it is still in the early stages of development, course teams are already finding that this method of providing feedback to students is improving their results. This approach has also enabled course teams to develop new, data-driven design methodologies; collaborative approaches are emerging for developing assessment criteria and feedback and staff have greater understanding of what data is of greatest use in different contexts.

As part of its on-going aim of improving the student experience, the University of Derby in the UK is working on integrating a range of internal data sources and systems so as to provide greater insight into how students are engaging with the university both pre- and post-enrolment. In addition to helping to enhance the student experience, these 'engagement analytics' are providing increased opportunities for cross-institutional development (MacNeill & Mutton, 2013). Focusing on the identification of key institutional systems that provide the touch points for developing students' digital footprints, e.g. library systems, learning environments, student record systems and through the holistic theme of student engagement, the team leading the work has been able to bring together key stakeholders (staff and students) and has focused discussions around the collection and use of data.

Currently, analytics developments are focused primarily at the macro and meso levels. Although the use of analytics may be increasing at the institutional level, there are still very few compelling examples of analytics being used at scale to benefit learners. There are a number of reasons why this may be case. Despite recent initiatives such as the advent of open courseware and MOOCs, that claim to be breaking down educational barriers, formal education is still institutionally focused. Furthermore, despite claims to the contrary, many commercial educational technology vendors develop tools that are primarily designed to meet the requirements of institutions in the first instance, with the needs of individual learners often appearing to be of secondary consideration. However, it is also important to acknowledge that capturing learner data from the myriad systems that students engage with throughout their learning journeys is a non-trivial task. It is considerably more problematic than surfacing data from large-scale institutional systems. In addition, students arguably lack the data literacy skills required to realise the potential benefits of the data that they generate through the process; and educational data is still widely regarded as belonging to institutions rather than to learners. Notwithstanding these issues, emerging activity suggests that both institutions and commercial vendors are beginning to lay foundations that may ultimately lead to the development of student-centric analytics tools.

Educational Content Analytics

In addition to being applicable to administrative and teaching and learning activities and data, analytics can also be applied to educational resources. Data about how learning resources are used, by whom and in what context, is sometimes referred to as paradata (Campbell & Barker, 2013). The term paradata was first used in this context[1] by the US National Science Digital Library (NSDL) in 2010 (McIlvain, 2013) to refer to data about user interactions with learning resources in its STEM Exchange. The concept was later adopted by the Learning Registry (*Paradata in 20 minutes or less*, 2011), an initiative funded initially by the U.S. Department of Education and the U.S. Department of Defense, which developed an open source decentralised content-distribution network for storing and sharing information about learning resources and their use.

The ability to gather and analyse data about how educational content is used in real-world learning contexts is potentially of considerable value, as it could help to address some of the problems that metadata standards have struggled to resolve. Systems, such as digital repositories, which are designed for managing and sharing information about learning resources generally rely on formal metadata application profiles to describe characteristics of the resources that are likely to be of relevance to their users. However, learning resources represent a diverse class of objects, used in a wide variety of contexts and, as a result, formal metadata standards and controlled vocabularies struggle to identify and describe all the characteristics that may be of interest or relevance to users (Barker & Campbell, 2010). While metadata generally attempts to record objective or authoritative descriptions of a resource, paradata can record the opinion of the users, together with how, where and with what outcome a resource has been used. By capturing the user activity related to a resource, paradata complements metadata by providing an additional layer of contextual information that can help to elucidate the potential educational utility of the resource (Campbell & Barker, 2013).

Paradata is generated as learning resources are used, reused, adapted, contextualised, favourited, tweeted and shared. Some paradata is deliberately created by users, e.g. likes and comments, while some is generated automatically as a result of the resource being used, e.g. hits and download statistics. On the simplest level, paradata can be used to record how users interact with learning resources by viewing, downloading, sharing, liking, commenting and tagging. Although paradata primarily refers to data about learning resources, it can also encompass information about users of a resource, e.g. age, educational level, geographical location. It can also record contextual information by linking resources with educational standards and curricula, course catalogues, pedagogic approaches and methodologies. In the context of decentralised content distribution networks, such as the Learning Registry, paradata can also be used to record complex aggregations of activities relating to a single resource, e.g. 'between January 2011 and January 2012 lecturers in Engineering, Physics and Maths, used this resource, six times for undergraduate teaching activities' (Thomas, Campbell, Barker, & Hawksey, 2012).

While the development of tools and systems to capture and analyse paradata has been driven by US initiatives, a small number of innovative projects have successfully experimented with the use of Learning Registry paradata within the context of the UK higher education sector. These include the JLeRN Experiment (*About the JLeRN Experiment*, n.d.) project, which successfully set up a Learning Registry test node, contributed data to it, including data from the national learning resource repository Jorum (*Jorum*, n.d.), developed an open source tool for exploring Learning Registry data and supported a special interest community of developers and practitioners from across the UK higher education sector (Campbell, Barker, Currier, & Syrotiuk, 2013). A second project, ENGrich, at the University of Liverpool, has developed Kritokos (*Kritikos*, n.d.), a custom search engine for visual media relevant to engineering education. Using Google Custom Search, with filters such as tags, file types and domains, as a primary search engine, Kritikos pushes and pulls corresponding metadata and paradata to and from the Learning Registry. A user interface enables academics and students to add comments and additional information about how resources and are being used. This additional paradata is then published to a Learning Registry node and used to order subsequent search results (Campbell & Barker, 2013).

Many institutional systems automatically generate paradata, including learning management systems, virtual learning environments, digital repositories, library systems and social media applications; however, it is not always simple to surface this data or query it in meaningful ways. The application of analytics to learning resources and the use of paradata is still in its infancy and although the Learning Registry potentially offers an innovative solution to surfacing and sharing this data, it has not yet been widely adopted outside the US and, as with learning analytics, applications have yet to emerge that are of real benefit to learners.

Ethical Issues

As institutional managers, administrators and researchers are well aware, any practice involving data collection and reuse has inherent legal and ethical implications. Most institutions have clear guidelines and policies in place governing the collection and use of research data. However, it is less common for institutions to have legal and ethical guidelines on the use of data gathered from internal systems (Prinsloo & Slade, 2013). As is often the case, the development of legal frameworks has not kept pace with the development of new technologies.

The Cetis Analytics Series paper on *Legal, Risk and Ethical Aspects of Analytics in Higher Education* (Kay, Korn, & Oppenheim, 2012) outlines a set of common principles that have universal application:

- Clarity—open definition of purpose, scope and boundaries, even if that is broad and in some respects extent open-ended.
- Comfort and care—consideration for both the interests and the feelings of the data subject and vigilance regarding exceptional cases.
- Choice and consent—informed individual opportunity to opt-out or opt-in.
- Consequence and complaint—recognition that there may be unforeseen consequences and therefore provision of mechanisms for redress.

In short, it is fundamental that institutions are aware of the legal and ethical implications of any activity requiring data collection before undertaking any form of data analysis activity.

Future Developments

Given the diversity of research strands that feed into the area of analytics in education, together with the increased ease of data storage, the field is expanding rapidly in a wide range of new directions. Until recently, the focus of most analytics developments to support teaching and learning has been on integrating tools with existing institutional learning management systems (Ferguson, 2013). This is primarily because such integration provides relatively easy access to available student data. However, the increased adoption of third party services such as social network tools and applications, and the emergence of MOOCs, has created new opportunities for large-scale experimentation with analytics. Recent examples of projects that are seeking to explore the use of data from MOOCs and social networks include Stanford University's Lytics Lab (Lytics, n.d.), which, amongst other work, runs randomised controlled trials of MOOC courses offered by Coursera. In addition to using analytics to identify potential 'threshold concepts' that might be exposed by tens of thousands of students taking multiple-choice tests, there are opportunities to identify, analyse and define wider engagement patterns within subpopulations of learners (Kizilcec, Piech, & Schneider, 2013).

Large-scale analytics initiatives are also taking place at a national level, with varying degrees of success. Launched in early 2013, inBloom is a US non-profit organisation backed by the Carnegie Corporation and the Bill and Melinda Gates Foundation that aims to create infrastructure to integrate, analyse and provide solutions to personalise student learning for schools at state and district level. By creating a common interface, inBloom set out to stimulate educational technology providers to develop new tools utilising the growing database and infrastructure around student data, without the cost of having to develop custom connections to existing local infrastructure such as student management systems (*inBloom*, 2013). Shortly after the project was launched, however, parents and civil liberties organisations began raising concerns about centralising sensitive student data in this manner and asking questions about who would have access to the data (Campbell, 2013). By August 2013 these concerns had resulted in a significant number of states pulling out of the project altogether, leaving only four school districts participating (Nelson, 2013).

Within the UK, the Department of Education launched an Analytical Review looking at the role of research, analysis and data within the Department. The Review focused on two key areas: data systems for the collection, sharing and retrieval of data generated by English schools; and the role of randomised controlled trials for 'building evidence into education' (Department for Education, 2013). Whilst it is still unclear what data exchange models will be adopted by the Department, the announcement, following the publication of two randomised controlled trials, is a clear indication that analytics is playing an increasingly significant role at all levels of education (Department for Education, 2013).

As analytics initiatives continue to develop, it is highly likely that commercial practices will continue to transfer into the educational sector. Recommendation systems and targeted advertising are the backbone of commercial giants such as Amazon and Google but they are increasingly finding their way into learning analytics systems. Emerging products in this area include Talis Aspire (*Talis Aspire*, 2013), which offers complete reading-list management solutions based on usage data to provide both staff and students with insights into catalogue use, thus creating opportunities for personalised learning.

Associated with these developments are 'analytics as a service' products offered by companies that specialise in providing analytic services for a fee. Companies such as Narrative Science, which specialises in automatically producing text-based summaries of numeric data, have already highlighted opportunities for creating personalised feedback with actionable insights by combining data from test results (Hammond, 2012).

Conclusion

There is undoubtedly potential for analytics-based approaches to provide new and increasingly nuanced data about users' interactions with content and systems in teaching and learning contexts. Such approaches have the potential to lead to greater understanding of patterns of learner behaviour and learner networks and interactions based on data that has previously been difficult or impossible to access.

The emergence of MOOCs could provide the context to leverage big data techniques, e.g. large-scale data warehousing of education-specific big data sets. How useful such data will be is unclear at present, as MOOCs are still in their infancy and their long-term viability is still to be established. Analysis of MOOC data sets may not progress far beyond current recommendation systems (similar to Amazon, Netflix etc.), or generic guidance and advice for learners. At this stage, it seems more likely that the most useful application of analytics approaches will be at the institutional or meso level, as this will provide greater contextual information for strategic planning and creativity in designing and teaching courses. It remains to be seen whether these developments will have a direct impact on students and lead to more successful learning experiences and outcomes.

It is important to recognise that access to data alone will not have a significant impact on the higher education sector; people are needed to contextualise, act upon and interpret the data. Consequently, developing staff and students' data literacies will be critical to enabling the cultural shift required to move towards data-driven design and decision-making approaches within education.

Acknowledgements

The authors would like to thank all their colleagues involved in producing the Cetis Analytics Series, in particular Adam Cooper and Stephen Powell, whose work they have drawn on extensively for this chapter.

Note

1 Not to be confused with survey paradata, which refers to administrative data about the processes by which survey data is collected.

References

Barker, P., & Campbell, L. M. (2010). Metadata for learning materials: An overview of existing standards and current developments. *Technology, Instruction, Cognition, and Learning, 7*(3–4), 225–243.

Bienkowski, M., Feng, M., & Means, B. (2012). *Enhancing teaching and learning through educational data mining and learning analytics: An issue brief.* US Department of Education, Office of Educational Technology. Retrieved from https://www.ed.gov/edblogs/ technology/files/2012/03/edm-la-brief.pdf.

Blackboard Learn. (n.d.). Retrieved from www.blackboard.com/Platforms/Learn/over-view.aspx.

Buckingham Shum, S. (2012). *Learning analytics.* UNESCO Policy Brief. Retrieved from http://iite.unesco.org/pics/publications/en/files/3214711.pdf.

Campbell, L. M. (2013). *Another perspective on inBloom.* Retrieved from http://blogs.cetis. ac.uk/lmc/2013/03/05/another-perspective-on-inbloom/.

Campbell, L. M., & Barker, P. (2013). *Activity data and paradata.* Cetis Briefing Paper, 2013: B01. Retrieved from http://publications.cetis.ac.uk/2013/808.

Campbell, L. M., Barker, P., Currier, S., & Syrotiuk, N. (2013). The Learning Registry: Social networking for open educational resources? *Open Educational Resources 13 Conference.* Retrieved from www.medev.ac.uk/oer13/108/view/.

Cetis Analytics Series. (2012). Retrieved from http://publications.cetis.ac.uk/c/analytics.

Cooper, A. (2012). What is analytics? Definition and essential characteristics. *Cetis Analytics Series, 1*(5). Retrieved from http://publications.cetis.ac.uk/2012/521.

Course Signals. (2013). Retrieved from www.itap.purdue.edu/learning/tools/signals/.

Department for Education. (2013). *Department of Education analytical review.* Corporate report. Retrieved from https://www.gov.uk/government/publications/department-for-education-analytical-review.

Department for Education. (2013). *New randomised controlled trials will drive forward evidence-based research.* [Press release]. Retrieved from https://www.gov.uk/government/news/ new-randomised-controlled-trials-will-drive-forward-evidence-based-research.

Ferguson, R. (2013). *Learning analytics for open and distance education.* CEMCA EdTechnotes. Retrieved from http://cemca.org.in/ckfinder/userfiles/files/EdTech%20Notes_LA_ Rebecca_15%20May.pdf.

Ferguson, R., & Buckingham Shum, S. (2012). Social learning analytics: Five approaches. *2nd International Conference on Learning Analytics & Knowledge, Vancouver, Canada.* Retrieved from http://oro.open.ac.uk/32910/.

Hammond, K. (2012). Transforming education [Blog post]. Retrieved from http:// khammond.blogspot.co.uk/2012/05/transforming-education.html.

inBloom. (2013). Retrieved from https://inbloom.org/.

Jorum. (n.d.). Retrieved from www.jorum.ac.uk/.

Kay, D., Korn, N., & Oppenheim, C. (2012). Legal, risk and ethical aspects of analytics in higher education. *Cetis Analytics Series, 1*(6). Retrieved from http://publications.cetis. ac.uk/2012/500.

Kizilcec, R. F., Piech, C., & Schneider, E. (2013). Deconstructing disengagements: Analyzing learner subpopulations in massive open online courses. *Proceedings of the Third International Conference on Learning Analytics and Knowledge, Leuven, Belgium.* Retrieved from http://hcibib.org/LAK13#S2.

Koulocheri, E., & Xenos, M. (2013). Considering formal assessment in learning analytics within a PLE: the HOU2LEARN case. *Proceedings of the Third International Conference on Learning Analytics and Knowledge, Leuven, Belgium.* Retrieved from http://hcibib.org/LAK13#S2.

Kritikos. (n.d.). Retrieved from http://engrich.liv.ac.uk/.

Long, P., & Siemens, G. (2011). Penetrating the fog: Analytics in learning and education. *EDUCAUSE Review, 46*(5). Retrieved from www.educause.edu/ero/article/penetrating-fog-analytics-learning-and-education.

Lytics (n.d.) http://lytics.stanford.edu/ (accessed 7 September 2013).

McIlvain, E. (2013). *What is Paradata?* NSDL Documentation Wiki. Retrieved from https://wiki.ucar.edu/display/nsdldocs/Paradata.

MacNeill, S. (2012). Analytics: What is changing and why does it matter? *Cetis Analytics Series, 1*(1). Retrieved from http://publications.cetis.ac.uk/2012/511.

MacNeill, S., & Ellis, C. (2013). Case study: Acting on assessment analytics. *Cetis Analytics Series, 2*(2). Retrieved from http://publications.cetis.ac.uk/2013/750.

MacNeill, S., & Mutton, J. (2013). Case study: Engaging with analytics. *Cetis Analytics Series, 2*(1). Retrieved from http://publications.cetis.ac.uk/2013/706.

Nelson, L. A. (2013). InBloom off the rose? *Politico Morning Education News*, 1 August 2013. Retrieved from www.politico.com/morningeducation/0813/morningeducation 11303.html?hp=l6_b1.

Paradata in 20 minutes or less (2011). Retrieved from https://docs.google.com/document/d/1 QG0lAmJ0ztHJq5DbiTGQj9DnQ8hP0Co0x0fB1QmoBco/edit?hl=en_US.

Powell, S., & MacNeill, S. (2012). Institutional readiness for analytics. *Cetis Analytics Series, 1*(8). Retrieved from http://publications.cetis.ac.uk/2012/527.

Prinsloo, P., & Slade, S. (2013). An evaluation of policy frameworks for addressing ethical considerations in learning analytics. *Proceedings of the Third International Conference on Learning Analytics, Leuven, Belgium.* Retrieved from http://hcibib.org/LAK13#S2

Quantified Self. (2012). Retrieved from http://quantifiedself.com/about/.

Talis Aspire. (n.d.). Retrieved from http://talisaspire.com/.

The JLeRN Experiment. (n.d.). Retrieved from http://jlernexperiment.wordpress.com/.

Thomas, A., Campbell, L. M., Barker, P., & Hawksey, M. (2012). *Into the wild: Technology for open educational resources.* Retrieved from http://publications.cetis.ac.uk/2012/601.

12

APPLYING AGILE METHODS IN RESEARCHING OPEN EDUCATION

Patrick McAndrew

Introduction

Research in academic terms has a pattern (Blaxter, Hughes, & Tight, 2010) of background, study, analysis, review and reporting. This pattern has served the research community well over a long period but may isolate research results from those that need them. Practitioners and policy makers can then appear to act without reference to research. The tendency to make policy while lacking evidence has been deplored by some in the community (Goldacre & Farley, 2009), with a call for greater use of trials and periods of reflection. However, the reality is that there is a growing desire to move quickly and to adapt to change within timeframes that cannot wait for slower processes to take place, leading to pressure for rapid research processes rather than considered reflection. In parallel, the ability to control research into learner and educator experience in education is reduced as access to open and free resources grows and spreads. Carefully planned and staged studies therefore become increasingly unrealistic and so there is a need to move to more agile processes.

There are probably few areas of education where the pace of change has been more apparent than in open and free approaches to providing resources. The concept of open educational resources (OERs) is relatively recent (UNESCO, 2002) and the term that caught the zeitgeist of 2012 and 2013, massive open online courses (MOOCs) (Daniel, 2012; EDUCAUSE, 2011), even more so. OERs are designed to be openly accessible, transferable and available to be used in ways chosen by the user. These characteristics all act against the idea that studies lead to fixed outcomes and that the behaviour of users can be tracked in and out of the system.

If we are to carry out research into OERs then we need methods and sources of data that can support the process of more rapid reaction. These methods favour automated data gathering (Long & Siemens, 2011), diverse feedback channels and collation of open behaviour and tools to accumulate collective intelligence (Malone et al., 2009, De Liddo et al., 2012). Researchers need to appreciate the different values of evidence that can be identified through these processes and develop timely approaches to working with multiple sources of data.

Agile Research

Inspiration for more rapid actions can be found in approaches to software engineering termed 'agile development' (Lindstrom & Jeffries, 2004). Agile development was a reaction against an unrealistic expectation of progression from one stage to another, described in software engineering as the waterfall model; activities flow from requirements, to design, to implementation, validation and then operation and maintenance. The waterfall model often ended up describing a fantasy where everything was apparently clear. In contrast, in the agile approach, rather than setting out a fixed set of requirements, the starting point is typically a prioritised list of things that need to be done, the time that is likely to be required to do them, and resources in place to tackle them. Progress checking then operates on a short time scale (for example one to two weeks), with adjustments to plans for the next stage based on results and measured achievements. Agile development has also been termed eXtreme Programming (XP) and began as an experimental approach. However, it has become a common and established method in the field of software engineering, no longer seen as extreme.

Agile development aims to quickly move practice forward so that everyone involved can appreciate the system that is being constructed and access working products that act as prototypes along the way to delivered systems. The endpoint may never be completely finalised; the perpetual beta of O'Reilly's Web2.0 (O'Reilly, 2005) or the continuous improvement cycle established as part of Microsoft's development philosophy (Turner, 2009) each imply that the current version will change and evolve. The culture of agile development is one of programming sprints, rapid feedback and getting out products that meet real and immediate needs rather than imagined and idealised ones.

Agile research, by analogy, is characterised by quickly setting out to bring together different pieces of information as evidence and provides an opportunity to take advantage of openness to allow researchers to engage more closely with the needs of practitioners and policy makers. This is ambitious, as the approach also needs to advocate realistic research with the intention to make simple statements that can be used as 'true' in most cases and then back them up with evidence and identify contexts in which they hold. The role of more formal research, such as comparison studies, can then be targeted at confirming and sometimes persuading. The skills demanded of the researcher become those of someone who is part of the digital landscape. Agile development has a strong motivational element; agile research can add to the excitement of being a researcher as specialisms become part of a greater picture that can combine for policy change.

Researching Education in the Open

Research in open education shares issues with other recent attempts to investigate technology and innovation in education. Piece-by-piece research of the complex situations found in education and learning has tended to lead to the identification of 'no-significant-difference' (Reeves, 2005). That is, for a particular intervention that we want to investigate, such as the introduction of a piece of technology into a classroom, there may well be some effect, but it is swamped by the other complexities that impact on the measurable outcomes of learning. Many factors outside the researcher's control can change what is happening, along with the changes associated with the planned intervention. Factors such as teacher attitudes, other people on the course, the cohort structure, researcher presence or even the weather can all have their influence on the learners' grades and performance. Often the best that can be said is that no-significant-difference is found in measurable outcomes, leaving the change to be justified by cost grounds, reported enjoyment or just that it is 'the future'. Given enough data that indicates a common direction, some of these uncertainties may be addressed; however, that takes time and a considerable volume of data. Time can be a luxury that is not available, given the pressure for more rapid research to support fast-changing circumstances and the political desire for instant policies.

While research is problematic for open education, there are also advantages emerging in how research on educational technologies can be carried out. Through online networks and connectivity: we can reach many people in a short time; individuals are sharing their opinions without prompting; large amounts of data can be gathered; and computers enable analysis and visualisation. Data and outputs can be shared online with ease to enable community involvement in the analysis, whether from experts or the broader population.

Measuring behaviour in open online environments is challenging but not impossible. For example, the experience across a range of projects which the UK Open University has been involved in with external partners (OpenLearn, iSpot, OLnet and OER Research Hub) shows that any single method has limitations but can provide a contribution to the overall picture. This approach is pragmatic, but also reflects ways to make 'legitimate the use of multiple approaches' (Johnson & Onwuegbuzie, 2004). For example, analytics, user tracking, survey questionnaires, monitoring of open user activity, interviews with individual learners and educators can act in combination (McAndrew, Godwin, & Santos, 2009). These methods have different strengths; for instance analytics helps to summarise use and quickly identifies patterns but generally lacks individual data and feedback. Working with educators helps to provide insight into use; however, in their responses their views of learner advances tend to be more optimistic than those of the learners themselves, and rich pictures gained by observing individual learners are inevitably a small sample amongst the larger numbers now engaged with learning in the open.

One element of research is to reach out to explore different situations and bring in a range of experiences. Openness gives a way to achieve those connections. The OLnet project and the subsequent OER Research Hub both make use of mechanisms to go beyond their core research teams. In OLnet, thirty fellowships were established. Fellows were drawn from across seventeen countries, from post-graduate student to established professorial staff and UNESCO OER fellows and bring in a diversity of experience as well as offering opportunities for professional development and sharing of methods. A typical fellowship included a visit to the research base at the Open University, followed by joint academic work and continuing remote collaboration (more details of the fellowships are available from www.olnet.org/content/about-olnet/olnet-fellows). The impact of the fellowship programme for the researchers was to bring in new perspectives on problems and ideas, both from experts and from practitioners. The impact on dissemination was to allow spread of ideas immediately by the fellows in follow-on work and, more subtly and pervasively, through their influence on others beyond the fellowship period. Both the diffusion of research and professional learning through fellowships were assisted by targeted use of conferences with 'key events' where a contingent of researchers and fellows attended a conference, providing a critical mass of presentations, posters and workshops. Presence at the conferences was also enhanced by joint use of online tools that provide a persistent record. A shared approach to blogging builds visibility for the conference and for the research team. In this role the Cloudworks tool, used in OLnet, provided a good mix of individual texts, integration of online media, commentary and tools to collate the works of others (Galley, Conole, & Alevizou, 2010).

Research 2.0 (Revisited)

New tools for research implies that research itself may need to evolve. Reflection on experience in previous research on OER, reported in McAndrew, Godwin and Santos (2009), set out the idea for Research 2.0 by analogy with O'Reilly's identification of the characteristics of Web 2.0 in 2005 (O'Reilly, 2005). While the fashion for adding 2.0 after every term has started to fade, those ideas provide a good list to review as a practical set of advice for combining information. They also encourage us to think more broadly about how we can adjust our approaches to make them more agile and responsive to the requirements of society. The principles for Research 2.0 (modified from McAndrew et al., 2009) are:

1. *Study the interesting things that happen.* Researchers need to spot the interesting and unpredictable in the unexpected actions of individuals as well as consider the mass actions at scale. Spotting the interesting behaviours of early adopters and 'lead users' (von Hippel, 2005) can help to identify emergent ideas.
2. *Look for patterns that can apply more widely.* Draw out patterns looking for shared characteristics and be open to signs of clustering behaviour by examining individual cases and see trends that can benefit others.

3. *Encourage all to be part of the experiment.* Extending an invitation to all involved, end-users and producers, helps to maximise the value in experiments and bring out routes to extra information.
4. *Build valuable activities that give data.* Activities that provide authentic outputs, especially if they are digital, mean that there is less need to request data solely for research purposes. For example, reflective logs help the learner but can also provide insight to the researcher, and badges (Knight & Casilli, 2012) that encourage progress can also help to track the overall performance of learners.
5. *Recognise that openness offers many benefits.* Openness encourages transfer between systems, providing the chance for early discussion, and expands dissemination.
6. *Draw conclusions, though you wish you had more data.* No computer system is ever completely finished or perfect, rather, it is always a beta release that can be refined. Similarly, no research project ever has all the data and can be sure of the results, but to be of value indicative results need to be available in early forms. This challenges the peer review process.
7. *Be prepared for the user who arrives from anywhere.* In researching openness it is important to recognise the reduced control inherent in open design. For such cases data gathering cannot depend on users reading advice or passing through other points such as login pages.
8. *Realise that there is no way to control all access.* Openness allows transfer of content, so it is likely that at some point there will be activity that we know nothing about. As researchers we must therefore operate with incomplete data, and partial knowledge in particular, where information can travel from site to site.

The Research 2.0 approach described above has influenced, and in turn been influenced by, work across several large-scale OER projects at the Open University. In the Open Learning network (OLnet) (McAndrew, 2011) a complex set of actions took place: nine strands of research, thirty fellowships, analysis of over 100 other externally funded international projects and work on methods and infrastructures that reached out to a collective intelligence. As the OLnet project progressed, the requirement to share and communicate its outcomes was a challenge in itself. Two related innovations were introduced to address this in an agile and open manner. First, a site was developed to encourage the gathering of information around the issues that were emerging. Second, key common challenges were identified from the issues and actions that were observed and reported. The issues were grouped into ten challenges that were then refined through open consultation, which led to expansion to twelve key challenges. The OLnet team and project were well placed to do this work; however, it is important not to over-claim on the resulting challenges. These were designed to be seen as open to question, often drawn from practice and only partly validated.

The development of the challenges clarified the work of the project, especially as a way to build on earlier research and analysis, and helped to communicate and discuss results and the areas of interest. The key challenges and the way in which they cover four different areas of concern are explored in more detail in McAndrew, Farrow, Law, and Elliott-Cirigottis (2012). While the content of the challenges is itself interesting, here the authors are looking at the way in which they came about and how the challenges were developed in further work.

A new site was configured for this later work as an 'OER Evidence Hub' built on software already used to allow individual researchers to make connections between items and reason and visualise how elements can combine to support or refute positions. This software, Compendium, has been applied in a range of contexts including to support learners and educators working with OERs (Buckingham Shum & Okada, 2008). A later collaborative development from Compendium, Cohere, also enables experienced researchers to build a system of labelled connections that can be shared with groups of other researchers to enable them to see the same views and add links to additional resources (De Liddo & Buckingham Shum, 2010). Cohere is very flexible in its approach and allows the user to build their own identification of links and meanings; within OLnet the requirement was a simplified interface that could allow the research team and others to match resources and findings against a common view of structure and meaning. The result was a pilot OER Evidence Hub, in its initial version applied to allow researchers to entered structured summaries of more than 100 projects funded by the Hewlett Foundation, drawing from their submitted annual project reports. (This work was also aided by automated text analysis that helped to identify key phrases and themes in the project reports (De Liddo, Sándor, & Buckingham Shum, 2012)). The system was then extended to permit general use by the research team for other categories of evidence, and entry of data by all who register with the system, to follow the model of open collective intelligence.

The OER Evidence Hub is described further in De Liddo, Buckingham Shum, McAndrew, and Farrow (2012) and the selection of challenges in McAndrew et al. (2012). In brief, a thematic coding based on the analysis of the reports (McAndrew & Cropper, 2010) helped categorise and cluster resources into the system, while an imposed structure of issues, claims, potential solutions and evidence that could support or refute them enabled grouping of particular arguments. A review in 2011, after a few months of using the system, led to the addition of key challenges which then acted to make the content and potential conclusions more manageable.

Reflection on this process highlights transferable points.

- *What you measure changes what you do.* The challenge approach changed the way the researchers thought about the outcomes of the research. Essentially the 'questions' become the answers in terms of focus. This is only partly satisfactory and needs to be interlinked with evidence to be more useful. Taking this forward, the researchers are moving from derived questions to more directly testable hypotheses (described further below).

- *The philosophy of evidence matters.* The software tool could act to take things only so far, but the way to think about the value of different pieces of work was more encompassing. The concept that each case, opinion and paper can provide a piece of evidence was a good communication device and structured work with other organisations.
- *Communication is an essential component.* Without the secondary work of a researcher dedicated to communicating results through curation and visualisation (as well as in more traditional ways such as papers and presentations), it was difficult to appreciate what is contained within collections of research output represented in the OER Evidence Hub.

The structure of the Evidence Hub in OLnet seems in many ways the right way to go: high-level messages, different types of evidence and collective input. However, it would be wrong to see this as having solved research problems with technology. In practice the 'public' who were given equal access to use the system made few direct contributions to the evidence base; rather, they used the system to enter factual information about organisations and to view the results once simplified into the key challenges. The lessons from this experience were to see the next stage in supporting the collation of evidence as having two distinct components. First to enable the researchers to assemble the pieces of evidence; second to allow easier actions such as comments or ordering by a wider group of users. The first of these elements became a focus for subsequent work in the OER Research Hub. The second has also been taken forward with further developments of the Evidence Hub software applied to larger groups with a shared agenda (De Liddo & Buckingham Shum, 2013).

Being Agile Researchers: The OER Research Hub

The evidence approach described above is valuable in setting out how to make use of diverse items of data. In the OER Research Hub (McAndrew & Farrow, 2013) the approach has been applied from the start to structure the work within the project. A set of eleven hypotheses have been set out in the project proposal and agreed within the team and with the funder. These hypotheses were then linked with eight external case studies. The research team is working with these other projects to align its case study findings with the hypotheses. At the same time information from other OER contacts, projects and papers all contributes to providing evidence in support of or against the hypotheses. Examples of the hypotheses include 'OERs improve student performance/satisfaction', 'OERs widen participation in education' and 'OERs use leads educators to reflect on their practice'. The first of these is an overarching hypothesis that applies in all projects, while the others are linked to specific cases. The use of hypotheses has also offered a further way to bring in collective views. The hypotheses serve as boundary objects for discussion and workshops (Figure 12.1).

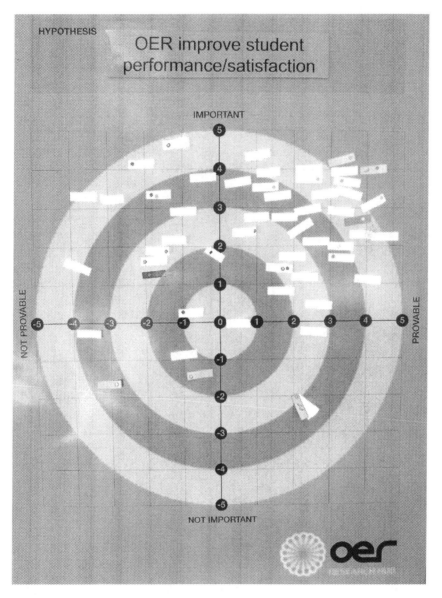

FIGURE 12.1 The Collective View of Participants in the OERchery Activity Marking the Provability and Significance of Different Hypotheses on Wall-Mounted Charts

The OER Research Hub built on the practical experience of OLnet to incorporate the three lessons learned of intelligent setting of measures, a philosophy of evidence and curation of collective input. These were then applied in ways that encourage agility. The use of hypotheses and collaborative projects with attached researchers addresses this at the macro level in the structure of the project and the targets it aims to meet. At the more micro level, implemented ideas were taken directly from agile development. These have found some success in terms of ways to address deadlines in the project, to get past critical stages and to build links between the team members and with those working within the collaborations.

In practice, we have found some differences between the approach to agile working advocated for software development, with its clearer focus on the final product, and the agile research approach suitable for team-based research. We adopted much of the terminology from agile software development (product backlog, sprints and scrum teams) and concentrated specific agile activity on key events—sprint events—to bring together work and align activities. Table 12.1 sets out the way in which we have implemented these sprint events.

The sprints in the project so far have helped to meet milestones and to extend activities to more easily include visiting fellows working with the core research team. They have also been intense and so, rather than a continuous sprint process, as is promoted for software development, our current view is that in the context of the OER Research Hub we are getting greatest benefit from running sprint events approximately monthly. With that pattern they act to give collective focus across the week in which they occur and provide synchronisation between members of the team. The sprint events have also helped to develop the philosophy of evidence that we consider necessary for the Evidence Hub to work in practice.

TABLE 12.1 Approach to Agile Working in OER Research Hub

1.	Clear aims established for things to be achieved in a short time. This is the 'product backlog.' For example in the 'Hypothesis sprint' a list was made of the papers, collaborations, survey results and connections that could feed into a review across each of the hypotheses. The target was to achieve shareable hypothesis reviews at the end of the sprint week. This product backlog was set out by the project leads.
2.	A sprint kickoff meeting agreed the scale of activities in the product backlog (using T-shirt size measures of Small, Medium, Large and eXtra Large), and then selected initial activities. The selections were owned by individual researchers.
3.	Progress was monitored by quick stand-up 'scrum meetings' where everyone said in turn what they had achieved, what they were about to do next and any issues that they needed help with. As the team involved team members who would be working away from base, or were joining from another organisation, this face-to-face activity was backed up with a shared online scrum document tracking things done, and things to do. This process was managed by the project coordinator acting as the 'scrummaster' to spot issues and find ways to solve them.
4.	A post-sprint review measured progress and planned how to ensure outputs were achieved.

Conclusions

This chapter has outlined a fundamental challenge of research: if it is to have impact, then it must be communicated to those who need it. This challenge has been recognised before (Wilson, Pettigrew, Cainan, & Nazareth, 2010), and indeed all researchers will have felt the dual pressures of complexity in findings and the need for simple-to-understand messages. In the field of OERs these pressures are particularly evident, driven by the potential to impact on practice and to influence policy. The Open Policy Network, for example, aims to meet the call for 'a central hub where open policies could be shared and discussed' (http://wiki.creativecommons.org/Open_Policy_Network) and seeks to connect to 'evidence of problem, evidence of benefits, barriers, . . . etc.'. The work on OLnet and the OER Research Hub looked at two different aspects of how to support the need to communicate and refine results from research. First, in OLnet, the use of the Evidence Hub as a way to bring in different levels of evidence, add in a wider range of views and highlight simplified conclusions. Later, in the OER Research Hub, the move to a more flexible, agile research model. Combining these approaches seems to be bringing benefits in allowing complex actions to give simpler messages.

The tools of the researcher are also changing as they become embedded as 'digital scholars' (Weller, 2011) in a more visible and connected world. The skills of the researcher as curator who can bring together, balance and mix from multiple sources, from primary to tertiary, needs to be valued. The agile approach outlined in this chapter provides a practical step in matching the environment now available to researchers with the demands that are made on them to provide greater impact and feed-through to policy.

Acknowledgements

The OLnet and OER Research Hub projects are supported by the William and Flora Hewlett Foundation.

References

Blaxter, L., Hughes, C., & Tight, M. (2010). *How to research*. Milton Keynes, UK: Open University Press.
Buckingham Shum, S., & Okada, A. (2008). Knowledge cartography for open sensemaking communities. *Journal of Interactive Media in Education, JIME Special Issue: Researching Open Content in Education*, 1–18. Retrieved from http://jime.open.ac.uk/jime/article/view/2008-10.
Daniel, J. (2012). Making sense of MOOCs: Musings in a maze of myth, paradox and possibility. *Journal of Interactive Media in Education*. Retrieved from http://jime.open.ac.uk/jime/article/view/2012-18.
De Liddo, A., & Buckingham Shum, S. (2010). Cohere: A prototype for contested collective intelligence. In *ACM Computer Supported Cooperative Work (CSCW 2010)—Workshop:*

Collective intelligence in organizations—Toward a research agenda. Retrieved from http://oro.open.ac.uk/19554/.

De Liddo, A., & Buckingham Shum, S. (2013). The Evidence Hub: harnessing the collective intelligence of communities to build evidence-based knowledge. In *Large Scale Ideation and Deliberation Workshop.* Retrieved from http://oro.open.ac.uk/38002/.

De Liddo, A., Buckingham Shum, S., McAndrew, P., & Farrow, R. (2012). The open education evidence hub: A collective intelligence tool for evidence based policy. In *Cambridge 2012: Joint OER12 and OpenCourseWare Consortium Global 2012 Conference.* Retrieved from www.ucel.ac.uk/oer12/abstracts/322.html.

De Liddo, A., Sándor, Á., & Buckingham Shum, S. (2012). Contested collective intelligence: Rationale, technologies, and a human–machine annotation study. *Computer Supported Cooperative Work (CSCW), 21*(4–5), 417–448. Retrieved from http://oro.open.ac.uk/31052/.

EDUCAUSE. (2011). 7 Things you should know about MOOCS. Retrieved from www.educause.edu/library/resources/7-things-you-should-know-about-moocs.

Galley, R., Conole, G., & Alevizou, P. (2010). Case study: Using cloudworks for an ppen literature review. Milton Keynes, UK: Open University. Retrieved from http://oro.open.ac.uk/26676/.

Goldacre, B., & Farley, R. (2009). *Bad science.* London: Fourth Estate.

Johnson, R., & Onwuegbuzie, A. J. (2004). Mixed methods research: A research paradigm whose time has come. *Educational Researcher, 33*(7), 14–26.

Knight, E., & Casilli, C. (2012). Mozilla open badges. In D. G. Oblinger (Ed.), *Game changers: Education and information technologies* (pp. 279–284). EDUCAUSE. Retrieved from http://net.educause.edu/ir/library/pdf/pub7203cs6.pdf.

Lindstrom, L., & Jeffries, R. (2004). Extreme programming and agile software development methodologies. *Information Systems Management, 21*(3), 41–52.

Long, P. and Siemens, G. (2011). Penetrating the Fog: Analytics in Learning and Education, *Educause Review, 46*(5), 31–40. Retrieved from: www.educause.edu/EDUCAUSE+Review/EDUCAUSEReviewMagazineVolume46/Penetratingthe FogAnalyticsinLe/235017.

McAndrew, P. (2011). Fostering open educational practices. *eLearning Papers*, 1–4. Retrieved from http://elearningpapers.eu/en/article/Fostering-Open-Educational-Practices?paper=72110.

McAndrew, P., & Cropper, K. (2010). Open Learning network: The evidence of OER impact. In *Open Ed 2010: The Seventh Annual Open Education Conference.* Retrieved from http://oro.open.ac.uk/23824/.

McAndrew, P., & Farrow, R. (2013). The ecology of sharing: Synthesizing OER research. In *OER13: Creating a virtuous circle, 26-27 March 2013.* Nottingham, UK. Retrieved from www.medev.ac.uk/oer13/67/view/.

McAndrew, P., Farrow, R., Law, P., & Elliott-Cirigottis, G. (2012). Learning the lessons of openness. *Journal of Interactive Media in Education.* Retrieved from http://jime.open.ac.uk/jime/article/view/2012-10.

McAndrew, P., Godwin, S., & Santos, A. (2009). Research 2.0: How do we know about the users that do not tell us anything? In G. Vavoula, N. Pachler, & A. Kukulska-Hulme (Eds.), *Researching mobile learning: Frameworks, tools and research designs* (pp. 277–288). Bern, Switzerland: Peter Lang. Retrieved from http://oro.open.ac.uk/23854/.

McAndrew, P., Santos, A., Lane, A., Godwin, S., Okada, A., Wilson, T., *et al.* (2009). *Learning from OpenLearn: Research report 2006–2008.* (P. McAndrew & A. I. Santos, Eds.). Milton Keynes, UK: Open University. Retrieved from http://oro.open.ac.uk/17513/

Malone, T., Laubacher, R., and Dellarocas, C. (2009) Harnessing crowds: Mapping the genome of collective intelligence. *MIT Sloan Research Paper No. 4732-09*, 1–21. Retrieved from http://dx.doi.org/10.2139/ssrn.1381502.

O'Reilly, T. (2005). What is Web 2.0: Design patterns and business models for the next generation of software. Retrieved from www.oreillynet.com/pub/a/oreilly/tim/news/2005/09/30/what-is-web-20.html.

Reeves, T. C. (2005). No significant differences revisited: A historical perspective on the research informing contemporary online learning. In G. Kearsley (Ed.), *Online learning: Personal reflections on the transformation of education* (pp. 299–308). Englewood Cliffs, NJ: Educational Technology Publications.

Turner, M. S. V. (2009). *Microsoft Solutions Framework Essentials*. Microsoft Press.

UNESCO. (2002). *Forum on the Impact of Open Courseware for Higher Education in Developing Countries—Final report*. Paris. Retrieved from http://portal.unesco.org/ci/en/files/2492/10330567404OCW_forum_report_final_draft.doc/OCW_forum_report_final_draft.doc.

von Hippel, E. (2005). *Democratizing innovation*. Cambridge, MA: MIT Press. Retrieved from http://web.mit.edu/evhippel/www/democ1.htm.

Weller, M. (2011). *The digital scholar: How technology is transforming scholarly practice*. London: Bloomsbury Publishing PLC.

Wilson, P. M., Pettigrew, M., Cainan, M. W., & Nazareth, I. (2010). Disseminating research findings: What should researchers do? A systematic scoping review of conceptual frameworks. *Implementation Science, 5*(91), 16. Retrieved from www.implementationscience.com/content/5/1/91.

INDEX